ISABELLA LUCY BIRD (1831-1904), the daughter of a clergyman, grew up in Tattenhall, Cheshire. Early in life she suffered from a spinal complaint and in 1854 she was sent by her doctor to America and Canada to improve her health. She published *The Englishwoman in America* in 1856 and *Aspects of Religion in the United States* in 1859. In 1860 her father died, and Isabella, with her mother and sister Henrietta, moved to Edinburgh. From there she made several excursions to the Outer Hebrides, writing articles on the island crofters and on subjects ranging from the poetry of John Donne to ragged schools. She continued to suffer from back trouble, insomnia and depression until, at the age of forty, she set off for Australia, continuing to Hawaii where her health miraculously improved. She wrote *Six Months in the Sandwich Islands* (1875) and climbed the world's largest volcano, Mauna Loa.

In 1873, Isabella Bird set off for the Rocky Mountains; her 'Letters from the Rocky Mountains' were published in the magazine *Leisure Hour* in 1878 and later published as *A Lady's Life in the Rocky Mountains* (1879). After a period at home she set off once more, this time to the northern Japanese island of Hokkaido and to the Native States of Malaya. As a result of these two journeys she published *Unbeaten Tracks in Japan* (1880) and *The Golden Chersonese* (1883).

In 1881 Isabella Bird married Dr John Bishop. He died in 1886, and three years later she set off on her travels to western Tibet and Ladakh, the deserts of Persia and Kurdistan, the Korean peninsula and the remote interior of China. These remarkable expeditions were recorded in *Journeys in Persia and Kurdistan* (1891), *Among the Tibetans* (1894), *Korea and Her Neighbours* (1898) and *The Yangtze Valley and Beyond* (1899).

Isabella Bird returned from the Far East in 1898; making her final journey at the age of seventy, she visited Morocco, touring the country on a black stallion given her by the Sultan. She died in Edinburgh in 1904.

ISABELLA L. BIRD

JOURNEYS
IN
PERSIA
AND
KURDISTAN

Volume I

WITH A NEW INTRODUCTION BY

PAT BARR

Published by VIRAGO PRESS Limited 1988
20-23 Mandela Street, London NW1 0HQ

First published by John Murray 1891
Virago Press edition reproduced from the John Murray edition

Introduction copyright © Pat Barr 1988

All rights reserved

British Library Cataloguing in Publication Data

A CIP catalogue record for this book
is available from the British Library

Printed in Great Britain by Cox & Wyman Ltd.,
Reading, Berkshire

TO

The Untravelled Many,

THESE VOLUMES

ARE CORDIALLY DEDICATED

INTRODUCTION

The group of foreigners travelling up the River Tigris from Basrah towards Baghdad on the steamer *Mejidieh* on a bright January day in 1890 were an ill-assorted bunch and, as one of their number, Mrs Isabella Bishop, wrote in a private letter, none of them 'could be guaranteed as non-explosive'. She, the only woman among them, was perhaps the least inflammable; certainly two of the other passengers, the Honourable George Curzon and Major Herbert Sawyer of the Indian Army, enjoyed a few skirmishes, though they shared similar views on the wretched hopelessness of the country round about them and its strategic importance to the British Empire. Curzon, later to make his most significant historical mark as an Indian Viceroy, was collecting material for his exhaustive work *Persia and the Persian Question* in which he urgently pressed the need to strengthen that ailing nation against what he saw as the growing threat of Russian aggression. Major Sawyer (called simply 'M. . . . ' in this book) was a military surveyor on a secret reconnaissance mission to ascertain both the extent of Russian infiltration in the Middle Eastern hinterlands and more precise geographical data about them.

Isabella had the Major to thank for being there at all, for she'd met him in Simla three months before and, when she expressed her keenness to visit the area (an exceptionally difficult one for an unaccompanied European woman at that time), he offered her his escort, at least as far as Tehran. The Major was a handsome widower of thirty-eight, Isabella a dumpy widow of fifty-nine, and, as she wryly commented to a friend, the Major's offer was considered 'the acme of my good fortune' by several Simla ladies. But, like all real travellers, she would greatly have preferred to go it alone – as she had before and would again – for she viewed any companion as 'an infringement on my liberty'.

Isabella had had to fight long and hard for her liberty. She'd spent a sheltered and conventional childhood in various English rectories, for her parents, Edward and Dora Bird, came from what the Victorians called 'good clerical stock'. Growing up in an atmosphere of devout highmindedness, she received every encouragement to pursue her wideranging studies and her practical philanthropy, but no clergyman's daughter was expected to go exploring the world's little-known countries on her own.

So, for many weary years, Isabella kept a tight rein on her deep hunger for adventurous liberty, and suffered, as a result, numerous physical and psychological illnesses, including spinal disease, headaches, disabling depressions. She directed her considerable energies into writing for scholarly magazines and working for charitable causes in Scotland, where she lived with her mother and younger sister, Henrietta, who was her closest companion and friend. But, in 1872, at the age of forty-one, she could no longer bear the constraints of this conventional, middle-class life and sailed for the Sandwich Isles (now called Hawaii), where she came fully alive for the first time. She cantered joyously through lush valleys, slept in native huts, climbed the 17,000-feet-high volcano Mauna Loa – all her ailments forgotten. She then visited the pioneering territories of the Colorado Rockies where she lived in settlers' cabins, made a dangerous excursion through the mountain passes in winter and had what was probably the most romantic encounter of her life, with trapper Jim Nugent, her 'dear desperado'.

On returning to England, Miss Bird wrote *Six Months in the Sandwich Isles* and *A Lady's Life in the Rocky Mountains* which first brought her recognition as a travel writer of originality, perception and courage. It was mainly the proceeds from these books (for she had no large source of private wealth) that enabled her to make the first of several expeditions to the East in 1878. The books about Japan and Malaya that resulted from it added considerably to her reputation as both a popular and reliably informative author. Soon afterwards, however, her beloved sister Henrietta died of typhoid and Isabella was utterly desolated. It must have been rather on the rebound from this bereavement that she suddenly agreed to marry John Bishop, a doctor ten years her junior, who'd long attended both sisters and had proposed to Isabella at least twice before. At this point (1881) Mrs Bishop, reduced to the role of dutiful doctor's wife in Edinburgh, might well have lapsed into middle-aged obscurity, except that John contracted erysipelas, a disease that led to his lingering death two days before their fifth wedding anniversary.

Bishop, by all accounts a considerate and devoted husband, is best remembered for his wry comment that his only formidable rival in his wife's heart was 'the high tableland of Central Asia'. And it must have been true, because Isabella, after a further period of deep mourning (for she'd grown to love John dearly in his last months of life), set her resolute and solitary steps in that direction. Reaching Kashmir early in 1889, she soon fled from the tourist-infested comforts of Srinigar to Ladakh where she rode over the mountain passes on an Arab steed called Gyalpo and then pushed onward through the even more remote Nubra province, riding on the back of a yak at altitudes of 18,000 feet where even the spirited Gyalpo couldn't carry her. It was on her return from this expedition that she met Major Sawyer, and her descriptions of its perils and hardships must have convinced him that

she was no ordinary traveller and would be a fit companion
for the trials of crossing the Persian deserts in winter.

Those trials proved even more severe than either of them
had imagined, and Isabella's account does not omit a single
horrendous detail of the cold, wet discomforts of the journey
which were occasionally alleviated by brief stays in the houses
of provincial officials – whose way of life she found fascinating ñ though often 'morally deplorable'. Isabella's determi-
nation to describe these little-known regions as they actually
existed in all their bleakness and squalor is typical of her later
work. To the average reader of the period the name 'Persia'
might conjure visions of marbled courts, jewelled magnificence, exquisite artifacts, but what she sees instead is the grim
reality of everyday life for the great majority of its population
– including its female peasantry who were seldom considered
worthy of mention by male European travellers. During her
enforced stay in Khannikin, for example, she gives us a
scrupulously drawn, indelible picture of one housewife's
monotonous and oppressed existence; and one wonders, inci-
dentally, to what extent it has changed since.

One might also wonder just why this plump little widow
from Edinburgh chose to be in such an unlikely and com-
fortless spot? And to that there is only one honest answer:
because it made her feel healthier and happier than she felt at
home. The extraordinary nature of her physical and psychological make-up, which made of her a depressed near-invalid
in Edinburgh and an extremely tough, lively, bold, optimistic
traveller through the world's remote places, was a lifelong
mystery to her – and to her doctors who wrote up her case in
medical journals after her death. She simply could not settle
anywhere for long, and only the challenges and serendipities
of constantly changing scenes could fully release her powers
of authorship, her indefatigable curiosity, her capacity for
real joy.

This had been the case from the moment she took her first

ride in the Sandwich Isles eighteen years before, and it was the same now. As soon as she left the confines of crowded Baghdad for 'the nameless charm of a nomadic life', she was a new woman. 'I felt better at once in the pure exhilarating air,' she writes, and 'even indulged in a gallop'. From then on she is in her element: relishing the practical problems of loading mules, obtaining supplies, setting up camps; carefully noting the habits of Persian officials, harem ladies, frontier tribes-men; able and willing to endure great extremes of cold and fatigue, to risk the considerable hazards of the way, in order to glory in yet another example of 'Nature's grandeur', to take yet another inspiriting canter across a free, empty landscape.

Not every day was given over to such indulgences, however, and though Isabella always approached centres of population with some reluctance, she did spend some time in Kum, Julfa (the suburb of Isfahan where all non-Moslem groups had to live) and Tehran. And how vividly she describes the nation's capital at that time, as a half-westernised, half-oriental city, ornate, squalid, corrupt and showy, its bazaars stuffed with shoddy foreign goods, its way of life still practically medieval. At Julfa she stayed with Dr Bruce, a missionary who'd also been a passenger on the *Mejidieh*, and whom Curzon (who had little love for the breed) dubbed 'a good example of a nineteenth-century Crusader'. In these later years, Mrs Bishop became an eloquent advocate of medical missions and, when in Srinigar, had founded one in memory of her late husband. But she was never tempted to become a missionary herself (how the discipline of labouring long in one small vineyard would have irked her!), and the sensible warning she voices here about the difficulties of mission life in the Middle East, especially for single women, was salutary, though little heeded by church societies at home.

This is the first book in which Isabella makes frequent reference to her strong Christian belief, perhaps because it was the first time she'd been confronted by so much evidence of the fanatical Moslem oppression of women. Nevertheless, she understood that the growth of European belief and influence in countries like Persia would inevitably result in the destruction of those traditional crafts and customs, the spoilation of those untamed regions, which constituted their main attraction for her. It was a dilemma she ponders here, but which neither she nor like-minded travellers of her calibre since have been able to resolve.

Certainly she believed that official corruption and general oppression of the populace were more prevalent in eastern countries like Persia than in western Europe, and she found little to admire in the national 'moral character' or in most of the individuals she met. Hadji, her crafty servant, comes in for very severe stricture, and yet emerges as a real personality for all that, with his exasperatingly pious phrases to cover all shortcomings, his jauntily ruffian looks and his indolent habits.

It is a pity that, due to the clandestine nature of Major Sawyer's mission, Isabella felt obliged to all but ignore his presence in this published account of their journey. But he was very much with her for most of the time and definitely made his presence felt. From letters written to friends at home we learn that he was as prickly and self-opinionated as Curzon, as stubborn, resourceful and courageous as she herself in the face of danger and hardship, and that he treated the 'natives' with such lordly impatience and disdain that she dubbed him The Sahib.

Yet this odd couple learned to respect and even like each other, for after parting in Tehran, they agreed to meet later in Julfa for a joint expedition to the Bakhtiari country. The Major's arrival in that introverted missionary community caused 'an immense sensation', Isabella wrote, and his 'splendid appearance, force of character' mingled with his 'brutal frankness, ability and kind-heartedness made a great breeze' there. For her part, she had long developed a brisk, no-nonsense manner of dealing with men which stood her in good stead with the Major. They became, she says, 'good comrades' and rubbed along well enough in the hinterlands where they could both indulge their eccentricities and Isabella enjoy the 'utter sartorial licence' which always suited her best. 'I am so much better as usual since I came into camp and have not to do company,' she explains.

This first volume of Mrs Bishop's Middle Eastern expedition ends in June on an optimistic note, with her and Sawyer still among the Bakhtiaris, still enjoying the 'romance of camp life' – though not in any sense of romantic togetherness. Indeed when they finally parted at Burujird, she privately expressed her relief that he would no longer rouse her at dawn with his call, 'To boot and saddle!' She journeyed on alone through parts of Kurdistan and Turkey to Trebizond, where she sailed for home, reaching London on Boxing Day, 1890. Immediately she busied herself with writing articles and delivering lectures about political and social conditions in the countries she'd visited, and then settled to write the book. Its progress was somewhat delayed because she'd agreed with Sawyer that her account of their joint travels be vetted by the Indian War Office, and this proved 'truly hampering'. Nevertheless it appeared in time for the next Christmas to considerable critical acclaim, and some reviewers expressed increasing astonishment that a member of the 'weaker sex' could endure so much privation and hardship, while travelling men tended 'to get writer's cramp and break down in health'. Isabella might have chuckled at that for, though she admired men more than women on the whole, she still liked to beat them at their own game.

At this stage in her career, when her reputation was growing, when even some men were prepared publicly to admire her toughness and talents, and when (as happened the following year) she was elected the first woman member of the Royal

Geographical Society, she would have been a substantial and valuable recruit to the feminist cause. But unfortunately she never was. Deeply imbued from youth with conventional social and moral Victorian standards, she viewed her own original life as something of an unnatural aberration for a mere woman; nor did she believe that the majority of her sex were either desirous or capable of the tough, bold exploits she enjoyed.

Political and social 'causes' were ever burdensome to her anyway, and it was to escape from such obligations that she again set out for the East in 1894. She spent the next three years travelling in Japan, Manchuria, outpost settlements of Siberia and the remote interiors of Korea and China, returning home reluctantly and for almost the last time at the age of sixty-six.

Though her reputation was thoroughly established by then and her books brought her a comfortable income, her last years were not particularly happy. She remained psychologically incapable of settling into routine domesticity, even when she became physically too frail for long-distance travel; nor did she form any binding emotional ties of the kind she'd lost. She certainly inspired affection in many friends, however, and they remained faithful to her till she died in Edinburgh in 1904.

Following her death, a few appreciative articles about her appeared, but (probably because she was a woman) she then sank into obscurity and no full-scale, serious assessment of her life and works was undertaken for many years. This account of her journeys in Persia and Kurdistan, though popular enough during her lifetime, is probably the least well known of all her works. I don't think this is because it is in any way inferior in quality to her others (though, as she says in her own introduction, it lacks the vivacity and spontaneity of her early letters to Henrietta that appeared in book form) but rather because its subject matter was less appealing to the average armchair traveller. But now, when the whole region of the Middle East is the subject of so much interest and speculation, would seem an appropriate time indeed to join Isabella Bird as she jogs along on various mules, donkeys, mettlesome Arab steeds and tells us exactly what it was all like nearly a hundred years ago.

Pat Barr
Norfolk, 1988

PREFACE

THE letters of which these volumes are composed embrace the second half of journeys in the East extending over a period of two years.[1] They attempt to be a faithful record of facts and impressions, but were necessarily written in haste at the conclusion of fatiguing marches, and often in circumstances of great discomfort and difficulty, and I relied for their correction in the event of publication on notes made with much care. Unfortunately I was robbed of nearly the whole of these, partly on my last journey in Persia and partly on the Turkish frontier,—a serious loss, which must be my apology to the reader for errors which, without this misfortune, would not have occurred.

The bibliography of Persia is a very extensive one, and it may well be that I have little that is new to communicate, except on a part of Luristan previously untraversed by Europeans ; but each traveller receives a different impression from those made upon his predecessors, and I hope that my book may be accepted as an honest attempt to make a popular contribution to the sum of knowledge of a country and people with which we are likely to be brought into closer relations.

[1] I left England with a definite object in view, to which others were subservient, but it is not necessary to obtrude it on the reader.

As these volumes are simply travels in Persia and Eastern Asia Minor, and are *not a book on either country,* the references to such subjects as were not within the sphere of my observation are brief and incidental. The administration of government, the religious and legal systems, the tenure of land, and the mode of taxation are dismissed in a few lines, and social customs are only described when I came in contact with them. The Ilyats, or nomadic tribes, form a very remarkable element of the population of Persia, but I have only noticed two of their divisions—the Bakhtiari and Feili Lurs. The antiquities of Persia are also passed over with hardly a remark, as well as many other subjects, which have been "threshed out" by previous writers with more or less of accuracy.

I make these omissions with all the more satisfaction, because most that is "knowable" concerning Persia will be accessible on the publication of a work now in the Press, *Persia and the Persian Question,* by the Hon. George N. Curzon, M.P., who has not only travelled extensively in the country, but has bestowed such enormous labour and research upon it, and has had such exceptional opportunities of acquiring the latest and best official information, that his volumes may fairly be described as "exhaustive."

It is always a pleasant duty to acknowledge kindness, and I am deeply grateful to several friends for the help which they have given me in many ways, and for the trouble which some of them have taken to recover facts which were lost with my notes, as well as for the careful revision of a portion of my letters in MS. I am indebted to the Indian authorities for the materials for a sketch map, for photographs from which many of the illustrations are taken, and for the use of a valuable geographical report, and to Mr. Thistleton Dyer, Director of the Royal

Botanic Gardens at Kew, for the identification of a few of my botanical specimens.

In justice to the many kind friends who received me into their homes, I am anxious to disclaim having either echoed or divulged their views on Persian or Turkish subjects, and to claim and accept the fullest responsibility for the opinions expressed in these pages, which, whether right or wrong, are wholly my own. It is from those who know Persia and Kurdistan the best that I am sure of receiving the most kindly allowance wherever, in spite of an honest desire to be accurate, I have fallen into mistakes.

The retention, not only of the form, but of the reality of diary letters, is not altogether satisfactory either to author or reader, for the author sacrifices the literary and artistic arrangement of his materials, and however ruthlessly omissions are made, the reader is apt to find himself involved in a multiplicity of minor details, treated in a fashion which he is inclined to term " slipshod," and to resent the egotism which persistently clings to familiar correspondence. Still, even with all the disadvantages of this form of narrative, I think that letters are the best mode of placing the reader in the position of the traveller, and of enabling him to share, not only first impressions in their original vividness, and the interests and enjoyments of travelling, but the hardships, difficulties, and tedium which are their frequent accompaniments !

For the lack of vivacity which, to my thinking, pervades the following letters, I ask the reader's indulgence. They were originally written, and have since been edited, under the heavy and abiding shadow, not only of the loss of the beloved and only sister who was the inspiration of my former books of travel, and to whose completely sympathetic interest they owed whatever of brightness they possessed, but of my beloved husband, whose able and careful revision accompanied my last volume through the Press.

Believing that these letters faithfully reflect what I saw of the regions of which they treat, I venture to ask for them the same kindly and lenient criticism with which my travels in the Far East and elsewhere were received in bygone years, and to express the hope that they may help to lead towards that goal to which all increase of knowledge of races and beliefs tends—a truer and kindlier recognition of the brotherhood of man, as seen in the light of the Fatherhood of God.

ISABELLA L. BISHOP.

November 12, 1891.

LIST OF ILLUSTRATIONS

IN VOLUME I.

A Gopher	*Page* 19
A Turkish Frontier Fort	*To face page* 78
Lodgings for Travellers	82
Persian Bread-making	159
The Shrine of Fatima	167
A Dervish	237
Castle of Ardal	318
Imam Kuli Khan	326
The Karun at Dupulan	*To face page* 351
Ali Jan	362
Armenian Women of Libasgun	366
Wall and Gate of Libasgun	*To face page* 368
A Perso-Bakhtiari Cradle	372
A Dastgird Tent	*To face page* 378

GLOSSARY

Abambar, a covered reservoir.

Agha, a master.

Andarun, women's quarters, a *haram.*

Arak, a coarse spirit.

Badgir, wind-tower.

Badragah, a parting escort.

Balakhana, an upper room.

Bringals, egg plants.

Chapar, post.

Chapar Khana, post-house.

Chapi, the Bakhtiari national dance.

Charvadar, a muleteer.

Farāsh, lit. a carpet-spreader.

Farsakh, from three and a half to four miles.

Gardan, a pass.

Gaz, a sweetmeat made from manna.

Gelims, thin carpets, drugget.

Gheva, a summer shoe.

Gholam, an official messenger or attendant.

Hākim, a governor.

Hakīm, a physician.

Hammam, a Turkish or hot bath.

Ilyats, the nomadic tribes of Persia.

Imam, a saint, a religious teacher.

Imamzada, a saint's shrine.

Istikbal, a procession of welcome.

Jul, a horse's outer blanket.

Kabob, pieces of skewered meat seasoned and toasted.

Kafir, an infidel, a Christian.

Kah, chopped straw.

Kajawehs, horse-panniers.

Kalian, a "hubble-bubble" or water-pipe for tobacco.

Kamarband, a girdle.

Kanaat, an underground water-channel.

Kanat, the upright side of a tent.

Karsi, a wooden frame for covering a fire-hole.

Katirgi (Turkish), a muleteer.

Ketchuda, a headman of a village.

Khan, lord or prince; a designation as common as esquire.

Khan (Turkish), an inn.

Khanjar, a curved dagger.

Khanji (Turkish), the keeper of a *khan.*

Khanum, a lady of rank.

Khurjins, saddle bags.

Kizik, a slab of animal fuel.

Kotal, lit. a ladder, a pass.

Kourbana (Syriac), the Holy Communion.

Kran, eightpence.

Kuh, mountain.

Lira (Turkish), about £1.

Malek (Syriac, *lit.* king), a chief or headman.

Mamachi, midwife.

Mangel, a brazier.

Mast, curdled milk.

Medresseh, a college.

Mirza, a scribe, secretary, or gentleman. An educated man.

Modakel, illicit percentage.

Mollah, a religious teacher.

Munshi, a clerk, a teacher of languages.

Namad, felt.

Nasr, steward.

Odah (Turkish), a room occupied by human beings and animals.

Piastre, a Turkish coin worth two-pence-halfpenny.

Pirahan, a chemise or shirt.

Pish-kash, a nominal present.

Qasha (Syriac), a priest.

Rayahs, subject Syrians.

Roghan, clarified butter.

Samovar, a Russian tea-urn.

Sartip, a general.

Seraidar, the keeper of a caravanserai.

Sharbat, a fruit syrup.

Shroff, a money-changer.

Shuldari (*Shooldarry*), a small tent with two poles and a ridge pole, but without *kanats.*

Shulwars, wide trousers.

Sowar, a horseman, a horse soldier.

Takchāh, a recess in a wall.

Taktrawan, a mule litter.

Tandūr, an oven in a floor.

Tang, a rift or defile.

Tufangchi, a foot soldier, an armed footman.

Tuman, seven shillings and sixpence.

Vakil, an authorised representative.

Vakil-u-Dowleh, agent of Government.

Yabu, a pony or inferior horse.

Yailaks, summer quarters.

Yekdan, a mule or camel trunk, made of leather.

Yohoort (Turkish), curdled milk.

Zaptieh (Turkish), a *gendarme.*

LETTER I

BASRAH, ASIATIC TURKEY, *Jan. 1, 1890*.

A *shamal* or N.W. wind following on the sirocco which had accompanied us up "the Gulf" was lashing the shallow waters of the roadstead into reddish yeast as we let go the anchor opposite the sea front of Bushire, the most important seaport in Persia. *The* Persian man-of-war *Persepolis*, officered by Germans, H.M. ship *Sphinx*, two big steamers owned in London, a British-built three-masted clipper, owned and navigated by Arabs, and a few Arab native vessels tugged at their anchors between two and three miles from the shore. Native *buggalows* clustered and bumped round the trading vessels, hanging on with difficulty, or thumped and smashed through the short waves, close on the wind, easily handled and sailing magnificently, while the Residency steam-launch, puffing and toiling, was scarcely holding her own against a heavy head sea.

Bushire, though it has a number of two-storied houses and a population of 15,000, has a most insignificant appearance, and lies so low that from the *Assyria's* deck it gave the impression of being below the sea-level. The *shamal* was raising a sand storm in the desert beyond; the sand was drifting over it in yellow clouds, the mountains which at a greater or less distance give a wild sublimity to the eastern shores of the Gulf were blotted out, and a blurred and windy shore harmonised with a blurred and windy sea.

The steam-launch, which after several baffled attempts succeeded in reaching the steamer's side, brought letters of welcome from Colonel Ross, who for eighteen years has filled the office of British. Resident in the Persian Gulf with so much ability, judgment, and tact as to have earned the respect and cordial esteem of Persians, Arabs, the mixed races, and Europeans alike. Of his kindness and hospitality there is no occasion to write, for every stranger who visits the Gulf has large experience of both.

The little launch, though going shorewards with the wind, was tossed about like a cork, shipping·deluges of spray, and it was so cold and generally tumultuous, that it was a relief to exchange the shallow, wind-lashed waters of the roadstead for the shelter of a projecting sea-wall below the governor's house. A curricle, with two fiery little Arab horses, took us over the low windy stretch of road which lies behind Bushire, through a part of the town and round again to the sea-shore, on which long yellow surges were breaking thunderously in drifts of creamy foam. The Residency, a large Persian house, with that sort of semi-fortified look which the larger Eastern houses are apt to have, is built round court-yards, and has a fine entrance, which was lined with well-set-up men of a Bombay marine battalion. As is usual in Persia and Turkey, the reception rooms, living rooms, and guest rooms are upstairs, opening on balconies, the lower part being occupied by the servants and as domestic offices. Good fires were a welcome adjunct to the genial hospitality of Colonel Ross and his family, for the mercury, which for the previous week had ranged from 84° to 93°, since the sunrise of that day had dropped to 45°, and the cold, damp wind suggested an English February. Even the Residency, thick as its walls are, was invaded

by sea sand, and penetrated by the howlings and shriek-
ings of the *shamal* and the low hiss at intervals of wind-
blown spray.

This miserable roadstead does a large trade,[1] though
every bale and chest destined for the cities of the interior
must be packed on mules' backs for carriage over the
horrible and perilous *kotals* or rock ladders of the inter-
vening mountain ranges. The chief caravan route in
Persia starts from Bushire *viâ* Shiraz, Isfahan, Kashan,
and Kûm, to Tihran. A loaded mule takes from thirty
to thirty-five days to Isfahan, and from Isfahan to
Tihran from twelve to sixteen days, according to the
state of the roads.

Bushire does not differ in appearance from an ordinary eastern town. Irregular and uncleanly alleys, dead
mud walls, with here and there a low doorway, bazars
in which the requirements of caravans are largely considered, and in which most of the manufactured goods
are English, a great variety in male attire, some small
mosques, a marked predominance of the Arab physiognomy
and costume, and ceaseless strings of asses bringing skins
of water from wells a mile from the town, are my impres-

[1] According to the returns for 1889, the British tonnage entering the
Bushire roadstead was 111,745 out of 118,570 tons, and the imports from
British territory amounted to a value of £744,018 out of £790,832. The
exports from Bushire in the same year amounted to £535,076, that of
opium being largely on the increase. Among other things exported are
pistachio nuts, gum, almonds, madder, wool, and cotton. Regarding gum,
the wars in the Soudan have affected the supply of it, and Persia is reaping
the benefit, large quantities now being collected from certain shrubs, especially from the wild almond, which abounds at high altitudes. The drawback is that firewood and charcoal are becoming consequently dearer and
scarcer. The gum exported in 1889 was 7472 cwts., as against 14,918 in
1888, but the value was more than the same.

The imports into Bushire, as comparing 1889 with 1888, have
increased by £244,186, and the exports by £147,862. The value of the
export of opium, chiefly to China, was £231,521, as against £148,523 in
1888.

sions of the first Persian city that I have seen. The Persian element, however, except in officialism and the style of building, is not strong, the population being chiefly composed of "Gulf Arabs." There are nearly fifty European residents, including the telegraph staff and the representatives of firms doing a very large business with England, the Persian Gulf Trading Company, Messrs. Hotz and Company, Messrs. Gray, Paul, and Company, and the British India Steam Navigation Company, which has enormously developed the trade of the Gulf.

Bushire is the great starting-point of travellers from India who desire "to go home through Persia" by Shiraz and Persepolis. *Charvadars* (muleteers) and the necessary outfit are obtainable, but even the kindness of the Resident fails to overcome the standing difficulty of obtaining a Persian servant who is both capable and trustworthy. Having been forewarned by him not to trust to Bushire for this indispensable article, I had brought from India a Persian of good antecedents and character, who, desiring to return to his own country, was willing to act as my interpreter, courier, and sole attendant. Grave doubts of his ability to act in the two latter capacities occurred to me before I left Karachi, grew graver on the voyage, and were quite confirmed as we tossed about in the Residency launch, where the "young Persian gentleman," as he styled himself, sat bolt upright with a despairing countenance, dressed in a tall hat, a beautifully made European suit, faultless tan boots, and snowy collar and cuffs, a man of truly refined feeling and manners, but hopelessly out of place. I pictured him helpless among the *déshabillé* and roughnesses of a camp, and anticipated my insurmountable reluctance to ask of him menial service, and was glad to find that the same doubts had occurred to himself.

I lost no time in interviewing Hadji,—a Gulf Arab, who has served various travellers, has been ten times to Mecca, went to Windsor with the horses presented to the Queen by the Sultan of Muscat, speaks more or less of six languages, knows English fairly, has some recommendations, and professes that he is "up to" all the requirements of camp life. The next morning I engaged him as "man of all work," and though a big, wild-looking Arab in a rough *abba* and a big turban, with a long knife and a revolver in his girdle, scarcely looks like a lady's servant, I hope he may suit me, though with these antecedents he is more likely to be a scamp than a treasure.

The continuance of the *shamal* prevented the steamer from unloading in the exposed roadstead, and knocked the launch about as we rejoined her. We called at the telegraph station at Fao, and brought off Dr. Bruce, the head of the Church Missionary Society's Mission at Julfa, whose long and intimate acquaintance with the country and people will make him a great acquisition on the Tigris.

"About sixty miles above the bar outside the Shat-el-Arab" (the united Tigris and Euphrates), "forty miles above the entrance to that estuary at Fao, and twenty miles below the Turkish port of Basrah, the present main exit of the Karun river flows into the Shat-el-Arab from the north-east by an artificial channel, whose etymology testifies to its origin, the Haffar" (dug-out) "canal. When this canal was cut, no one knows. . . . Where it flows into the Shat-el-Arab it is about a quarter of a mile in width, with a depth of from twenty to thirty feet.

"The town of Mohammerah is situated a little more than a mile up the canal on its right bank, and is a filthy place, with about 2000 inhabitants, and consists

mainly of mud huts and hovels, backed by a superb
fringe of date palms." [1]   In the rose flush of a winter
morning we steamed slowly past this diplomatically
famous confluence of the Haffar and Shat-el-Arab, at
the angle of which the Persians have lately built a
quay, a governor's house, and a large warehouse, in
expectation of a trade which shows few signs of development.

A winter morning it was indeed, splendid and invigorating after the ferocious heat of the Gulf.   To-day
there has been frost!

The Shat-el-Arab is a noble river or estuary.   From
both its Persian and Turkish shores, however, mountains
have disappeared, and dark forests of date palms inter-
sected by canals fringe its margin heavily, and extend
to some distance inland.   The tide is strong, and such
native boats as *belems*, *buggalows*, and dug-outs, loaded
with natives and goods, add a cheerful element of busy
life.

We anchored near Basrah, below the foreign settlement, and had the ignominy of being placed for twenty-
four hours in quarantine, flying the degrading yellow
flag.   Basrah has just been grievously ravaged by the
cholera, which has not only carried off three hundred of
the native population daily for some time, but the British
Vice-Consul and his children.   Cholera still exists in
Turkey while it is extinct in Bombay, and the imposition
of quarantine on a ship with a " clean bill of health "
seems devised for no other purpose than to extract fees,
to annoy, and to produce a harassing impression of
Turkish officialism.

After this detention we steamed up to the anchorage,
which is in front of a few large bungalows which lie

[1] "The Karun River," Hon. G. Curzon, M.P., *Proceedings of R.G.S.*,
September 1890.

between the belt of palms and the river, and form the
European settlement of Margil. A fever-haunted swamp,
with no outlet but the river; canals exposing at low
water deep, impassable, and malodorous slime separating
the bungalows; a climate which is damp, hot, malarious,
and prostrating except for a few weeks in winter, and a
total absence of all the resources and amenities of civilisation, make Basrah one of the least desirable places to
which Europeans are exiled by the exigencies of commerce. It is scarcely necessary to say that the few
residents exercise unbounded hospitality, which is the
most grateful memory which the stranger retains of the
brief halt by the " River of Arabia."

This is the dead season in the " city of dates." An
unused river steamer, a large English trader, two Turkish
ships-of-war painted white, the *Mejidieh*, one of two
English-owned steamers which are allowed to ply on the
Tigris, and the *Assyria* of the B.I.S.N. Co., constitute the
fleet at anchor. As at Bushire, all cargo must be loaded and
unloaded by boats, and crowds of native craft hanging
on to the trading vessels give a little but not much
vivacity.

October, after the ingathering of the date harvest, is
the busiest month here. The magnitude of the date
industry may be gathered from the fact that in 1890,
60,000 tons of dates were exported from Basrah, 20,000
in boxes, and the remainder in palm-leaf mats, one
vessel taking 1800 tons. The quantity of wood imported
for the boxes was 7000 tons in cut lengths, with iron
hooping, nails, and oiled paper for inside wrapping,
brought chiefly from England.

A hundred trees can be grown on an acre of ground.
The mature tree gives a profit of 4s., making the profit
on an acre £20 annually. The Governor of Mohammerah has lately planted 30,000 trees, and date palms to

the number of 60,000 have been recently planted on Persian soil.

It is said that there are 160 varieties of dates, but only a few are known to commerce. These great sombre date forests or "date gardens," which no sunshine can enliven, are of course artificial, and depend upon irrigation. The palms are propagated by means of suckers taken from the female date. The young trees begin to bear when they are about five years old, reach maturity at nine, and may be prolific for two centuries. Mohammed said wisely, "Honour the palm, it is your paternal aunt." One soon learns here that it not only provides the people with nutritious food, but with building materials, as well as with fuel, carpets, ropes, and mats. But it is the least beautiful of the palms, and the dark monotonous masses along the river contrast with my memories of the graceful coco palm fringing the coral islands of the Pacific.

I left the *Assyria* with regret. The captain and officers had done all that intelligence and kindness could do to make the voyage an agreeable one, and were altogether successful. On shore a hospitable reception, a good fire, and New Year's Day come together appropriately. The sky is clear and cloudless, and the air keen. The bungalows belonging to the European firms are dwelling-houses above and offices below, and are surrounded by packing-yards and sheds for goods. In line with them are the Consulates.

The ancient commercial glories of Basrah are too well known to need recapitulation. Circumstances are doing much to give it something of renewed importance. The modern Basrah, a town which has risen from a state of decay till it has an estimated population of 25,000, is on the right bank of the river, at some distance up a picturesque palm-fringed canal. Founded by Omar soon

after the death of Mohammed, and tossed like a shuttlecock
between Turk and Persian, it is now definitely Turkish,
and the great southern outlet of Chaldæa and Mesopotamia, as well as the port at which the goods passing to
and from Baghdad "break bulk." A population more
thoroughly polyglot could scarcely be found, Turks, Arabs,
Sabeans, Syrians, Greeks, Hindus, Armenians, Frenchmen,
Wahabees, Britons, Jews, Persians, Italians, and Africans,
and there are even more creeds than races.

S.S. Mejidieh, River Tigris, Jan. 4.—Leaving Basrah
at 4 P.M. on Tuesday we have been stemming the strong
flood of the Tigris for three bright winter days, in which
to sit by a red-hot stove and sleep under a pile of
blankets have been real luxuries after the torrid heat of
the "Gulf." The party on board consists of Dr. Bruce,
Mr. Hammond, who has been for some months pushing
British trade at Shuster, the Assistant Quartermaster-
General for India, a French-speaking Jewish merchant,
the Hon. G. Curzon, M.P., and Mr. Swabadi, a Hungarian
gentleman in the employment of the Tigris and Euphrates
Steam Navigation Company, a very scholarly man, who in
the course of a long residence in Southern Turkey has
acquainted himself intimately with the country and its
peoples, and is ever ready to place his own stores of
information at our disposal. Mr. Curzon has been
"prospecting" the Karun river, and came on board from
the *Shushan,* a small stern-wheel steamer with a carrying
capacity of 30 tons, a draught when empty of 18 inches,
and when laden of from 24 to 36. She belongs to the
Messrs. Lynch Brothers, of the Tigris and Euphrates
S.N. Co. They run her once a fortnight at a considerable
loss between Mohammerah and Ahwaz. Her isolated
position and diminutive size are a curious commentary
on the flourish of trumpets and *blether* of exultation with
which the English newspapers announced the very poor

concession of leave to run steamers on the Karun between the Shat-el-Arab and Ahwaz.

[Since this letter was written, things have taken rather a singular turn, and the development of trade on the Karun has partly fallen into the hands of a trading corporation of Persians, the *Nasiri* Company. By them, and under their representative partner, Haja Mahomad, a man of great energy, the formidable rapids at Ahwaz are being circumvented by the construction of a tramway 2400 yards long, which is proceeding steadily. A merchants' caravanserai has already been built on the river bank at the lower landing-place and commencement of the tramway, and a bakery, butchery, and carpentry, along with a *café* and a grocery and general goods stores, have already been opened by men brought to Ahwaz by H. Mahomad.

A river face wall, where native craft are to lie, is being constructed of hewn stone blocks and sections of circular pillars, remains of the ancient city.

The *Nasiri* Company has a small steamer, the *Nasiri*, plying on the lower Karun, chiefly as a tug, taking up two Arab boats of twenty-seven tons each, lashed alongside of her. On her transference at the spring floods of this year to the river above Ahwaz, the *Karun*, a steam launch of about sixty tons, belonging to the Governor of Mohammerah, takes her place below, and a second steamer belonging to the same company is now running on the lower stream. Poles from Zanzibar have been distributed for a telegraph line from Mohammerah to Ahwaz. The Messrs. Lynch have placed a fine river steamer of 300 tons on the route; but this enterprising firm, and English capitalists generally, are being partially "cut out" by the singular "go" of this Persian company, which not only appears to have strong support from Government quarters, but has gained the co-operation of the well-known and wealthy Sheikh Mizal, whose personal influence in Arabistan is very great, and who has hitherto been an obstacle to the opening of trade on the Karun.

A great change for the better has taken place in the circumstances of the population, and villages, attracted by trade, are springing up, which the *Nasiri* Company is doing its best to encourage. The land-tax is very light, and the cultivators are receiving every encouragement. Much wheat was exported last year, and there is a brisk demand for river lands on leases of sixty years for the cultivation of cotton, cereals, sugar-cane, and date palms.

Persian soldiers all have their donkeys, and at Ahwaz a brisk and amusing competition is going on between the soldiers of a fine regiment stationed there and the Arabs for the transport of goods past the rapids, and for the conveyance of tramway and building materials. This competition is enabling goods to pass the rapids cheaply and expeditiously.

One interesting feature connected with these works is the rapidly increased well-being of the Arabs. In less than a year labour at 1 *kran* (8d.) a day has put quite a number of them in possession of a pair of donkeys and a plough, and seed-corn wherewith to cultivate Government lands on their own account, besides leaving a small balance in hand on which to live without having to borrow on the coming crop at frightfully usurious rates.

Until now the sheikhs have been able to command labour for little more than the poorest food; and now many of the very poor who depended on them have started as small farmers, and things are rapidly changing.

The careful observer, from whose report on Persia to the Foreign Office, No. 207, I have transferred the foregoing facts, wrote in January 1891: " It was a sight to see the whole Arab population on the river banks hard at work taking advantage of the copious rain which had just fallen ; every available animal fit for draught was yoked to the plough—horses, mules, bullocks, and donkeys, and even mares, with their foals following them up the furrows."

This, which is practically a Persian opening of the trade of the Karun, is not what was expected, however much it was to be desired. After a journey of nine months through Persia, I am strongly of opinion that if the Empire is to have a solid and permanent resurrection, it must be through the enterprise of Persians, aided it may be by foreign skill and capital, though the less of the latter that is employed the more hopefully I should regard the Persian future. The *Nasiri* Company and the Messrs. Lynch may possibly unite, and the New Road Company may join with them in making a regular transport service by river and road to Tihran, by which England may pour her manufactured goods even into Northern Persia, as this route would compete successfully both with the Baghdad and Trebizond routes.

Already, owing to the improved circumstances of the people, the import of English and Indian cotton goods and of sugar has increased; the latter, which is French, from its low price, only $2\frac{1}{2}$d. a pound in the Gulf, pushing its way as far north as Sultanabad. Unfortunately the shadow of Russia hangs over the future of Persia.]

At present two English and four Turkish boats run on the Tigris. They are necessarily of light draught, as the river is shallow at certain seasons and is full of shifting sand-banks. The *Mejidieh* is a comfortable boat, with a superabundance of excellent food. Her saloon, state-rooms, and engines are on the main deck, which is open fore and aft, and has above it a fine hurricane deck, on the fore part of which the deck passengers, a motley crowd, encamp. She is fully loaded with British goods.

The first object of passing interest was Kornah, reputed among the Arabs to be the site of the Garden of Eden, a tongue of land at the junction of the Tigris and Euphrates. The "Garden of Eden" contains a village, and bright fires burned in front of the mat-and-mud houses. Women in red and white, and turbaned men in brown, flitted across the firelight; there was a mass of vegetation, chiefly palms with a number of native vessels moored to their stems, and a leaning minaret. A frosty moonlight glorified the broad, turbid waters, Kornah and the Euphrates were left in shadow, and we turned up the glittering waterway of the Tigris. The night was too keenly frosty for any dreams of Paradise, even in this classic Chaldæa, and under a sky blazing down to the level horizon with the countless stars which were not to outnumber the children of "Faithful Abraham."

Four hours after leaving Kornah we passed the reputed tomb of Ezra the prophet. At a distance and in the moonlight it looked handsome. There is a buttressed river wall, and above it some long flat-roofed buildings, the centre one surmounted by a tiled dome. The Tigris is so fierce and rapid, and swallows its alluvial banks so greedily, that it is probable that some of the buildings described by the Hebrew traveller Benjamin of Tudela as existing in the twelfth century were long since carried away. The tomb is held in great veneration not only by Jews and Moslems but also by Oriental Christians. It is a great place of Jewish pilgrimage, and is so venerated by the Arabs that it needs no guard.[1]

[1] Sir A. H. Layard describes the interior of the domed building as consisting of two chambers, the outer one empty, and the inner one containing the Prophet's tomb, built of bricks covered with white stucco, and enclosed in a wooden case or ark, over which is thrown a large blue cloth, fringed with yellow tassels, the name of the donor being inscribed in Hebrew characters upon it. — Layard's *Early Adventures*, vol. i. p. 214.

Hadji brought my breakfast, or as he called it, "the grub," the next morning, and I contemplated the Son of Abraham with some astonishment. He had discarded his turban and *abba*, and looked a regular uncivilised desert Ishmaelite, with knives and rosaries in his belt, and his head muffled in a *kiffiyeh*, a yellow silk shawl striped with red, with one point and tassels half a yard long hanging down his back, and fastened round his head by three coils of camel's-hair rope. A loose coat with a gay girdle, "breeks" of some kind, loose boots turned up at the toes and reaching to the knees, and a striped under-garment showing here and there, completed his costume.

The view from the hurricane deck, though there are no striking varieties, is too novel to be monotonous. The level plains of Chaldæa, only a few feet higher than the Tigris, stretch away to the distant horizon, unbroken until to-day, when low hills, white with the first snows of winter, are softly painted on a pure blue sky, very far away. The plains are buff and brown, with an occasional splash, near villages as buff and brown as the soil out of which they rise, of the dark-green of date gardens, or the vivid green of winter wheat. With the exception of these gardens, which are rarely seen, the vast expanse is un-broken by a tree. A few miserable shrubs there are, the *mimosa agrestis* or St. John's bread, and a scrubby tamarisk, while liquorice, wormwood, capers, and some alkaline plants which camels love, are recognisable even in their withered condition.

There are a few villages of low mud hovels enclosed by square mud walls, and hamlets of mat huts, the mats being made of woven sedges and flags, strengthened by palm fronds, but oftener by the tall, tough stems of growing reeds bent into arches, and woven together by the long leaves of aquatic plants, chiefly rushes. The hovels, so ingeniously constructed, are shared indiscriminately by the Arabs and their animals, and crowds of women and children emerged from them as we passed. Each village has its arrangement for raising water from the river.

Boats under sail, usually a fleet at a time, hurry down-stream, owing more to the strong current than to the breeze, or are hauled up laboriously against both by their Arab crews.

The more distant plain is sparsely sprinkled with clusters of brown tents, long and low, and is dotted over with flocks of large brown sheep, shepherded by Arabs in *kiffiyehs*, each shepherd armed with a long gun slung over his shoulder. Herds of cattle and strings of camels move slowly over the brown plain, and companies of men on horseback, with long guns and lances, gallop up to the river bank, throw their fiery horses on their haunches, and after a moment of gratified curiosity wheel round and gallop back to the desert from which they came. Occasionally a stretch of arable land is being ploughed up by small buffaloes with most primitive ploughs, but the plains are pastoral chiefly, tents and flocks are their chief features—features which have changed little since the great Sheikh Abraham, whose descendants now people them, left his "kindred" in the not distant Ur of the Chaldees, and started on the long march to Canaan.

Reedy marshes, alive with water-fowl, arable lands, bare buff plains, brown tents, brown flocks, mat huts, mud and brick villages, groups of women and children, flights of armed horsemen, alternate rapidly, — the unchanging features are the posts and wires of the telegraph.

The Tigris in parts is wonderfully tortuous, and at one great bend, "The Devil's Elbow," a man on foot can walk the distance in less than an hour which takes the steamer four hours to accomplish. The current is very

strong, and the slow progress is rendered slower at this
season of low water by the frequent occurrence of sand-
banks, of which one is usually made aware by a jolt, a
grinding sound, a cessation of motion, some turns astern,
and then full speed ahead, which often overcomes the
obstacle.   Some hours' delay and the floats of one paddle-
wheel injured were the most serious disasters brought
about; and in spite of the shallows at this season, the
Tigris is a noble river, and the voyage is truly fascinating.
Not that there are many remarkable objects, but the
desert atmosphere and the desert freedom are in themselves delightful, the dust and *débris* are the dust and
débris of mighty empires, and there are countless
associations with the earliest past of which we have any
records.

Aimarah, a rising Turkish town of about 7000 people,
built at a point where the river turns at a sharp angle
to the left, is interesting as showing what commerce can
create even here, in less than twenty years.   A caravan
route into Persia was opened and Aimarah does a somewhat busy trade.   Flat-faced brick buildings, with projecting lattice windows, run a good way along the left
bank of the river, which is so steep and irregular that
the crowd which thronged it when the steamer made
fast was shown to great advantage—Osmanlis, Greeks,
Persians, Sabeans, Jews of great height and superb
physique, known by much-tasselled turbans, and a predominating Arab element.

We walked down the long, broad, covered bazar,
with a broken water channel in the middle, where there
were crowds, solely of men, meat, game, bread, fruit,
grain, lentils, horse-shoes, pack saddles, Manchester
cottons, money-changers, silversmiths, and scribes, and
heard the roar of business, and the thin shouts of boys
unaccustomed to the sight of European women.   The

crowds pressed and followed, picking at my clothes, and singing snatches of songs which were not complimentary. It had not occurred to me that I was violating rigid custom in appearing in a hat and gauze veil rather than in a *chadar* and face cloth, but the mistake was made unpleasantly apparent. In Moslem towns women go about in companies and never walk with men.

We visited an enclosed square, where there are barracks for *zaptiehs* (gendarmes), the Kadi's court, and the prison, which consists of an open grating like that of a menagerie, a covered space behind, and dark cells or dens opening upon it, all better than the hovels of the peasantry. There were a number of prisoners well clothed, and apparently well fed, to whom we were an obvious diversion, but the guards gesticulated, shouted, and brandished their side-arms, making us at last understand that our presence in front of the grating was forbidden. After seeing a large barrack yard, and walking, still pursued by a crowd, round the forlorn out-skirts of Aimarah, which include a Sabean village, we visited the gold and silversmiths' shops where the Sabeans were working at their craft, of which in this region they have nearly a monopoly, not only settling temporarily in the towns, but visiting the Arab encampments on the plains, where they are always welcome as the makers and repairers of the ornaments with which the women are loaded. These craftsmen and others of the race whom I have seen differ greatly from the Arabs in appearance, being white rather than brown, very white, *i.e.* very pale, with jet-black hair; large, gentle, intelligent eyes; small, straight noses, and small, well-formed mouths. The handsome faces of these "Christians of St. John" are very pleasing in their expression, and there was a dainty cleanliness about their persons and white cloth-ing significant of those frequent ablutions of both which are so remarkable a part of their religion. The children at Aimarah, and generally in the riparian villages, wear very handsome chased, convex silver links, each as large as the top of a breakfast cup, to fasten their girdles.

The reedy marshes, the haunts of pelicans and pigs, are left behind at Aimarah, and tamarisk scrub and liquorice appear on the banks. At Kut-al-Aimarah, a small military post and an Arab town of sun-dried bricks on the verge of a high bank above the Tigris, we landed again, and ragamuffin boys pressed very much upon us, and ragamuffin *zaptiehs*,[1] grotesquely dressed in clothes of different European nationalities, pelted them with stones. To take up stones and throw them at unwelcome visitors is a frequent way of getting rid of them in the less civilised parts of the East.

A *zaptieh* station, barracks, with a large and badly-kept parade ground, a covered bazar well supplied, houses with blank walls, large *cafés* with broad matted benches, asafœtida, crowds of men of superb *physique,* picturesque Arabs on high-bred horses, and a total invisibility of women, were the salient features of Kut-al-Aimarah. Big-masted, high-stemmed boats, the broad, turbid Tigris with a great expanse of yellowish sand on its farther shore, reeds " shaken with the wind," and a windy sky, heavily overcast, made up the view from the bank. There were seen for the first time by the new-comers the most venerable boats in the world, for they were old even when Herodotus mentions them—*kufas* or *gophers*, very deep round baskets covered with bitumen, with incurved tops, and worked by one man with a paddle. These remarkable tubs are used for the conveyance of passengers, goods, and even animals.

---

[1] A year later in Kurdistan, the *zaptiehs,* all time-expired soldiers and well set up soldierly men, wore neat, serviceable, dark blue braided uniforms, and high riding-boots.

Before leaving we visited the Arab Khan or Sheikh in his house. He received us in an upper room of difficult access, carpeted with very handsome rugs, and with a divan similarly covered, but the walls of brown mud were not even plastered. His manner was dignified and courteous, and his expression remarkably shrewd. A number of men sitting on the floor represented by

A GOPHER.

their haughty aspect and magnificent *physique* the royalty of the Ishmaelite descent from Abraham. This Khan said that his tribe could put 3000 fighting men into the field, but it was obvious that its independence is broken, and that these tribal warriors are reckoned as Osmanli irregulars or Bashi Bazouks. The Khan remarked that "the English do not make good friends, for," he added, "they back out when difficulties arise."

On board the steamer the condition of the Arabs is

much discussed, and the old residents describe it as steadily growing worse under the oppression and corruption of the Osmanli officials, who appear to be doing their best to efface these fine riparian tribes by merciless exactions coming upon the top of taxation so heavy as to render agriculture unprofitable, the impositions actually driving thousands of them to seek a living in the cities and to the Persian shores of the Gulf, where they exchange a life of hereditary freedom for a precarious and often scanty subsistence among unpropitious surroundings. Still, the Arab of the desert is not conquered by the Turks.

LETTER I (*Continued*)

BAGHDAD, *Jan. 5.*

THE last day on the Tigris passed as pleasantly as its predecessors. There was rain in the early morning, then frost which froze the rain on deck, and at 7 A.M. the mercury in my cabin stood at 28°.

In the afternoon the country became more populous, that is, there were *kraals* of mat huts at frequent intervals, and groups of tents to which an external wall of mats gave a certain aspect of permanence. Increased cultivation accompanied the increased population. In some places the ground was being scratched with a primitive plough of unshod wood, or a branch of a tree slightly trimmed, leaving a scar about two inches deep. These scars, which pass for furrows, are about ten inches apart, and camel thorn, tamarisk, and other shrubs inimical to crops stand between them. The seed is now being sown. After it comes up it grows apace, and in spite of shallow scratches, camel thorn, and tamarisk the tilth is so luxuriant that the husbandmen actually turn cattle and sheep into it for two or three weeks, and then leave it to throw up the ear! They say that there are from eighteen to thirty-five stalks from each seed in consequence of this process! The harvest is reaped in April, after which water covers the land.

Another style of cultivation is adopted for land, of which we saw a good deal, very low lying, and annually overflowed, usually surrounding a nucleus of permanent marsh. This land, after the water dries up, is destitute of vegetation, and presents a smooth, moist surface full of cracks, which scales off later. No scratching is needed for this soil. The seed is sown broadcast over it, and such of it as is not devoured by birds falls into the cracks, and produces an abundant crop. All this rich alluvial soil is stoneless, but is strewn from Seleucia to Babylon with fragments of glass, bricks, and pottery. Artificial mounds also abound, and remains of canals, all denoting that these fertile plains in ancient days supported a large stationary population. Of all that once was, this swirling river alone remains, singing in every eddy and ripple—

> " For men may come and men may go,
>   But I go on for ever."

As we were writing in the evening we were nearly thrown off our chairs by running aground with a thump, which injured one paddle wheel and obliged us to lie up part of the night for repairs near the ruins of the ancient palace of Ctesiphon. Seleucia, on the right bank of the river, is little more now than a historic name, but the palace of Tak-i-Kasr, with its superb archway 100 feet in height, has been even in recent times magnificent enough in its ruin to recall the glories of the Parthian kings, and the days when, according to Gibbon, " Khosroes Nushirwan gave audience to the ambassadors of the world " within its stately walls. Its gaunt and shattered remains have even still a mournful grandeur about them, but they have suffered so severely from the barbarous removal of the stones and the fall of much of the front as to be altogether disappointing.

Soon after leaving Ctesiphon there is increased cultivation, and within a few miles of Baghdad the banks

of the river, which is its great high road, become
populous. " Palatial residences," in which the women's
apartments are indicated by the blankness of their walls,
are mixed up with mud hovels and goat's-hair tents;
there are large farmhouses with enclosures for cattle and
horses; date gardens and orange groves fringe the
stream, and arrangements for drawing water are let into
its banks at frequent intervals. Strings of asses laden
with country produce, companies of horsemen and innumerable foot passengers, all moved citywards.

The frosty sun rose out of an orange sky as a disc
of blood and flame, but the morning became misty and
overcast, so that the City of the Arabian Nights did not
burst upon the view in any halo of splendour. A few
tiled minarets, the blue domes of certain mosques,
handsome houses,—some of them European Consulates,
half hidden by orange groves laden with their golden
fruitage,—a picturesque bridge of boats, a dense growth
of palms on the right bank, beyond which gleam the
golden domes of Kazimain and the top of Zobeide's tomb,
the superannuated British gun-boat *Comet*, two steamers,
a crowd of native craft, including *kufas* or *gophers*, a
prominent Custom-house, and decayed alleys opening on
the water, make up the Baghdad of the present as seen
from the *Mejidieh's* deck.

As soon as we anchored swarms of *kufas* clustered
round us, and swarms of officials and *hamals* (porters)
invaded the deck. Some of the passengers had landed
two hours before, others had proceeded to their destina-
tions at once, and as my friends had not come off I was
alone for some time in the middle of a tremendous
Babel, in which every man shouted at the top of his
voice and all together, Hadji assuming a deportment of
childish helplessness. Certain officials under cover of
bribes lavished on my behalf by a man who spoke

English professed to let my baggage pass unopened, then a higher official with a sword knocked Hadji down, then a man said that everything would be all right if I would bestow another gold *lira*, about £1, on the officers, and I was truly glad when kind Captain Dougherty with Dr. Sutton came alongside in the *Comet's* boat, and brought me ashore. The baggage was put into another of her boats, but as soon as we were out of sight it was removed, and was taken to the Custom-house, where they insisted that some small tent poles in a cover were guns, and smashed a box of dates in the idea that it was tobacco !

The Church Mission House, in which I am receiving hospitality, is a "native" house, though built and decorated by Persians, as also are several of the Consulates. It is in a narrow roadway with blank walls, a part of the European quarter; a door of much strength admits into a small courtyard, round which are some of the servants' quarters and reception rooms for Moslem visitors, and within this again is a spacious and handsome courtyard, round which are kitchens, domestic offices, and the *serdabs*, which play an important part in Eastern life.

These *serdabs* are semi-subterranean rooms, usually with arched fronts, filled in above-ground with lattice-work. They are lofty, and their vaulted roofs are supported in rich men's houses on pillars. The well of the household is often found within. The general effect of this one is that of a crypt, and it was most appropriate for the Divine Service in English which greeted my arrival. The cold of it was, however, frightful. It was only when the Holy Communion was over that I found that I was wearing Hadji's revolver and cartridge belt under my cloak, which he had begged me to put on to save them from confiscation ! In these vaulted chambers both Europeans and natives spend the hot season, sleeping at night on the roofs.

Above this lower floor are the winter apartments, which open upon a fine stone balcony running round three sides of the court.   On the river side of the house there is an orange garden, which just now might be the garden of the Hesperides, and a terrace, below which is the noble, swirling Tigris, and beyond, a dark belt of palms.   These rooms on the river front have large projecting windows, six in a row, with screens which slide up and down, and those which look to the court-yard are secluded by very beautiful fretwork.   The drawing-room, used as a dormitory, is a superb room, in which exquisitely beautiful ceiling and wall decorations in shades of fawn enriched with gold, and fretwork windows, suggest Oriental feeling at every turn.   The plaster-work of this room is said to be distinctively Persian and is very charming.   The house, though large, is inconveniently crowded, with the medical and clerical mission families, two lady missionaries, and two guests. Each apartment has two rows of vaulted recesses in its walls, and very fine cornices above.   It is impossible to warm the rooms, but the winter is very short and brilliant, and after ulsters, greatcoats, and fur cloaks have been worn for breakfast, the sun mitigates the temperature.

I. L. B.

LETTER II

BAGHDAD, *Jan. 9.*

BAGHDAD is too well known from the careful descriptions given of it by Eastern travellers to justify me in lingering upon it in detail, and I will only record a few impressions, which are decidedly *couleur de rose,* for the weather is splendid, making locomotion a pleasure, and the rough, irregular roadways which at other seasons are deep in foul and choking dust, or in mud and pestilential slime, are now firm and not remarkably dirty.

A little earlier than this the richer inhabitants, who have *warstled* through the summer in their dim and latticed *serdabs,* emerge and pitch their tents in the plains of Ctesiphon, where the men find a stimulating amusement in hunting the boar, but it is now the "season" in the city, the liveliest and busiest time of the year. The cholera, which is believed to have claimed 6000 victims, has departed, and the wailing of the women, which scarcely ceased day or night for a month, is silent. The Jewish troubles, which apparently rose out of the indignation of the Moslems at the burial within the gates, contrary to a strict edict on the subject, of a Rabbi who died of cholera, have subsided, and the motley populations and their yet more motley creeds are for the time at peace.

In the daytime there is a roar or hum of business, mingled with braying of asses, squeals of belligerent horses, yells of camel-drivers and muleteers, beating of drums, shouts of beggars, hoarse-toned ejaculations of fakirs, ear-splitting snatches of discordant music, and in short a chorus of sounds unfamiliar to Western ears, but the nights are so still that the swirl of the Tigris as it hurries past is distinctly heard. Only the long melancholy call to prayer, or the wail of women over the dead, or the barking of dogs, breaks the silence which at sunset falls as a pall over Baghdad.

Under the blue sunny sky the river view is very fine. The river itself is imposing from its breadth and volume, and in the gorgeous sunsets, with a sky of crimson flame, and the fronds of the dark date palms mirrored in its reddened waters, it looks really beautiful. The city is stately enough as far as the general *coup-d'œil* of the river front goes, and its river *façade* agreeably surprises me. The Tigris, besides being what may be called the main street, divides Baghdad into two unequal parts, and though the city on the left bank has almost a monopoly of picturesque and somewhat stately irregularity in the houses of fair height, whose lattices and oriel windows overhang the stream from an environment of orange gardens, the dark date groves dignify the meaner buildings of the right bank. The rush of a great river is in itself attractive, and from the roof of this house the view is fascinating, with the ceaseless movements of hundreds of boats and *kufas*, the constant traffic of men, horses, asses, and caravans across the great bridge of boats, and the long lines of buildings which with more or less picturesqueness line the great waterway.

Without the wearisomeness of sight-seeing there is much to be seen in Baghdad, and though much that would be novel to a new-comer from the West is familiar to me after two years of Eastern travel, there is a great deal that is really interesting. The *kufas* accumulating

at their landing, freighted with the products of the Upper
Tigris, the transpontine city, in which country produce
takes the foremost place ; the tramway to Kazimain constructed during the brief valiship of Midhat Pasha, on
which the last journey of the day is always performed at
a gallop, *coûte que coûte* ; the caravans of asses, each one
with a huge fish, the " Fish of Tobias," hanging across its
back ; the strings of the same humble animal, carrying
skins of water from the river throughout the city ; the
tombs, the mosques, the churches, the great caravans of
mules and camels, almost monopolising the narrow roadways, Arabs and Osmanlis on showy horses, Persians,
Turks, Arabs, Jews, Armenians, Chaldæans, in all the
variety of their picturesque national costumes, to which
the niggardly clothing of a chance European acts as an
ungraceful foil ; Persian dead, usually swaddled, making
their last journey on mule or horseback to the holy
ground at Kerbela, and the occasional march of horse or
foot through the thronged bazars, are among the hourly
sights of a city on which European influence is scarcely
if at all perceptible.

Turkish statistics must be received with caution, and
the population of Baghdad may not reach 120,000 souls,
but it has obviously recovered wonderfully from the
effects of war, plague, inundation, and famine, and looks
busy and fairly prosperous, so much so indeed that the
account given of its misery and decay in Mr. Baillie
Fraser's charming *Travels in Kurdistan* reads like a story
of the last century.   If nothing remains of the glories of
the city of the Caliphs, it is certainly for Turkey a busy,
growing, and passably wealthy nineteenth-century capital.
It is said to have a hundred mosques, twenty-six minarets,
and fifteen domes, but I have not counted them !

Its bazars, which many people regard as the finest in
the East outside of Stamboul, are of enormous extent and

very great variety. Many are of brick, with well-built domed roofs, and sides arcaded both above and below, and are wide and airy. Some are of wood, all are covered, and admit light scantily, only from the roof. Those which supply the poorer classes are apt to be ruinous and squalid—"*ramshackle*," to say the truth, with an air of decay about them, and their roofs are merely rough timber, roughly thatched with reeds or date tree fronds. Of splendour there is none anywhere, and of cleanliness there are few traces. The old, narrow, and filthy bazars in which the gold and silversmiths ply their trade are of all the most interesting. The trades have their separate localities, and the buyer who is in search of cotton goods, silk stuffs, carpets, cotton yarn, gold and silver thread, ready-made clothing, weapons, saddlery, rope, fruit, meat, grain, fish, jewellery, muslins, copper pots, etc., has a whole alley of contiguous shops devoted to the sale of the same article to choose from.

At any hour of daylight at this season progress through the bazars is slow. They are crowded, and almost entirely with men. It is only the poorer women who market for themselves, and in twos and threes, at certain hours of the day. In a whole afternoon, among thousands of men, I saw only five women, tall, shapeless, badly-made-up bundles, carried mysteriously along, rather by high, loose, canary-yellow leather boots than by feet. The face is covered with a thick black gauze mask, or cloth, and the head and remainder of the form with a dark blue or black sheet, which is clutched by the hand below the nose. The walk is one of tottering decrepitude. All the business transacted in the bazars is a matter of bargaining, and as Arabs shout at the top of their voices, and buyers and sellers are equally keen, the roar is tremendous.

Great *cafés*, as in Cairo, occur frequently. In the

larger ones from a hundred to two hundred men are seen lounging at one time on the broad matted seats, shouting, chaffering, drinking coffee or *sharbat* and smoking *chibouks* or *kalians*. Negro attendants supply their wants. These *cafés* are the clubs of Baghdad. Whatever of public opinion exists in a country where the recognised use of words is to "conceal thought," is formed in them. They are centres of business likewise, and much of the noise is due to bargaining, and they are also manufactories of rumours, scandals, and fanaticism. The great caravan-serais, such as the magnificent Khan Othman, are also resorts of merchants for the display and sale of their goods.

Europeans never make purchases in the bazars. They either have the goods from which they wish to make a choice brought to their houses, or their servants bargain for them, getting a commission both from buyer and seller.

The splendour of the East, if it exists at all, is not to be seen in the bazars. The jewelled daggers, the cloth of silver and gold, the diaphanous silk tissues, the brocaded silks, the rich embroideries, the damascened sword blades, the finer carpets, the inlaid armour, the cunning work in brass and inlaid bronze, and all the articles of *vertu* and *bric-à-brac* of real or spurious value, are carefully concealed by their owners, and are carried for display, with much secrecy and mystery, to the houses of their ordinary customers, and to such European strangers as are reported to be willing to be victimised.

Trade in Baghdad is regarded by Europeans and large capitalists as growing annually more depressed and unsatisfactory, but this is not the view of the small traders, chiefly Jews and Christians, who start with a capital of £5 or upwards, and by buying some cheap lot in Bombay, — gay handkerchiefs, perfumery, shoes, socks, buttons, tin boxes with mirror lids, scissors, pocket-knives, toys, and the like,—bid fair to make small fortunes. The amount of perfumery and rubbish piled in these ramshackle shops is wonderful. The trader who picks up a desert Arab for a customer and sells him a knife, or a mirror box, or a packet of candles is likely to attract to himself a large trade, for when once the unmastered pastoral hordes of Al Jazīra, Trak, and Stramīya see such objects, the desire of possession is aroused, and the refuse of Manchester and Birmingham will find its way into every tent in the desert.

The best bazars are the least crowded, though once in them it is difficult to move, and the strings of asses laden with skins of water are a great nuisance. The foot-passenger is also liable at any moment to be ridden down by horsemen, or squeezed into a jelly by the passage of caravans.

It is in the meat, vegetable, cotton, oil, grain, fruit, and fish bazars that the throngs are busiest and noisiest, and though cucumbers, the great joy of the Turkish palate, are over, vegetables "of sorts" are abundant, and the slant, broken sunbeams fall on pyramids of fruit, and glorify the warm colouring of melons, apples, and pomegranates.

A melon of 10 lbs. weight can be got for a penny, a sheep for five or six shillings, and fish for something like a farthing per pound, that is the " Fish of Tobias," the monster of the Tigris waters, which is largely eaten by the poor. Poultry and game are also very cheap, and the absolute necessaries of life, such as broken wheat for porridge, oil, flour, and cheese, cost little.

Cook-shops abound, but their viands are not tempting, and the bazars are pervaded by a pungent odour of hot sesamum oil and rancid fat, frying being a usual mode of cooking in these restaurants. An impassive Turk, silently smoking, sits cross-legged on a platform at each Turkish shop door. He shows his goods as if he had no interest in them, and whether he sells or not seems a matter of indifference, so that he can return to his pipe. It is not to him that the overpowering din is owing, but to the agitated eagerness of the other nationalities.

The charm of the bazars lies in the variety of race and costume and in the splendid *physique* of the greater number of the men. The European looks "nowhere." The natural look of a Moslem is one of *hauteur*, but no words can describe the scorn and lofty Pharisaism which sit on the faces of the Seyyids, the descendants of Mohammed, whose hands and even garments are kissed reverently as they pass through the crowd ; or the wrathful melancholy mixed with pride which gives a fierceness to the dignified bearing of the magnificent beings who glide through the streets, their white turbans or shawl headgear, their gracefully flowing robes, their richly embroidered under-vests, their Kashmir girdles, their inlaid pistols, their silver-hilted dirks, and the predominance of red throughout their clothing aiding the general effect. Yet most of these grand creatures, with their lofty looks and regal stride, would be accessible to a bribe, and would not despise even a perquisite. These are the *mollahs*, the scribes, the traders, and the merchants of the city.

The Bedouin and the city Arabs dress differently, and are among the marked features of the streets. The under-dress is a very coarse shirt of unbleached homespun cotton, rarely clean, over which the Sheikhs and richer men wear a robe of striped silk or cotton with a Kashmir girdle of a shawl pattern in red on a white ground. The poor wear shirts of coarse hair or cotton, without a robe. The invariable feature of Arab dress is the *abba*—a long cloak, sleeveless, but with holes through which to pass the arms, and capable of many adaptations. It conceals all superabundance and deficiency of attire, and while it has the dignity of the *toga* by day it has the utility of a blanket by night. The better-class *abba* is very hard, being made of closely-woven worsted, in broad brown and white or black and white perpendicular stripes. The poorest *abba* is of coarse brown worsted, and even of goat's-hair. I saw many men who were destitute of any clothing but tattered *abbas* tied round their waists by frayed hair ropes. The *abba* is the distinctive national costume of the Arabs. The head-gear is not the turban but a shawl of very thick silk woven in irregular stripes of yellow and red, with long cords and tassels depending, made of the twisted woof. This handsome square is doubled triangularly, the double end hangs down the back, and the others over the shoulders. A loosely-twisted rope of camel's-hair is wound several times round the crown of the head. When the weather is cold, being like all Orientals very sensitive in their heads, they bring one side of the shawl over the whole of the face but the eyes, and tuck it in, in great cold only exposing one eye, and in great heat also. Most Moslems shave the head, but the Arabs let their hair grow very long, and wear it in a number of long plaits, and these elf-locks mixed up with the long coloured tassels of the *kiffiyeh*, and the dark glittering eyes looking out from under the yellow silk, give them an appearance of extreme wildness, aided by the long guns which they carry and their long desert stride.

The Arab moves as if he were the ruler of the country, though the grip of the Osmanli may be closing on him. His eyes are deeply set under shaggy eyebrows, his nose is high and sharp, he is long and thin, his profile suggests a bird of prey, and his demeanour a fierce independence.

The Arab women go about the streets unveiled, and with the *abba* covering their very poor clothing, but it is not clutched closely enough to conceal the extraordinary tattooing which the Bedouin women everywhere regard as ornamental.　There are artists in Baghdad who make their living by this mode of decorating the person, and vie with each other in the elaboration of their patterns. I saw several women tattooed with two wreaths of blue flowers on their bosoms linked by a blue chain, palm fronds on the throat, stars on the brow and chin, and bands round the wrists and ankles.　These disfigurements, and large gold or silver filigree buttons placed outside one nostril by means of a wire passed through it, worn by married women, are much admired.　When these women sell country produce in the markets, they cover their heads with the ordinary *chadar*.

The streets are narrow, and the walls, which are built of fire-burned bricks, are high.　Windows to the streets are common, and the oriel windows, with their warm brown lattices projecting over the roadways at irregular heights, are strikingly picturesque.　Not less so are latticework galleries, which are often thrown across the street to connect the two houses of wealthy residents, and the sitting-rooms with oriel windows, which likewise bridge the roadways.　Solid doorways with iron-clasped and iron-studded doors give an impression of security, and suggest comfort and to some extent home life, and sprays of orange trees, hanging over walls, and fronds of date palms give an aspect of pleasantness to the courtyards.

The best parts of the city, where the great bazars, large dwelling-houses, and most of the mosques are, is surrounded by a labyrinth of alleys, fringing off into streets growing meaner till they cease altogether among open spaces, given up to holes, heaps, rubbish, the slaughter of animals, and in some favoured spots to the production of vegetables. Then come the walls, which are of kiln-burned bricks, and have towers intended for guns at intervals. The wastes within the walls have every element of decay and meanness, the wastes without, where the desert sands sweep up to the very foot of the fortifications, have many elements of grandeur.

Baghdad is altogether built of chrome-yellow kiln-dried bricks. There are about twenty-five kilns, chiefly in the hands of Jews and Christians in the wastes outside the city, but the demand exceeds the supply, not for building only, but for the perpetual patchings which houses, paths, and walls are always requiring, owing to the absorption of moisture in the winter.

Bricks at the kilns sell for 36s. per thousand twelve inches square, and 18s. per thousand seven inches square. They are carried from the kilns on donkeys, small beasts, each taking ten large or twenty-five small bricks.

Unskilled labour is abundant. Men can be engaged at 9d. a day, and boys for 5d.

This afternoon, in the glory of a sunset which reddened the yellow waste up to the distant horizon, a caravan of mules, mostly in single file, approached the city. Each carried two or four white bales slung on his sides, or two or more long boxes, consisting of planks roped rather than nailed together. This is the fashion in which thousands of Persian Moslems (Shiahs or "Sectaries") have been conveyed for ages for final burial at Kerbela, the holiest place of the Shiahs, an easy journey from Baghdad, where rest the ashes of Ali, regarded as scarcely second to Mohammed, and of Houssein and Hassan his sons, whose "martyrdom" is annually commemorated by a Passion Play which is acted in every town and village in Persia. To make a pilgrimage to Kerbela, or to rest finally in its holy dust, or both,

constitutes the ambition of every Shiah. The Sunnis, or
"Orthodox," who hate the Shiahs, are so far kept in check
that these doleful caravans are not exposed to any worse
molestation than the shouts and ridicule of street Arabs.

The mode of carrying the dead is not reverent. The
katirgis, who contract for the removal, hurry the bodies
along as goods, and pile them in the yards of the
caravanserais at night, and the mournful journey is
performed, oftener than not, without the presence of
relations, each body being ticketed with the name once
borne by its owner. Some have been exhumed and are
merely skeletons, others are in various stages of decomposition, and some are of the newly dead.[1]

Outside the walls predatory Arabs render the roads
unsafe for solitary travellers, and at times for feeble caravans; but things in this respect are better than they were.

Visits to the Armenian and Chaldæan Churches, to
the Mosque of Abdel Kader, with its courts thronged by
Afghan pilgrims, and to the Jewish quarter, have been
very interesting. There are said to be 30,000 Jews
here, and while a large proportion of them are in
poverty, on the whole they are an influential nationality,
and some of them are very rich.

Through the liberality of Sir Albert Sassoon a Jewish
High School has been opened, where an admirable education
is given. I was extremely pleased with it, and with the
director, who speaks French fluently, and with the pro-
ficiency in French of the elder students. He describes
their earnestness and energetic application as being most
remarkable.

The French Carmelite monks have a large, solid

---

[1] I heard that the Shah had prohibited this "Dead March" to Kerbela,
on account of the many risks to the public health involved in it, but
nearly a year later, in Persian Kurdistan, I met, besides thousands of
living pilgrims, a large caravan of the dead.

" Mission Church " or Cathedral with a fine peal of bells, and a very prosperous school attached, in which are boys belonging to all the many creeds professed in Baghdad. The sisters of St. Joseph have a school for girls, which Turkish children are not slow to avail themselves of. The sisters find a remarkable unhandiness among the women. Few, if any, among them have any idea of cutting out or repairing, and rich and poor are equally incapable of employing their fingers usefully.

The people here are so used to the sight of Europeans that it is quite easy for foreign ladies to walk in this quarter only attended by a servant, and I have accompanied Mrs. Sutton on visits to several Armenian houses. The Armenians are in many cases wealthy, as their admirably-designed and well-built houses testify. The Christian population is estimated at 5000, and its wealth and energy give it greater importance than its numbers warrant. One of the houses which we visited was truly beautiful and in very good taste, the solidity of the stone and brickwork, the finish of the wood, and the beauty of the designs and their execution in hammered iron being quite remarkable. The lofty roofs and cornices are elaborately worked in plaster, and this is completely concealed by hundreds or thousands of mirrors set so as to resemble facets, so that roof and cornices flash like diamonds. This is a Persian style of decoration, and is extremely effective in large handsome rooms. Superb carpets and divans and tea tables inlaid with mother-of-pearl furnish the reception and smoking rooms, and the bedrooms and nurseries over which we were taken were simply arranged with French bedsteads and curtains of Nottingham mosquito net. As in other Eastern houses, there were no traces of occupation, no morning room or den sacred to litter; neither was there anything to look at—the opposite extreme from our overloaded drawing-rooms—or any library. Cigarettes and black coffee in minute porcelain cups, in gold filigree receptacles, were presented on each occasion, and the kind and courteous intention was very pleasing.

The visits which I paid with Dr. Sutton were very different. He has worked as a medical missionary here for some years, and his unaffected benevolence and quiet attention to all suffering persons, without distinction of race or creed, and his recent extraordinary labours by night and day among the cholera-smitten people, have won for him general esteem and confidence, and he is even allowed to enter Moslem houses and prescribe for the women in some cases.

The dispensary, in which there is not half enough accommodation, is very largely attended by people of all creeds, and even Moslem women, though exclusively of the poorer classes, avail themselves of it. Yesterday, when I was there, the comfortable seats of the cheerful matted waiting-room were all occupied by Armenian and Chaldæan women, unveiled and speaking quite freely to Dr. Sutton; while a few Moslem women, masked rather than veiled, and enveloped in black sheets, cowered on the floor and scarcely let their voices be heard even in a tremulous whisper.

I am always sorry to see any encroachment made by Christian teachers on national customs where they are not contrary to morality, and willingly leave to Eastern women the *pardah* and the veil, but still there is a wholesomeness about the unveiled, rosy, comely, frank faces of these Christian women. But—and it is a decided but—though the women were comely, and though some of the Armenian girls are beautiful, every one has one or more flattish depressions on her face—scars in fact—the size of a large date stone. Nearly the whole population is thus disfigured. So universal is it among the fair-

skinned Armenian girls, that so far from being regarded as
a blemish, it is viewed as a token of good health, and it is
said that a young man would hesitate to ask for the
hand of a girl in marriage if she had not a "date mark"
on her face.

These "date boils," or "Baghdad boils," as they are
sometimes called, are not slow in attacking European
strangers, and few, if any, escape during their residence
here. As no cause can reasonably be assigned for them,
so no cure has been found. Various remedies, including
cauterisation, have been tried, but without success, and
it is now thought wisest to do nothing more than keep
them dry and clean, and let them run their natural course,
which lasts about a year. Happily they are not so painful as ordinary boils. The malady appears at first as a
white point, not larger than a pin's head, and remains
thus for about three months. Then the flesh swells,
becomes red and hard and suppurates, and underneath
a rough crust which is formed is corroded and eaten
away as by vitriol. On some strangers the fatal point
appears within a few days of their arrival.

In two years in the East I have not seen any
European welcomed so cordially as Dr. Sutton into
Moslem homes. The *Hakīm*, exhibiting in "quiet continuance in well-doing" the legible and easily-recognised
higher fruits of Christianity, while refraining from harsh
and irreverent onslaughts on the creeds of those whose
sufferings he mitigates, is everywhere blessed.[1]

To my thinking, no one follows in the Master's foot-
prints so closely as the medical missionary, and on
no agency for alleviating human suffering can one look

[1] Six months later a Bakhtiari chief, a bigoted Moslem, said to me at
the conclusion of an earnest plea for European medical advice, "Yes,
Jesus was a great prophet ; *send us a Hakīm in His likeness*," and doubtless
the nearer that likeness is the greater is the success.

with more unqualified satisfaction. The medical mission is the outcome of the living teachings of our faith. I have now visited such missions in many parts of the world, and never saw one which was not healing, helping, blessing; softening prejudice, diminishing suffering, making an end of many of the cruelties which proceed from ignorance, restoring sight to the blind, limbs to the crippled, health to the sick, telling, in every work of love and of consecrated skill, of the infinite compassion of Him who came "not to destroy men's lives, but to save them."

In one house Dr. Sutton was welcome because he had saved a woman's life, in another because a blind youth had received his sight, and so on. Among our visits was one to a poor Moslem family in a very poor quarter. No matter how poor the people are, their rooms stand back from the street, and open on yards more or less mean. It is a misnomer to call this dwelling a house, or to write that it *opens*, for it is merely an arched recess which can never be shut !

In a hole in the middle of an uneven earthen floor there was a fire of tamarisk root and animal fuel, giving off a stinging smoke. On this the broken wheat porridge for supper was being cooked in a copper pot, supported on three rusty cannon-balls. An earthenware basin, a wooden spoon, a long knife, a goat-skin of water, a mallet, a long hen-coop, which had served as the bed for the wife when she was ill, some ugly hens, a clay jar full of grain, two heaps of brick rubbish, and some wadded quilts, which had taken on the prevailing gray-brown colour, were the plenishings of the arch.

Poverty brings one blessing in Turkey—the poor man is of necessity a monogamist. Wretched though the place was, it had the air of home, and the smoky hole in the floor was a fireside. The wife was unveiled and

joined in the conversation, the husband was helping her
to cook the supper, and the children were sitting round
or scrambling over their parents' knees. All looked as
happy as people in their class anywhere. It is good to
have ocular demonstration that such homes exist in
Turkey. God be thanked for them! The man, a fine
frank-looking Turk, welcomed Dr. Sutton jovially. He had
saved the wife's life and was received as their best friend.
Who indeed but the medical missionary would care for
such as them and give them of his skill " without money
and without price " ? The hearty laugh of this Turk was
good to hear, his wife smiled cordially, and the boys
laughed like their father. The eldest, a nice, bright
fellow of nine, taught in the mosque school, was proud to
show how well he could read Arabic, and read part of a
chapter from St. John's Gospel, his parents looking on
with wonder and admiration.

Among the Christian families we called on were those
of the dispenser and catechist—people with very small
salaries but comfortable homes. These families were
living in a house furnished like those of the rich Armenians, but on a very simple scale, the floor and daïs
covered with Persian carpets, the divan with Turkish
woollen stuff, and there were in addition a chair or two,
and silk cushions on the floor. In one room there were
an intelligent elderly woman, a beautiful girl of seventeen, married a few days ago, and wearing her bridal
ornaments, with her husband ; another man and his wife,
and two bright, ruddy-cheeked boys who spoke six
languages. All had " date marks " on their faces. After
a year among Moslems and Hindus, it was startling to
find men and women sitting together, the women unveiled, and taking their share in the conversation merrily
and happily. Even the young bride took the initiative
in talking to Dr. Sutton.

Of course the Christian women cover their faces in the streets, but the covering is of different material and arrangement, and is really magnificent, being of very rich, stiff, corded silk—self-coloured usually—black, heliotrope, or dark blue, with a contrasting colour woven in deep vandykes upon a white ground as a border. The silk is superb, really capable of standing on end with richness. Such a sheet costs about £5. The ambition of every woman is to possess one, and to gratify it she even denies herself in the necessaries of life.

The upper classes of both Moslem and Christian women are rarely seen on foot in the streets except on certain days, as when they visit the churches and the mosques and burial-grounds. Nevertheless they go about a great deal to visit each other, riding on white asses, which are also used by *mollahs* and rich elderly merchants. All asses have their nostrils slit to improve their wind. A good white ass of long pedigree, over thirteen hands high, costs as much as £50. As they are groomed till they look as white as snow, and are caparisoned with red leather trappings embroidered with gold thread and silks, and as a rider on a white ass is usually preceded by runners who shout and brandish sticks to clear the way, this animal always suggests position, or at least wealth.

Women of the upper classes mounted on these asses usually go to pay afternoon visits in companies, with mounted eunuchs and attendants, and men to clear the way. They ride astride with short stirrups, but the rider is represented only by a shapeless blue bundle, out of which protrude two yellow boots. Blacks of the purest negro type frequently attend on women, and indeed consequence is shown by the possession of a number of them.

Of the Georgian and Circassian *belles* of the harams, a single lustrous eye with its brilliancy enhanced by the

use of *kohl* is all that one sees. At the bottom of the
scale are the Arab women and the unsecluded women of
the lower orders generally, who are of necessity drudges,
and are old hags before they are twenty, except in the
few cases in which they do not become mothers, when
the good looks which many of them possess in extreme
youth last a little longer. If one's memories of Baghdad
women were only of those to be seen in the streets, they
would be of leathery, wrinkled faces, prematurely old,
figures which have lost all shape, and henna-stained
hands crinkled and deformed by toil.

Baghdad is busy and noisy with traffic. Great quantities of British goods pass through it to Persia, avoiding
by doing so the horrible rock ladders between Bushire
and Isfahan. The water transit from England and
India, only involving the inconvenience of transhipment
at Basrah, makes Baghdad practically into a seaport, with
something of the bustle and vivacity of a seaport, and
caravans numbering from 20,000 to 26,000 laden mules
are employed in the carriage of goods to and from the
Persian cities. A duty of one per cent is levied on
goods in transit to Persia.[1]

The trade of Baghdad is not to be despised. The
principal articles which were imported from Europe
amounted in 1889 to a value of £621,140, and from
India to £239,940, while the exports from Baghdad to

---

[1] The entire trade of Baghdad is estimated at about £2,500,000, of
which the Persian transit trade is nearly a quarter. The Persian imports
and exports through Baghdad are classified thus : Manufactured goods,
including Manchester piece goods, and continental woollens and cottons,
7000 to 8000 loads. Indian manufactures, 1000 loads. Loaf sugar,
chiefly from Marseilles, 6000 loads. Drugs, pepper, coffee, tea, other
sugars, indigo, cochineal, copper, and spelter, 7000 loads. The Persian
exports for despatch by sea include wool, opium, cotton, carpets, gum,
and dried fruits, and for local consumption, among others, tobacco, *roghan*
(clarified butter), and dried and fresh fruits, with a probable bulk of from
12,000 to 15,000 loads.

Europe and America were valued in the same year at
£469,200, and to India by British India Company
steamers only at £35,150. In looking through the
Consular list of exports, it is interesting to notice that
13,400 cwts. of gum of the value of £70,000 were
exported in 1889. Neither the Indian postage stamps
nor ours should suffer from the partial failure of the
Soudan supply.

Liquorice roots to the value of £7800 were exported
in 1888, almost solely to America, to be used in the
preparation of quid tobacco and " fancy drinks " !

The gall nuts which grow in profusion on the dwarf
oaks which cover many hillsides, were exported last year
to the value of £35,000, to be used chiefly in the production of ink, so closely is commerce binding countries
one to the other.

Two English firms have concessions for pressing wool
and making it into bales suitable for shipment. There
are five principal English firms here, three French, and
six Turkish, not including the small fry. There are five
foreign Consulates.

The carriage of goods is one of the most important of
Persian and Turkish industries, and the breeding of mules
and the manufacture of caravan equipments give extensive
employment; but one shudders to think of the amount
of suffering involved in sore backs and wounds, and of
exhausted and over-weighted animals lying down forlornly
to die, having their eyes picked out before death.

The mercury was at 37° at breakfast-time this morning. Fuel is scarce and dear, some of the rooms are
without fireplaces, and these good people study, write,
and work cheerfully in this temperature in open rooms,
untouched by the early sun.

The preparations for to-morrow's journey are nearly
complete. Three mules have been engaged for the

baggage—one for Hadji, and a saddle mule for myself; stores, a revolver, and a *mangel* or brazier have been bought; a permit to travel has been obtained, and my hosts, with the most thoughtful kindness, have facilitated all the arrangements. I have bought two mule *yekdans*, which are tall, narrow leather trunks on strong iron frames, with stout straps to buckle over the top of the pack saddle. On the whole I find that it is best to adopt as far as possible the travelling equipments of the country in which one travels. The muleteers and servants understand them better, and if any thing goes wrong, or wears out, it can be repaired or replaced. I have given away *en route* nearly all the things I brought from England, and have reduced my camp furniture to a folding bed and a chair. I shall start with three novelties—a fellow-traveller,[1] a saddle mule, and an untried saddle.

It is expected that the journey will be a very severe one, owing to the exceptionally heavy snowfall reported from the Zagros mountains and the Persian plateau. The Persian post has arrived several days late. I. L. B.

---

[1] I had given up the idea of travelling in Persia, and was preparing to leave India for England, when an officer, with whom I was then unacquainted, and who was about to proceed to Tihran on business, kindly offered me his escort. The journey turned out one of extreme hardship and difficulty, and had it not been for his kindness and efficient help I do not think that I should have accomplished it.

LETTER III [1]

YAKOBIYEH, ASIATIC TURKEY, *Jan. 11.*

WHETHER for "well or ill" the journey to Tihran is begun. I am ashamed to say that I had grown so nervous about its untried elements, and about the possibilities of the next two months, that a very small thing would have made me give it up at the last moment; but now that I am fairly embarked upon it in splendid weather, the spirit of travel has returned.

Much remained for the last morning,—debts to be paid in complicated money, for Indian, Turkish, and Persian coins are all current here; English circular notes to be turned into difficult coin, and the usual "row" with the muleteers to be endured. This disagreeable farce attends nearly all departures in the East, and I never feel the comfortable assurance that it means nothing.

The men weighed my baggage, which was considerably under weight, the day before, but yesterday three or four of them came into the courtyard, shouting in Arabic at the top of their loud harsh voices that they would not carry the loads. Hadji roared at them, loading his revolver all the time, calling them "sons of burnt fathers," and other choice names. Dr. Bruce and Dr. Sutton reasoned with them from the balcony, when, in the very

---

[1] I present my diary letters much as they were written, believing that the details of travel, however wearisome to the experienced traveller, will be interesting to the "Untravelled Many," to whom these volumes are dedicated.

height of the row, they suddenly shouldered the loads
and went off with them.

Two hours later the delightful hospitalities of Dr. and
Mrs. Sutton were left behind, and the farewell to the
group in the courtyard of the mission house is a long
farewell to civilisation. Rumours of difficulties have
been rife, and among the various dismal prophecies the
one oftenest repeated is that we shall be entangled in
the snows of the Zagros mountains; but the journey
began propitiously among oranges and palms, bright sunshine and warm good wishes. My mule turns out a fine,
spirited, fast-walking animal, and the untried saddle
suits me. My marching equipment consists of two large
holsters, with a revolver and tea-making apparatus in
one, and a bottle of milk, and dates in the other. An
Afghan sheepskin coat is strapped to the front of
the saddle, and a blanket and stout mackintosh behind.
I wear a cork sun-helmet, a gray mask instead of a veil,
an American mountain dress with a warm jacket over it,
and tan boots, scarcely the worse for a year of Himalayan
travel. Hadji is dressed like a wild Ishmaelite.

Captain Dougherty of H.M.S. *Comet* and his chief
engineer piloted us through the narrow alleys and
thronged bazars,—a *zaptieh*, or gendarme, with a rifle
across his saddle-bow, and a sheathed sabre in his hand,
shouting at the donkey boys, and clearing the crowd to
right and left. Through the twilight of the bazars,
where chance rays of sunshine fell on warm colouring,
gay merchandise, and picturesque crowds; along narrow
alleys, overhung by brown lattice windows; out under the
glorious blue of heaven among ruins and graves, through
the northern gateway, and then there was an abrupt exchange
of the roar and limitations of the City of the Caliphs for
the silence of the desert and the brown sweep of a limit-
less horizon. A walled Eastern city has no suburbs. It

is a literal step from a crowded town to absolute solitude. The contrast is specially emphasised at Baghdad, where the transition is made from a great commercial city with a crowded waterway, to an uninhabited plain in the nudity of mid-winter.

A last look at gleaming domes, coloured minarets, and massive mausoleums, rising out of an environment of palms and orange groves, at the brick walls and towers of the city, at the great gate to which lines of caravans were converging from every quarter, a farewell to the kindly pilots, and the journey began in earnest.

The "Desert" sweeps up to the walls of Baghdad, but it is a misnomer to call the vast level of rich, stoneless, alluvial soil a desert. It is a dead flat of uninhabited earth; orange colocynth balls, a little wormwood, and some alkaline plants which camels eat, being its chief products. After the inundations reedy grass grows in the hollows. It is a waste rather than a desert, and was once a populous plain, and the rich soil only needs irrigation to make it " blossom as the rose." Traces of the splendid irrigation system under which it was once a garden abound along the route.

The mid-day and afternoon were as glorious as an un-clouded sky, a warm sun, and a fresh, keen air could make them. The desert freedom was all around, and the nameless charm of a nomadic life. The naked plain, which stretched to the horizon, was broken only by the brown tents of Arabs, mixed up with brown patches of migrating flocks, strings of brown camels, straggling caravans, and companies of Arab horsemen heavily armed. An expanse of dried mud, the mirage continually seen, a cloudless sky, and a brilliant sun—this was all. I felt better at once in the pure, exhilarating desert air, and nervousness about the journey was left behind. I even indulged in a gallop, and except for her impetuosity, which carried me into the middle of a caravan, and turning round a few times, the mule behaved so irreproachably that I forgot the potential possibilities of evil. Still, I do not think that there can ever be that perfect correspondence of will between a mule and his rider that there is between a horse and his rider.

The mirage was almost continual and grossly deceptive. Fair blue lakes appeared with palms and towers mirrored on their glassy surfaces, giving place to snowy ranges with bright waters at their feet, fringed by tall trees, changing into stately processions, all so absolutely real that the real often seemed the delusion. These deceptions, continued for several hours, were humiliating and exasperating.

Towards evening the shams disappeared, the waste purpled as the sun sank, and after riding fifteen miles we halted near the mud village of Orta Khan, a place with brackish water and no supplies but a little brackish sheep's milk. The caravanserai was abominable, and we rode on to a fine gravelly camping-ground, but the headman and some of the villagers came out, and would not hear of our pitching the tents where we should be the prey of predatory hordes, strong enough, they said, to overpower an officer, two *zaptiehs*, and three orderlies! Being unwilling to get them into trouble, we accepted a horrible camping-ground, a mud-walled "garden," trenched for dates, and lately irrigated, as damp and clayey as it could be. My *dhurrie* will not be dry again this winter. The mules could not get in, the baggage was unloaded at some distance, and was all mixed up, and Hadji showed himself incapable; my tent fell twice, remained precarious, and the *kanats* were never pegged down at all.

The *dhurrie* was trampled into the mud by clayey feet. Baggage had to be disentangled and unpacked after dark, and the confusion apt to prevail on the first night of a march was something terrible. It opened my eyes to the thorough inefficiency of Hadji, who was so dazed with opium this morning that he stood about in a dream, ejaculating " *Ya Allah* ! " when it was suggested that he should bestir himself, leaving me to do all the packing, groaning as he took up the tent pegs, and putting on the mule's bridle with the bit hanging under her chin !

The night was very damp, not quite frosty, and in the dim morning the tent and its contents were wet. Tea at seven, with Baghdad rusks, with a distinctly " native taste," two hours spent in standing about on the damp, clayey ground till my feet were numb, while the men, most of whom were complaining of rheumatism, stumbled through their new work; and then five hours of wastes, enlivened by caravans of camels, mules, horses, or asses, and sometimes of all mixed, with their wild, armed drivers. The leader of each caravan carries a cylinder-shaped bell under his throat, suspended from a red leather band stitched with cowries, another at his chest, and very large ones, often twenty-four inches long by ten in diameter, hanging from each pack. Every other animal of the caravan has smaller bells, and the tones, which are often most musical, reach from the deep note of a church bell up to the frivolous jingle of sleigh bells; jingle often becomes jangle when several caravans are together. The *katirgis* (muleteers) spend large sums on the bells and other decorations. Among the loads we met or overtook were paraffin, oranges, pomegranates, carpets, cotton goods, melons, grain, and chopped straw. The waste is covered with tracks, and a guide is absolutely necessary.

The day has been still and very gloomy, with flakes of snow falling at times. The passing over rich soil, once cultivated and populous, now abandoned to the antelope

and partridge, is most melancholy.   The remains of
canals and water-courses, which in former days brought
the waters of the Tigris and the Diyalah into the fields
of the great grain-growing population of these vast levels
of Chaldæa and Mesopotamia, are everywhere, and at
times create difficulties on the road.   By road is simply
meant a track of greater or less width, trodden on the
soil by the passage of caravans for ages.   On these two
marches not a stone has been seen which could strike a
ploughshare.

Great ancient canals, with their banks in ruins and
their deep beds choked up and useless, have been a
mournful feature of rather a dismal day's journey.   We
crossed the bed of the once magnificent Nahrwan canal,
the finest of the ancient irrigation works to the east of
the Tigris, still in many places from twenty-five to forty
feet deep and from 150 to 200 feet in breadth.

For many miles the only permanent village is a
collection of miserable mud hovels round a forlorn caravanserai, in which travellers may find a wretched refuge
from the vicissitudes of weather.   There is a remarkable
lack of shelter and provender, considering that this is
not only one of the busiest of caravan routes, but is
enormously frequented by Shiah pilgrims on their way
from Persia to the shrines of Kerbela.

After crossing the Nahrwan canal the road keeps
near the right bank of the Diyalah, a fine stream, which
for a considerable distance runs parallel with the Tigris
at a distance of from ten to thirty miles from it, and falls
into it below Baghdad ; and *imamzadas* and villages with
groves of palms break the line of the horizon, while on
the left bank for fully two miles are contiguous groves
of dates and pomegranates.   These groves are walled,
and among them this semi-decayed and ruinous town is
situated, miserably shrunk from its former proportions.

We entered Yakobiyeh after crossing the Diyalah by a pontoon bridge of twelve boats, and found one good house with projecting lattice windows, and a large entrance over which the head and ears of a hare were nailed; narrow, filthy lanes, a covered bazar, very dark and ruinous, but fairly well supplied, an archway, and within it this caravanserai in which the baggage must be waited for for two hours.

This first experience of a Turkish inn is striking. There is a large square yard, heaped with dirt and rubbish, round which are stables and some dark, ruinous rooms. A broken stair leads to a flat mud roof, on which are some narrow "stalls,"—*rooms* they cannot be called,—with rude doors fastening only from the outside, for windows small round holes mostly stuffed with straw near the roof, for floors sodden earth, for fireplaces holes in the same, the walls slimy and unplastered, the corners full of ages of dusty cobwebs, both the walls and the rafters of the roof black with ages of smoke, and beetles and other abominations hurry into crannies, when the doors are opened, to emerge as soon as they are shut. A small hole in the wall outside each stall serves for cooking. The habits of the people are repulsive, foul odours are only hybernating, and so, mercifully, are the vermin.

While waiting for the "furniture" which is to make my "unfurnished apartment" habitable, I write sitting on my camp stool with its back against the wall, wrapped up in a horse-blanket, a heap of saddles, swords, holsters, and gear keeping the wind from my feet. The Afghan orderly smokes at the top of the stair. Plumes of palms and faintly-seen ridges of snowy hills appear over the battlements of the roof. A snow wind blows keenly. My fingers are nearly numb, and I am generally stiff and aching, but so much better that discomforts are only an amusement. Snow is said to be impending.

I have lunched frugally on sheep's milk and dates, and feel everything but my present surroundings to be very far off, and as if I had lived the desert life, and had heard the chimes of the great caravans, and had seen the wild desert riders, and the sun sinking below the level line of the desert horizon, for two months instead of two days.

Yakobiyeh is said to have 800 houses. It has some small mosques and several caravanserais, of which this is the best! It was once a flourishing place, but repeated ravages of the plague and chronic official extortions have reduced it to decay. Nevertheless, it grows grain enough for its own needs on poorly irrigated soil, and in its immense gardens apples, pears, apricots, walnuts, and mulberries flourish alongside of the orange and palm.

Kizil Robat, Jan. 14.—It was not very cold at Yakobiyeh. At home few people would be able to sit in a fireless den, with the door open, on a January night, but fireless though it was, my slender camp equipage gave it a look of comfort, and though rats or mice ate a bag of rusks during the night, and ran over my bed, there were no other annoyances. Hadji grows more dazed and possibly more unwilling every day, as he sees his vista of perquisites growing more limited, and to get off, even at nine, I have to do the heavy as well as the light packing myself.

There was a great "row," arising out of an alleged delinquency of the *katirgis* concerning payment, when we left Yakobiyeh the following morning. The owners of the caravanserai wanted to detain us, and the archway was so packed with a shouting, gesticulating, scowling, and not kindly crowd, mostly armed, that it was not easy for me to mount. The hire of mules always includes their fodder and the keep of the men, but in the first day or two the latter usually attempt to break their bargain, and compel their employer to provide for them.   So long as Arabic is spoken Hadji acts as sole interpreter, and though soldiers and *zaptiehs* were left with him he was scared at being left behind with the baggage. The people stormed and threatened at the top of their voices, but doubtless it was not so bad as it sounded, for we got through the bazars without molestation, and then into a perplexing system of ancient water-courses whose high broken banks and deep waterless beds intersect each other and the road.   In contrast to this magnificent irriga-tion system there are modern water-channels about a foot wide, taken from the river Diyalah, which, small as they are, turn the rich deep soil into a " fruitful field."

After these glimpses of a prosperity which once was and might be again (for these vast alluvial plains, which extend from the Zagros mountains to the Euphrates and up to the Syrian desert, are capable with irrigation and cultivation of becoming the granary of Western Asia), the road emerges on a level and somewhat gravelly waste, on which after a long ride we were overtaken by a *zaptieh* sent by the Persian agent in Yakobiyeh, to say that the baggage and servants were being forcibly de-tained, but shortly afterwards with a good glass the caravan was seen emerging from the town.

The country was nearly as featureless as on the pre-ceding day, and on the whole quite barren ; among the few caravans on the road there were two of immense value, the loads being the best description of Persian carpets.   There were a few families on asses, migrating with all their possessions, and a few parties of Arab horsemen picturesquely and very fully armed, but no dwellings, till in the bright afternoon sunshine, on the dreariest stretch of an apparently verdureless waste, we came on the caravanserai of Wiyjahea, a gateway with a room above it, a square court with high walls and arched recesses all round for goods and travellers, and large stables. A row of reed huts, another of Arab tents, and a hovel opposite the gateway, where a man with two guns within reach sells food, tobacco, and hair ropes, make up this place of horror. For, indeed, the only water is a brackish reedy pool, with its slime well stirred by the feet of animals, and every man's hand is against his brother.

We proposed to pitch my tent in a ruined enclosure, but the headman was unwilling, and when it was suggested that it should be placed between the shop and the caravanserai, he said that before sunset all the predatory Arabs for ten miles round would hear that "rich foreigners were travelling," and would fall upon and plunder us, so we must pitch, if at all, in the filthy and crowded court of the caravanserai. The *balakhana*, or upper room, was too insecure for me, and had no privacy, as the fodder was kept in it, and there was no method of closing the doors, which let in the bitterly cold wind.

We arrived at 3 P.M., and long before sunset a number of caravans came in, and the courtyard was full of horses, mules, and asses. When they halted the loads were taken off and stacked in the arched recesses; next, the great padded pack-saddles, which cover nearly the whole back, were removed, revealing in most cases deep sores and ulcers. Then the animals were groomed with box curry-combs, with "clatters" like the noise of a bird-scarer inside them. Fifty curry-combs going at once is like the din of the cicada. Then the beasts were driven in batches to the reedy pool, and came flying back helter-skelter through the archway, some fighting, others playing, many rolling. One of them nearly pulled my tent over by rolling among the tent ropes. It had been pitched on damp and filthy ground in a corner of the yard, among mules, horses, asses, dogs, and the roughest of rough men, but even there the damp inside looked like home.

After this brief hilarity, the pack-saddles, which serve as blankets, were put on, the camels were made to lie down in rows, most of the mules and horses were tethered in the great stable, where they neighed, stamped, and jangled their bells all night, and others were picketed in the yard among the goats and donkeys and the big dogs, which wandered about yelping. Later, the small remaining space was filled up with sheep. It was just possible to move, but no more, and sheep and goats were even packed under the *flys* of my tent. The muleteers and travellers spread their bedding in the recesses, lighted their fires of animal fuel, and cooked their food.

At sunset the view from the roof was almost beautiful. Far away, in all directions, stretched the level desert purpling in the purple light. Very faintly, on the far horizon to the north-east, mountain ranges were painted in amethyst on an orange sky. Horsemen in companies galloped to tents which were not in sight, strings of camels cast their long shadows on the purple sand, and flocks of big brown sheep, led by armed shepherds, converged on the reedy pool in long brown lines. The evening air was keen, nearly frosty.

The prospects for the night were not encouraging, and on descending the filthy stair on which goats had taken up their quarters, I found the malodorous, crowded courtyard so blocked, that shepherds, with much pushing, shouting, and barking of big dogs, with difficulty made a way for me to pass through the packed mass of sheep and goats into the cold, damp tent, which was pitched on damp manure, two or three feet deep, into which heavy feet had trampled the carpet. The uproar of *katirgis* and travellers went on for another two hours, and was exchanged later for sounds of jangling bells, yelping and quarrelling dogs, braying asses, bleating sheep, and coarsely-snoring men.

At 9 P.M. the heavy gates, clamped with iron, were closed and barred, and some belated travellers, eager to get in from the perils of the outside, thundered at them long and persistently, but "the door was shut," and they encountered a hoarse refusal. The *seraidar* said that 400 horses and mules, besides camels and asses, 2000 sheep, and over 70 men were lodged in the caravanserai that night.

The servants were in a recess near, and Hadji professed that he watched all night, and said that he fired at a man who tried to rob my tent after the light went out, but I slept too soundly to be disturbed, till the caravans and flocks left at daybreak, after a preliminary uproar of two hours. It was bitterly cold, and my tent and its contents were soaked with the heavy dew, nearly doubling their weight.

I started at 9 A.M., before the hoar-frost had melted, and rode with the *zaptieh* over flat, stoneless, alluvial soil, with some irrigation and the remains of some fine canals. There are villages to be seen in the distance, but though the soil is rich enough to support a very large population, there are no habitations near the road except a few temporary reed huts, beside two large caravanserais. There was little of an interesting kind except the perpetual contrast between things as they are and things as they were and might be. Some large graveyards, with brick graves, a crumbling *imamzada*, a pointed arch of brick over the Nahrud canal, a few ass caravans, with a live fowl tied by one leg on the back of each ass, and struggling painfully to keep its uneasy seat, some cultivation and much waste, and then we reached the walled village of Sheraban, once a town, but now only possessing 300 houses.

Passing as usual among ruinous dwellings and between black walls with doors here and there, by alleys foul with heaps of refuse, and dangerous from slimy pitfalls, in the very foulest part we turned into the caravanserai, its great courtyard reeking with filth and puddles, among which are the contaminated wells from which we are supposed to drink. The experience of the night before was not repeated. There were fairly good rooms, mine looking into a palm garden, through a wooden grating, cold truly, but pleasant. I fear we may never have such "luxury" again. I remarked to my fellow-traveller that our early arrival had fortunately given us the "choice of rooms," and he replied, "choice of pig-styes,—choice of dens!" but my experience at Wiyjahea has deprived me of the last remnants of fastidiousness!

I walked through the ruinous, wretched town, and its poor bazar, where the very fine *physique* of the men was in marked contrast with their wretched surroundings, and gives one the impression that under honest officials they might be a fine people. They are not genial to strangers, however. There was some bad language used in the bazar, and on the roads they pass one in silence at the best, so unlike the Tibetans with their friendly *Tzu*. At Sheraban one of the muleteers forced his way into my room, and roughly turned over my saddle and baggage, accusing me of having taken his blanket! Hadji is useless under such circumstances. He blusters and fingers his revolver, but carries no weight. Indeed his defects are more apparent every day. I often have to speak to him two or three times before I can rouse him from his opium dream, and there is a growing inclination to shirk his very light work when he can shift it upon somebody else. I hope that he is well-meaning, as that would cover a multitude of faults, but he is very rough and ignorant, and is either unable or unwilling to learn anything, even how to put up my trestle bed!

Open rooms have sundry disadvantages. In the night a

cat fell from the roof upon my bed, and was soon joined by more, and they knocked over the lamp and milk bottle, and in the darkness had a noisy quarrel over the milk.

The march of eighteen miles here was made in six hours, at a good caravan pace. The baggage animals were sent off in advance, and the *zaptieh* led a mule loaded with chairs, blankets, and occupations. I ride with the *zaptieh* in front of me till I get near the halting-place, when M—— and his orderly overtake me, as it might be disagreeable for a European woman to enter a town alone.

The route lies over treeless levels of the same brown alluvial soil, till it is lifted on a gentle gravelly slope to a series of low crumbling mounds of red and gray sandstone, mixed up with soft conglomerate rocks of jasper and porphyry pebbles. These ranges of mounds, known as the Hamrin Hills, run parallel to the great Kurdistan ranges, from a point considerably below Baghdad, nearly to Mosul and the river Zab. They mark the termination in this direction of the vast alluvial plains of the Tigris and Euphrates, and are the first step to the uplifted Iranian plateau.

Arid and intricate ravines, dignified by the name of passes, furrow these hills, and bear an evil reputation, as Arab robbers lie in wait, "making it very unsafe for small caravans." A wild, desolate, ill-omened-looking region it is. When we were fairly within the pass, the *zaptieh* stopped, and with much gesticulation and many repetitions of the word *effendi*, made me understand that it was unsafe to proceed without a larger party. We were unmolested, but it is a discredit to the administration of the province that an organised system of pillage should be allowed to exist year after year on one of the most frequented caravan routes in Turkey. There were several companies of armed horsemen among the ranges, and some camels browsing, but we met no caravans.

From the top of the descent there was a striking view over a great brown alluvial plain, watered by the Beladruz and the Diyalah, with serrated hills of no great height, but snow-covered; on its east side a silent, strange, weird view, without interest or beauty as seen under a sullen sky. There are no villages on this march, but ancient canals run in all directions, and fragments of buildings, as well as of brick and pottery, scattered over the unploughed surface, are supposed by many to mark the situation of Dastagird, the residence of Khosroe Parviz in the seventh century. I have no books of reference with me, and can seldom write except of such things as I see and hear.

Farther on a multitude of irrigation ditches have turned a plain of dry friable soil into a plain of mud, through which it was difficult to struggle. Then came a grove of palms, and then the town or village of Kizil Robat (Red Shrine), with its *imamzada*, whose reputation for sanctity is indicated by the immense number of graves which surround it. The walls of this decayed and wretched town are of thick layers of hardened but now crumbling earth, and on the east side there is an old gateway of burned brick. There are said to be 400 houses, which at the lowest computation would mean a population of 2000, but inhabited houses and ruins are so jumbled up together that one cannot form any estimate.

So woe-begone and miserable a place I never saw, and the dirt is appalling even in this dry weather. In spring the alleys of the town are impassable, and people whose business calls them out cross from roof to roof on boards. Pools of filthy water, loathsome ditches with broad margins of trodden slime full of abominations, ruins of houses, yards foul with refuse, half-clothed and wholly unwashed children, men of low aspect standing in melancholy groups, a well-built brick bazar, in which Manchester cottons are prominent, more mud and dirt, some ruinous caravanserais, and near the extremity of the town or village is the horrible one in which I now am, said to be the best, with a yard a foot deep in manure and slush, in the midst of which is the well, and around which are stables and recesses for travellers.

At first it seemed likely that I should fall so low as to occupy one of these, but careful investigation revealed a ruinous stair leading to the roof, up which were two rooms, or shall I say three?—an arched recess such as coals are kept in, a small room within it, and a low wood hole. The open arch, with a *mangel* or iron pan of charcoal, serves as the "parlour" this January night, M—— occupies the wood hole, and I the one room, into which Hadji, with many groans and ejaculations of "*Ya Allah!*" has brought up the essential parts of my baggage. The evening is gray and threatening, and low, snow-covered hills look grimly over the bare brown plain which lies outside this mournful place.

Khannikin, Jan. 15.—This has been a hard, rough march, but there will be many worse ahead. Rain fell heavily all night, converting the yard into a lake of trampled mud, and seemed so likely to continue that it was difficult to decide whether to march or halt. Miserable it was to see mules standing to be loaded, up to their knees in mud, bales of tents and bedding lying in the quagmire, and the shivering Indian servants up to their knees in the swamp. In rain steadily falling the twelve animals were loaded, and after the usual scrimmage at starting, in which the *bakhsheesh* is often thrown back at us, we rode out into a sea of deep mud, through which the mules, struggling and floundering, got on about a mile an hour.

After a time we came to gravel, then relapsed into deep alluvial soil, which now means deep mire, then a

low range of gravelly hills on which a few sheep and
camels were browsing on artemisia and other aromatic
herbs gave a temporary respite, then again we floundered
through miles of mud, succeeded by miles of gravel and
stones. The rain fell in torrents, and there was a cold
strong wind to fight against. There was that amount of
general unpropitiousness which is highly stimulating and
inspiriting.

When noon came, there was not a rock or bush for
shelter, and turning our backs to the storm we ate our
lunch in our saddles. There was nothing to look at but
brown gravel, or brown mud, brooded over by a gray mist.
So we tramped on, hour after hour, in single file, the
zaptieh leading, everything but his gun muffled in his
brown *abba*, splashing through mud and water, the water
pouring from my hat and cloak, the six woollen thicknesses
of my mask dripping, seeing neither villages nor caravans,
for caravans of goods do not travel in such rain as this.
Then over a slope we went down into a lake of mud,
where the *aide-de-camp* of the Governor of Khannikin, in
a fez and military frock-coat and trousers, with a number
of Bashi Bazouks or irregulars, met M—— with courtesies
and an invitation.

From the top of the next slope there was a view of
Khannikin, a considerable-looking town among groves of
palms and other trees. Then came a worse sea of mud,
and a rudely cobbled causeway, so horrible that it diverted
us back into the mud, which was so bottomless that it
drove us back to the causeway, and the causeway back to
the mud, the rain all the time coming down in sheets.
This causeway, without improvement, is carried through
Khannikin, a town with narrow blind alleys, upon which
foul courtyards open, often so foul as to render the recent
ravages of cholera (if science speaks truly) a matter of
necessity. The mud and water in these alleys was up to

the knees of the mules. Not a creature was in the streets. No amount of curiosity, even regarding the rare sight of a Frank woman, could make people face the storm in flimsy cotton clothes.

Where the road turns to the bridge a line of irregular infantry was drawn up, poorly dressed, soaked creatures, standing in chilly mud up to their ankles, in soaked boots reaching to their knees. These joined and headed the cavalcade, and I fell humbly in the rear. Poor fellows! To keep step was impossible when it was hard work to drag their feet out of the mire, and they carried their rifles anyhow. It was a grotesque procession. A trim officer, forlorn infantry, wild-looking Bashi Bazouks, Europeans in stout mackintoshes splashed with mud from head to foot, mules rolling under their bespattered loads, and a *posse* of servants and orderlies crouching on the top of baggage, muffled up to the eyes, the asses which carry the *katirgis* and their equipments far behind, staggering and nearly done up, for the march of seventeen miles had taken eight and a half hours.

An abrupt turn in the causeway leads to the Holwan, a tributary of the Diyalah, a broad, rapid stream, over which the enterprise of a Persian has thrown a really fine brick bridge of thirteen heavily-buttressed arches, which connects the two parts of the town and gives some dignity and picturesqueness to what would otherwise be mean. On the left bank of the Holwan are the barracks, the governor's house, some large caravanserais, the Custom-house, and a quarantine station, quarantine having just been imposed on all arrivals from Persia, giving travel and commerce a decided check.

After half a mile of slush on the river bank we entered by a handsome gateway a nearly flooded court-yard, and the Governor's house hospitably engorged the whole party.

The fully-laden mules stuck in the mud a few miles off, and did not come in for two hours, and in spite of covers everything not done up in waterproof was very wet. The servants looked most miserable, and complained of chills and rheumatism, and one of the orderlies is really ill. We cannot move till the storm is over.

The rain falls heavily still, the river is rising, the alleys are two feet deep in slush, travel is absolutely suspended, and it is not possible without necessity to go out. It was well indeed that we decided to leave the shelterless shelter of Kizil Robat. Nothing can exceed the wretchedness of Khannikin or any Turkish town in such rain as this. Would that one could think that it would be washed, but as there are no channels to carry off the water it simply lodges and stagnates in every depression, and all the accumulations of summer refuse slide into these abominable pools, and the foul dust, a foot deep, becomes mud far deeper; buried things are half uncovered; torrents, not to be avoided, pour from every roof, the courtyards are knee-deep in mud, the cows stand disconsolately in mud; not a woman is to be seen, the few men driven forth by the merciless exigences of business show nothing but one eye, and with "loins girded" and big staffs move wearily, stumbling and plunging in the mire.

After some hours the flat mud roofs begin to leak, water finds out every weak place in the walls, the bazars, only half open for a short time in the day, are deserted by buyers, and the patient sellers crouch over *mangels*, muffled up in sheepskins, the caravanserais are crammed and quarrelsome; the price of fodder and fuel rises, and every one is drowned in rain and wretchedness. Even here, owing to the scarcity of fuel, nothing can be dried; the servants in their damp clothes come in steaming;

Hadji in his misshapen "jack-boots," which he asserts he cannot take off, spreads fresh mud over the carpets whenever he enters; I shift from place to place to avoid the drip from the roof—and still the rain comes down with unabated vigour!

LETTER III (*Continued*)

THE house consists of two courtyards, with buildings round them. The larger and handsomer is the *haram* or women's house, which is strictly enclosed, has no exterior windows, and its one door into the men's house is guarded by a very ancient eunuch. The courtyard of this house is surrounded partly by arched *serdabs*, with green lattice fronts, and partly by a kitchen, bakery, wood-house, *hammam* or hot bath, and the servants' quarters. The *haram* has a similar arrangement on the lower floor. A broad balcony, reached by a steep and narrow stair, runs round three sides of the upper part of this house. There are very few rooms, and some of them are used for storing fruit. The wet baggage is mostly up here, and under the deep roof the servants and orderlies camp, looking miserable. The *haram* has a balcony all round it, on which a number of reception and living rooms open, and though not grand or elaborately decorated, is convenient and comfortable.

The Turkish host evidently did not know what to do with such an embarrassing guest as a European woman, and solved the difficulty by giving me the guest-chamber in the men's house, a most fortunate decision, as I have had quiet and privacy for three days. Besides, this room has a projecting window, with panes of glass held in by nails, and there is not only a view of the alley with its slush, but into the house of some poor folk, and over that to the Holwan, sometimes in spate, sometimes falling, and through all the hours of daylight frequented by grooms for the purpose of washing their horses. Some shingle banks, now overflowed, sustain a few scraggy willows, and on the farther side is some low-lying land. There may be much besides, but the heavy rain-clouds blot out all else.

My room is whitewashed, and is furnished with Persian rugs, Austrian bent-wood chairs, and a divan in the window, on which I sleep. Lamps, *samovars*, and glasses are kept in recesses, and a black slave is often in and out for them. Otherwise no one enters but Hadji. I get my food somewhat precariously. It is carved and sent from table at the beginning of meals, chiefly pillau, curry, *kabobs*, and roast chicken, but apparently it is not etiquette for me to get it till after the men have dined, and it is none the better for being cold.

The male part of the household consists of the Governor and his brother-in-law, a Moslem judge, and the quarantine doctor, a Cretan, takes his meals in the house. The Governor and doctor speak French. My fellow-traveller lives with them.

The night we arrived, the Governor in some agitation asked me to go and see his wife, who is very ill. The cholera has only just disappeared, and the lady had had a baby, which died of it in three days, and " being a boy her heart was broken," and " something had come under her arm." So I went with him into the *haram*, which seemed crowded with women of various races and colours, peeping from behind curtains and through chinks of doors, tittering and whispering. The wife's room is richly carpeted and thoroughly comfortable, with a huge charcoal brazier in the centre, and cushions all over the floor, except at one end, where there is a raised alcove with a bed in it.

On this the lady sat—a rather handsome Kurdish

woman, about thirty-five, dressed in a silk quilted jacket, and with a black gauze handkerchief round her head, and a wadded quilt over her crossed legs. She was supported by a pile of pillows. Since then I have been sent for to see her several times every day, and found her always in the same position. There is surely something weird about it. She says she sits there all night, and has not lain down for two months. A black slave was fanning her, and two women, shrouded in veils of tinselled gauze, sat on the bed combing her luxuriant hair. She is not really beautiful at all, but her husband assures me constantly that she is "*une femme savante.*" She has property and the consideration which attaches to it. She was burning with fever and very weak.

I had scarcely returned to my room when my host sent again, begging that I would go back and see the doctor. I found that it was expected that I should persuade the lady to consent to have the abscess, or whatever it is, reopened. The room was full of women and eunuchs, and the chief eunuch, an elderly Arab, sat on the bed and supported her while the doctor dressed the wound, and even helped him with it. Her screams were fearful, and five people held her with difficulty. Her husband left the room, unable to bear her cries.

Quite late I was sent for again, and that time by the lady, to know if I thought she would die. It appears that her brother, the judge, remains here to see that she is not the victim of foul play, but I don't like to ask to whom the suspicion points, or whether our host, although the civil governor, keeps him here that he may not be suspected in case his rich wife dies.

Except for the repeated summonses to the sick-room, a walk on the slime of the roof when the rain ceases for a time, and on the balcony of the *haram* when it does not, and a study of the habits of my neighbours over the

way, it is very dull.   I have patched and mended everything that gave any excuse for either operation, have
written letters which it is not safe to post, and have
studied my one book on Persia till I know it throughout,
and still the rain falls nearly without cessation and the
quagmires outside deepen.

So bad is it that, dearly as Orientals love bazars and
hammams, Hadji refuses leave to go to either.   I remarked to him that he must be glad of such a rest, and
he replied in his usual sententious fashion : "They who
have to work must work.   God knows all."   I fear he
is very lazy, and he has no idea of making one comfortable or of keeping anything clean.   He stamps the mud
of the courtyard into the carpets, and wipes my plates
without washing them, with his shirt.   He considers that
our host has attained the height of human felicity.
"What is there left to wish for ?" he says.   "He has
numbers of slaves, and he's always buying more, and he's
got numbers of women and eunuchs, and everything, and
when he wants money he just sends round the villages.
God is great !   *Ya Allah !*"

Khannikin, being the nearest town to the Persian
frontier, should be a place of some importance.   It is
well situated at an altitude of 1700 feet among groves of
palms, on both banks of the Holwan, and having plenty
of water, the rich alluvium between it and Yakobiyeh
is able to support its own population, though it has to
import for caravans.   Most of the Persian trade with
Baghdad and thousands of Shiah pilgrims annually pass
through it.   It is a customs station, and has a regiment
of soldiers.   Nevertheless, it is very ruinous, and its
population has diminished of late years from 5000 to
about 1800 (exclusive of the troops), and of this number
a fifth have been carried off by cholera within the last
few weeks.   It has no schools, and no special industries.

The stamp of decay rests upon it. Exactions, crushing hope out of the people, the general insecurity of property, and the misrule which has blighted these fine Asiatic provinces everywhere, sufficiently explain its decadence.

The imposition of quarantine on arrivals from Persia has all but stopped the supply of charcoal, and knowing the scarcity in the house, I am going without a fire, as most of the inhabitants are doing. A large caravanserai outside the walls is used as a quarantine station, and three others are taken as lazarettos. Out of these arrangements the officials make a great deal of money in fees, but anything more horrible than the sanitary state of these places cannot be conceived. The water appears to be the essence of typhoid fever and cholera, and the unfortunate *détenus* are crowded into holes unfit for beasts, breathing pestiferous exhalations, and surrounded by such ancient and modern accumulations of horrors that typhus fever, cholera, and even the plague might well be expected to break out.

Yesterday, for a brief interval, hills covered with snow appeared through rolling black clouds, and a change seemed probable, but rain fell in torrents all night; there is a spate in the river, and though we were ready to start at eight this morning, the *katirgis* declined to move, saying that the road could not be travelled because of the depth of the fords and the mud.

The roof, though a good one, is now so leaky that I am obliged to sleep under my waterproof cloak, and the un-puttied window-frames let in the rain. Early this morning a gale from the south-west came on, and the howling and roaring have been frightful, the rain falling in sheets most of the time. Sensations are not wanting. One of the orderlies is seriously ill, and has to be left behind under medical care till he can be sent to India,—

the second man who has broken down.   A runner came in
with the news that all caravans are stopped in the Zagros
mountains by snow, which has been falling for five days,
and that the road is not expected to be open for a fortnight.   Later, the Persian agent called to say that on the
next march the road, which is carried on a precipice above
the river, has slid down bodily, and that there are fifteen
feet of water where there should be only two.   Of course
this prolonged storm is " exceptional."   The temperature
is falling, and it is so cold without a fire that though
my bed is only a blanket-covered dais of brick and
lime, dripped upon continually, in a window with forty
draughts, I am glad to muffle myself up in its blankets
and write among wraps.

The Governor, recognising the craze of Europeans for
exercise, sent word that M—— might walk in the
balcony of the *haram* if I went to chaperon him, and this
great concession was gladly accepted, for it was the only
possible way of getting warm.   The apparition of a
strange man, and a European, within the precincts of the
haram was a great event, and every window, curtain, and
doorway was taken advantage of by bright dark eyes
sparkling among folds of cotton and gauze.   The enjoyment was surreptitious, but possibly all the more keen,
and sounds of whispering and giggling surged out of
every crevice.   There are over thirty women, some of
them negresses.   Some are Kurds and very handsome,
but the faces of the two handsomest, though quite young,
have something fiendish in their expression.   I have seldom
seen a *haram* without its tragedies of jealousy and hate,
and every fresh experience makes me believe that the
system is as humiliating to men as it is to women.

The *haram* reception-rooms here are large and bright,
with roofs and cornices worked daintily in very white
plaster, and there are superb carpets on the floors, and

divans covered with Damascus embroidery in gold silk on cream muslin.

Each day the demands for my presence in the sick-room are more frequent, and though I say that I can scarcely aspire to be a nurse, they persist in thinking that I am a *Hakīm*, and possibly a useful spy on the doctor. I have become aware that unscrupulous jealousy of the principal wife exists, and, as is usual in the East, everybody distrusts everybody else, and prefers to trust strangers. The husband frequently asks me to remove what seems a cancerous tumour, and the doctor says that an operation is necessary to save the lady's life, but when I urge him to perform it, and offer a nurse's help, he replies that if she were to die he would be at once accused of murder, and would run a serious risk.

The Governor to-day was so anxious that I should persuade the lady to undergo an operation that he even brought Hadji into the room to interpret what I said in Arabic. His ceaseless question is, " Will she die ? " and she asks me the same many times every day. She insists that I shall be present each day when the wound is dressed, and give help, lest the doctor without her leave should plunge a knife into the swelling. These are most distressing occasions, for an hour of struggle and suffering usually ends in delirium.

This afternoon, however, she was much freer from pain, and sent for me to amuse her. She wore some fine jewels, and some folds of tinselled gauze round her head, and looked really handsome and intelligent. Her husband wished that we could converse without his imperfect interpreting, and repeated many times, " She is a learned woman, and can write and read several languages." The room was as usual full of women, who had removed their veils at their lord's command. I showed the lady some

Tibetan sketches, but when I came to one of a man the women replaced their veils!

When I showed some embroidery, the Governor said he had heard that the Queen of England employed herself with her needle in leisure hours, but that it is not *comme il faut* here for ladies to work. It seems that the making of sweetmeats is the only occupation which can be pursued without loss of dignity. Is it wonderful that intolerable *ennui* should be productive of the miserable jealousies, rivalries, intrigues, and hatreds which accompany the system of polygamy?

The host, although civil governor of a large district, also suffers from *ennui*. The necessary official duties are very light, and the accounts and reports are prepared by others. If money is wanted he makes "an exaction" on a village, and subordinates screw it out of the people. Justice, or the marketable commodity which passes for such, is administered by a *kadi*. He clatters about the balconies with slippered feet, is domestic, that is, he spends most of the day in the *haram*, smokes, eats two meals of six or seven courses each, and towards evening takes a good deal of wine, according to a habit which is becoming increasingly common among the higher classes of Moslems. He is hospitable, and is certainly anything but tyrannical in his household.

The customs and ways of the first Turkish house I have visited in would be as interesting to you as they were to myself, but it would be a poor return for hospitality to dwell upon anything, unless, like the difficulties regarding the illness of the principal wife, it were a matter of common notoriety.

It is a punishable act in Persia, and possibly here also, to look into a neighbour's house, but I cannot help it unless I were to avoid the window altogether. Wealth and poverty are within a few feet of each other, and as Moslems are charitable to a degree and in a manner which puts us to shame, the juxtaposition is advantageous.

My neighbour's premises consist of a very small and mean yard, now a foot deep in black mire, a cow-shed, and a room without door or windows, with a black uneven floor, and black slimy rafters—neither worse nor better than many hovels in the Western Isles of Scotland. A man in middle life, a woman of dubious age, two girls from eight to ten years old, and a boy a little older are the occupants. The furniture consists of some wadded quilts, a copper pot, an iron girdle, a clay ewer or two, a long knife, a wooden spoon, a clay receptacle for grain, two or three earthenware basins, glazed green, and a wicker tray. The cow-shed contains—besides the cow, which is fed on dried thistles—a spade, an open basket, and a baggage pad. A few fowls live in the house, and are disconcerted to find that they cannot get out of it without swimming.

The weather is cold and raw, fuel is enormously dear, work is at a standstill, and cold and *ennui* keep my neighbours in bed till the day is well advanced. " Bed " consists of a wadded quilt laid on the floor, with another for a covering. The man and boy sleep at one end of the room, the woman and girls at the other, with covered heads. None make any change in their dress at night, except that the man takes off the *pagri* of his turban, retaining only a skull cap.

The woman gets up first, lights a fire of tamarisk twigs and thistles in a hole in the middle of the floor, makes porridge of some coarse brownish flour and water, and sets it on to warm—to *boil* it, with the means at her disposal, is impossible. She wades across the yard, gives the cow a bunch of thistles, milks it into a basin, adds a little leaven to the milk, which she shakes in a goat skin till it is thick, carries the skin and basket to the house, feeds the fowls from the basket, and then rouses her lord. He rises, stretches himself, yawns, and places himself cross-legged by the fire, after putting on his *pagri*. The room is dense with pungent wood smoke, which escapes through the doorway, and only a few embers remain. The wife hands him an earthen bowl, pours some porridge into it, adds some "thick milk" from the goat skin, and stands before him with her arms crossed while he eats, then receives the bowl from his hands and kisses it, as is usual with the slaves in a household.

Then she lights his pipe, and while he enjoys it she serves her boy with breakfast in the same fashion, omitting the concluding ceremony, after which she and the girls retire to a respectful distance with the big pot, and finish its contents simultaneously. The pipe over, she pours water on her lord's hands, letting it run on the already damp floor, and wipes them with her *chadar*. No other ablution is customary in the house.

Poor as this man is, he is a Hadji, and having brought from Mecca a " prayer stone," with the Prophet's hand upon it, he takes it from his girdle, puts it on the floor, bows his forehead on it, turning Mecca-ward, and says his prayers, repeating his devotions towards evening. The first day or two he went out, but the roads now being almost impassable, he confines himself to the repairing of a small dyke, which keeps the water from running into the room, which is lower than the yard, and performs its duty very imperfectly, the soak from the yard and the drip from the roof increasing the sliminess hourly. These repairs, an occasional pipe, and much sleep are the record of this man's day till an hour before sunset, when the meal of the morning is repeated with the addition of some cheese.

The children keep chiefly in bed. Meanwhile the woman, the busy bee of the family, contrives to patter about nearly all day in wet clothing, carrying out rubbish in single handfuls, breaking twigs, cleaning the pot, and feeding the cow.　The roof, which in fine weather is the scene of most domestic occupations, is reached by a steep ladder, and she climbs this seven times in succession, each time carrying up a fowl, to pick for imaginary worms in the slimy mud.　Dyed yarn is also carried up to steep in the rain, and in an interval of dryness some wool was taken up and carded.　An hour before sunset she lights the fire, puts on the porridge, and again performs seven journeys with seven fowls, feeds them in the house, attends respectfully to her lord, feeds her family, including the cow, paddles through mire to draw water from the river, and unrolls and spreads the wadded quilts.　By the time it is dark they are once more in bed, where I trust this harmless, industrious woman enjoys a well-earned sleep.

The clouds are breaking, and in spite of adverse rumours it is decided *coûte que coûte* to start to-morrow. For my own part I prefer the freedom even with the " swinishness " of a caravanserai to receiving hospitality for which no fitting return can be made.　　　I. L. B.

LETTER IV

SARIPUL-I-ZOHAB, *Jan. 21.*

THE rain at last ceased, and after the *katirgis* had squabbled for an hour over the baggage, we got off at ten, two days ago, very grateful for shelter and hospitality under such untoward circumstances. Six Bashi Bazouks and two *zaptiehs* on foot in ragged and incongruous uniforms escorted us to the Turkish frontier.

The streets were in a terrible condition, and horse and footmen, after an attempt to march in pairs, fell perforce into a floundering and disorderly single file, the footmen occasionally pulling themselves out of mud holes by the tails of the horses. Outside the town there was an expanse of mud and flooded water-channels which broke up the last attempt at a procession, and led to a general *sauve qui peut.* The mire was tenacious and up to the horses' knees, half the mules were down with their loads, Hadji rolled into the mud, my capable animal snorted and struggled, some went on banks and some took to streams, the asses had to be relieved of their loads, and the air was full of shouts and objurgations, till after much delay the forlorn rabble all struggled to the *terra firma* of a gravelly slope, splashed from head to foot.

The road crosses low, rolling, gravelly hills, with an occasional outcrop of red sandstone, and ascends on the whole. The sun was bright, but the wind was strong and very cold. The Bashi Bazouk escort was altogether harum-scarum and inconsequent, careering in circles, and firing at birds (which they never hit) from the saddle, and when we reached some low hills bearing a bad reputation, the officer, in order to represent danger and his vigilant care, threw them out in all directions scouting for robbers, till we came to a steepish hill crowned by a round tower with a mushroom top, a few ruinous mud buildings, and a tattered tent. Here the escort formed into one line, and the ragged garrison into another, with an officer facing them, and were photographed as they shivered in the biting wind. This tower is a Turkish frontier fort.

Soon afterwards the Persian frontier is crossed, the hills increase considerably in size, and mud was exchanged for firm, rough gravel. A feature of the otherwise featureless landscape is the frequent occurrence of towers like martello towers, on hill-tops, placed there for the shelter of the guards who formerly kept a lookout for robbers. In the uninteresting gravel lie pebbles of jasper and agate, emerald green, red, yellow, and purple. The first object of the slightest interest in this new country was a village of Ilyats, built of reed screens, with roofs of goat's-hair cloth, and with small yards with reed walls in front. The women, who wore full trousers and short jackets, were tall, somewhat striking-looking, and unveiled. Their hair hung down in long plaits, and they wore red handkerchiefs knotted at the back of the head.

There an escort of four Persian *sowars* joined us. The type of face was that with which we are familiar on Sasanian coins and sculptured stones, the brow and chin receding considerably, and the nose thin and projecting, the profile suggesting a beak rather than a human face, and the skin having the appearance of being drawn so tightly over the bones as to force the eyes into singular prominence.

A TURKISH FRONTIER FORT.

A six hours' march ended at the wildly-situated village of Kasr-i-Shirin, high on the right bank of the Holwan, with a plantation of dates on the left bank and considerable cultivation in the valley. It has only eighty houses of the most wretched construction, rivalled in height and size by middens, the drainage of which wastes itself on the wretched roadway. A caravanserai of the most miserable description, a square fort with a small garrison, and some large graveyards with domed tombs and curious obelisks, are the salient features of this village. Its wretched aspect is accounted for by its insecurity. It has been destroyed by robber tribes as often as there was anything worth destroying, and it has been so tossed to and fro between Turkey and Persia as not to have any of the special characteristics of either empire.

We stopped short of the village, at a great pile of building on a height, in massiveness and irregularity resembling a German medieval castle, in which a letter had secured accommodation. It has been unoccupied since its owner, Jan Mir, a sheikh of a robber tribe, and the terror of the surrounding neighbourhood, was made away with by the Persian Government.

The accommodation consisted of great, dark, arched, vaulted rooms, with stone-flagged floors, noble in size, but needing fifty candles and huge log fires to light up and warm their dark recesses, and gruesome and damp with one candle and a crackle of twigs. They were clean, however, and their massive walls kept out the cold. The village is at an elevation of 2300 feet, and the temperature has greatly changed.

The interest of Kasr-i-Shirin is that it lies among masses of ancient rubble, and that the slopes which surround it are completely covered with hewn and unhewn stones of all sizes, the relics of a great city, at the western extremity of which the present wretched hamlet stands.[1] The walls, which are easily traced, enclose an irregular square, the shortest front of which is said to be three miles long. They are built of roughly-hewn blocks of gray and red sandstone, and very hard mortar or concrete. The blocks are so huge in many places as to deserve the often misused epithet Cyclopean.

Within this enclosure are remains of houses built of water-worn round stones, which lie in monstrous heaps, and of a large fort on an eminence. In another direction are the ruins of an immense palace of quadrangular form, with only one entrance, and large underground rooms now nearly choked up. There are remains of what must have been very fine archways, but as the outer coating of hewn stone and all the decorations have fallen off, leaving only the inner case of rough rubble and concrete, the architectural forms are very badly defined, and the aspect of what must once have been magnificent is now forbidding and desolate. The remains of an aqueduct cut in the rock, and of troughs and stone pipes by which water was brought into the palace and city, from a distance of fifteen miles, are still traceable among the desolations, but of the beautiful gardens which they watered, and with which Khosroe surrounded the beautiful Shirin, not a trace remains. There was a pale sunset, flushing with

[1] Another interest, however, is its connection with many of the romantic legends still told of Khosroe Parviz and his beautiful queen, complicated with love stories concerning the sculptor Farhad, to whom the Persians attribute some of their most famous rock sculptures. One of the most romantic of these legends is that Farhad loved Shirin, and that Khosroe was aware of it, and promised to give her to him if he could execute the impossible task of bringing to the city the abundant waters of the mountains. Farhad set himself to the Herculean labour, and to the horror of the king nearly accomplished it, when Khosroe, dreading the advancing necessity of losing Shirin or being dishonoured, sent to inform him of her death. Being at the time on the top of a precipice, urging on the work of the aqueduct, the news filled him with such ungovernable despair that he threw himself down and was killed.

pale pink distant leagues of sodden snow, and right across
a lurid opening in a heavy mass of black clouds the great
ruined pile of the palace of Khosroe the Magnificent stood
out, a dismal commentary on splendour and fame.

The promise of the evening was fulfilled the next day
in windy rain, which began gently, but afterwards fell in
persistent torrents, varied by pungent swirls of sleet and
snow. Leaving the gash through cliffs with curious
stratification in white and red, formed by the Holwan,
the day was spent in skirting or crossing low hills.
The mud was very deep and tenacious, and the rate of
progress barely two miles an hour. There were no
caravans, travellers, or population, and no birds or beasts.
The rain clouds hung low and heavy, mists boiled up
from among the folds of the hills, the temperature fell
perceptibly. It was really inspiriting for people pro-
tected by good mackintoshes.

After riding for six hours the rain changed into sleet
and wet snow, blotting out the hills and creating an
unnatural twilight, in which we floundered in mud up to
the mules' knees into the filthiest village I have ever
seen, a compound of foul, green ditches, piles of dissolving
manure, mud hovels looking as if they were dissolving too,
reed huts, and an Ilyat village, grouped round the vilest
of caravanserais, the entrance to which was knee-deep in
mire. To lodge in it was voted impossible, and the
escort led us in the darkening mist and pelting sleet to
an adjacent mud hamlet as hopeless-looking on the other
side of the bridge, where, standing up to the knees of the
mules in liquid manure, we sought but vainly for shelter,
forded the Holwan, and returned to the caravanserai
through almost impassable slush.

It was simply loathsome, with its stench, its foulness,
and its mire, and was already crowded and noisy with
men and beasts. There was a great courtyard with arched

recesses all round, too abominable to be occupied, too
exposed and ruinous, even had they been cleaned, to give
shelter from the driving sleet. The last resource was to pass
through an archway into the great, lofty mule stable, on
both sides of which are similar recesses or mangers, about
ten feet by seven and about eight feet high. The stable
was of great size and height with a domed roof. Probably
it runs half-way round the quadrangle at the back of the
uninhabitable recesses. There were at least four hundred
mules in this place, jangling their great bells, and crowds

LODGINGS FOR TRAVELLERS.

of *katirgis*, travellers, and *zaptiehs*, all wet and splashed
over their heads with mud, some unloading, others making fires and feeding their mules, all shouting when they
had anything to say, the Babel aggravated by the clatter
of the rattles of a hundred curry-combs and the squeals
of fighting horses.

The floor was deep with the manure of ages and piled
with bales and boxes. In the side recesses, which are
about the height of a mule's back, the muleteers camped
with their fires and their goods, and laid the provender
for their beasts in the front. These places are the
mangers of the eastern caravanserai, or *khan*, or inn.
Such must have been the inn at Bethlehem, and surely

the first step to the humiliation of "the death of the cross" must have been the birth in the manger, amidst the crowd and horrors of such a stable.

The odour was overpowering and the noise stunning, and when our wet, mud-covered baggage animals came in, adding to the din, there was hardly room to move, far less for the roll in which all mules indulge when the loads are taken off; and the crush resulted in a fight, and one mule got his fore-feet upon my "manger," and threatened to share it with me.   It was an awful place to come to after a six hours' march in rain and snow, but I slid off my mule into the recess, had it carpeted, put down my chair, hung a blanket up in front, and prepared to brave it, when the inhabitants of this room, the one place which has any pretensions to being a room in the village, were bribed by an offer of six *krans* (about four shillings) to vacate it for me.   Its "pretensions" consist in being over a gateway, and in having a door, and a square hole looking on the street; a crumbling stair slippery with mud leads up to it.   The roof leaks in every direction, and the slimy floor is full of pools, but it is luxury after the caravanserai stable, and with one waterproof sheet over my bed and another over myself I have fared well, though the door cannot be shut, and the rest of the party are in the stable at an impassable distance.

Our language happily has no words in which the state of this village can be described.   In front of this room is a broken ditch full of slimy greenish water, which Hadji took for my tea!   There has been a slight snowfall during the night, and snow is impending.   We have now reached a considerable altitude, and may expect anything.   Hadji has just climbed the stair with groans of " *Ya Allah*," and has almost wailed out, " Colonel says we go—God help us."

Kirrind, Jan. 23.—From Saripul-i-Zohab we are
taking the most southerly of the three routes to Kirmanshah traversed by Sir H. Rawlinson in 1836.[1]   A sea of
mud varied by patches of sodden snow, walls of rock
with narrow passes, great snow-covered mountains, seen
spectrally for a minute at a time through swirling snow-
clouds, black tents of nomads, half-drowned villages, and
a long, cold, steep ascent, among scrub oaks and dwarf
ash, to snow which was not melting, and the hospitalities
of a Kurdish village, comprise the interests of the march
from Saripul to Myan Tak, so far as they lie on the
surface, but in various ways this part of Kurdistan has
many interests, not to be absolutely ignored even in a
familiar letter.

Here the Ilyats, who are supposed to constitute a fifth
of the rural population of Persia, are met with in large
numbers, and their brown flocks and herds are still
picking up a scanty subsistence.   The great chief of this,
the Gurān tribe, holds the region on an annual payment
to the Persian Government, gives grain to his tribesmen,
and receives from them, of corn one-half, and of rice two-
thirds of the crop.   These people sow their grain in early
spring, and then move up with their flocks to the
mountain pastures, leaving behind only a few men to
harvest the crops.   They use no manure, this being
required for fuel, and in the case of rice they allow a
fallow of at least seven years.   There are very few
cultivators resident upon these lands, but Ilyat camps
occur frequently.

The region is steeped in history.   The wretched
village of Saripul is the Calah of Asshur and the Halah
of the Israelitish captivity,[2] and gave to the surrounding

---

[1] The Pashalik of Zohab, now Persian territory, is fully described by
Major Rawlinson in a most interesting paper in *The Journal of the Royal
Geographical Society*, vol. ix. part 1, p. 26.

[2] Gen. x. 11 ; 2 Kings xviii. 11 ; 1 Chron. v. 26.

country the name of Chalonitis, which we have on our old maps. A metropolitan See in the fifth century A.D., soon after the institution of the Nestorian hierarchy, it was called Calah, Halah, and Holwan. If the Diyalah be the ancient Gyndes, noteworthy for the singular delay of Cyrus on his march to Babylon, and Saripul the ancient Holwan, and if in addition to the numerous Chaldæan and Sasanian remains there are relics of Semiramis and of the fire-temples of the Magi, the crowd of historic associations is almost too much for one day, and I will return to the insignificant details of the journey.

We left at nine, crossed the Holwan by a four-arched brick bridge, and in falling snow and deep mud rode over fairly level ground till we came to an abrupt range of limestone rock, with a natural rift, across which the foundations of a wall still remain. The clouds were rolling low, and the snow was driving wildly, so as to make it impossible to see the sculptured tablet described by Rawlinson and Layard, on which a high-priest of the Magi is represented, with one hand raised in benediction, and the other grasping a scroll, the dress being the pontifical robe worn by the Zoroastrian priests, with a square cap, pointed in front, and lappets covering the mouth. Above this is a tomb with an ornamented entrance.

We were now among a very strange and mysterious people, of whose ancestry and actual beliefs very little is known. They are Ali-Ilahis, but Europeans often speak of them as " Davidites," from their special veneration for King David. This tomb in the rift is called Dukkani-Daoud, or David's shop, and the people believe that he still dwells there, and come on pilgrimages and to offer animals in sacrifice from all parts of Kurdistan. He is believed to work as a smith, and the *katirgis* say that he makes suits of fine armour. A part of the tomb which

is divided from the rest by a low partition is believed to
be a reservoir containing the water which he uses to
temper his metal. A great mound with some building
in the centre, on the right of the road near this gorge,
though properly it bears another name, is called by the
people "David's Fort." Jewish traditions abound, specially
concerning David, who is regarded by the tribes as their
great tutelar prophet.

The Gurāns and Kalhurs, who are the nomadic
inhabitants of this district, are of a very marked type of
physiognomy, so Israelitish indeed that, taken along with
certain traditions of their origin, their Jewish names, and
their veneration for David, they have been put forward
as claimants to the dignity of being the "lost tribes."
The great Hebrew traveller of the twelfth century, to
whom I have referred before, believed that the whole of
the Ali-Ilahis were Jews, and writes of 100 synagogues
in the Zagros mountains, and of 50,000 Jewish families
in the neighbourhood.

As we shall be for some days among these people, I
will abbreviate Sir H. Rawlinson's sketch of their tenets.
He considers that Ali-Ilahism bears evident marks of
Judaism, mixed up with Moslem, Christian, and Sabæan
legends. The Ali-Ilahis believe in 1001 incarnations of
the Godhead in a series; among them Benjamin, Moses,
Elias, David, Jesus Christ, Ali and Salman his tutor, the
Imam Houssein and the Haftān (or seven bodies), the
chief spiritual guides in the early ages of Islam, "and
each, worshipped as a Deity, is an object of adoration
in some locality of Kurdistan." The tomb of one of
these, Bābā Yadgār, is their holy place, and this was
regarded as the dwelling of Elijah at the time when the
Arabs invaded Persia. All these incarnations are regarded
as of one and the same person. All that changes is the
bodily form of the Divine manifestation. There are

degrees in the perfection of the development, and the most perfect forms are Benjamin, David, and Ali.

Practically, however, the metaphysical speculations involved in this creed of successive incarnations are unknown, and the Imam Ali, the cousin of Mohammed, is the great object of worship. Though professing Mohammedanism the Ali-Ilahis are held in great horror by "believers," and those of this region lie under the stigma of practising unholy rites as a part of their religion, and have received the name of "Chiragh Sonderan," the putters-out of lights.[1] This accusation, Sir A. H. Layard observes, may be only a calumny invented, like many another, to justify persecution.

Passing through the rift in the Dukkani-Daoud range which has led to this digression, we entered an ascending valley between the range through which we had passed and some wild mountains covered with snow, which were then actively engaged in brewing a storm. Farther on there was irrigation and cultivation, and then the wretched village of Pai Tak, and the ruins of a bridge. There, the people told us, we must halt, as the caravanserai at the next place was already full, and we plunged about in the snow and mud looking for a hovel in which to take shelter, but decided to risk going on, and shortly began the ascent of the remarkable pass known as "The Gates of Zagros," on the ancient highway between Babylonia and Media, by which, in a few hours, the mountain barrier of Zagros is crossed, and the plain of Kirrind, a part of the great Iranian plateau, is reached.

This great road, which zigzags steeply up the pass, is partly composed of smoothed boulders and partly of natural rock, somewhat dressed, and much worn by the continual passage of shod animals. It is said to be much like a torrent bed, but the snow was lying heavily upon

[1] See Sir A. H. Layard's *Early Adventures*, vol. i. p. 217.

it, filling up its inequalities.   Dwarf oaks, hawthorn, ash, and other scrub find root-hold in every crevice.   All that may be ugly was draped in pure white, and looking back from the surrounding glitter, the view of low ranges lying in indigo gloom was very striking.   On the ascent there is a remarkable arch of great blocks of white marble, with a vaulted recess, called the "Tak-i-Girreh," "the arch holding the road," which gives the popular name of Gardan-i-Tak-i-Girreh (the pass of Tak-i-Girreh) to the ascent, though the geographers call it Akabah-i-Holwan (the defile of Holwan).

After the deep mud of the earlier part of the march it was a pleasure to ride through pure, deep, powdery snow, and to find the dirt of the village of Myan Tak, a Kurdish hamlet situated on a mountain torrent among steep hills and small trees, covered with this radiant mantle. The elevation of the pass is 4630 feet, but Myan Tak is at a lower altitude an hour farther on.

The small and ruinous caravanserai was really full of caravans detained by the snowstorm, and we lodged in a Kurdish house, typical of the style of architecture common among the settled tribes.   Within a wide doorway without a door, high enough for a loaded mule to enter, is a very large room, with a low, flat mud roof, supported on three rows of misshapen trunks of trees, with their branches cut off about a foot from the stem, all black and shiny with smoke.   Mud and rubble platforms, two feet high, run along one side and one end, and on the end one there is a clay, beehive-shaped fireplace, but no chimney.   Under this platform the many fowls are shut in at night by a stone at the hole by which they enter.   Within this room is a perfectly dark stable of great size.   Certainly forty mules, besides asses and oxen, were lodged in it, and the overflow shared the living-room with a number of Kurds, *katirgis,* servants, dogs, soldiers, and Europeans. The furniture consisted of guns and swords hanging on the walls.

The owner is an old Kurd with some handsome sons with ruddy complexions and auburn hair. The big house is the patriarchal roof, where the patriarch, his sons, their wives and children, and their animals, dwell together. The women, however, had all been got rid of somehow. The old Kurd made a great fire on the dais, wood being plentiful, and crouched over it. My bed was pitched near it, and enclosed by some reed screens. With chairs and a table, with routes, maps, writing materials, and a good lantern upon it, an excellent dinner of soup and a leg of mutton, cooked at a bonfire in the middle of the floor, and the sight of all the servants and *katirgis* lying round it, warm and comfortable, and the knowledge that we were above the mud, the clouds of blinding smoke which were the only drawback scarcely affected the cheerfulness and comfort of the blazing, unstinted fire. The doorway gave not only ample ventilation but a brilliant view of snow, and of myriads of frosty stars.

It was infinitely picturesque, with the fitful firelight falling on the uncouth avenues of blackened tree-stumps, on big dogs, on mild-eyed ox faces and long ass ears, on turbaned Indian heads, and on a confused crowd of Turks, Kurds, and Persians, some cooking, some sleeping, some smoking, while from the black depth beyond a startling bray of an ass or the abortive shriek of a mule occasionally proceeded, or a stray mule created a commotion by rushing in from the snow outside.

I slept comfortably, till I was awakened early by various country sounds—the braying of an ass into my ear (for I was within a few inches of the stable), the crowing of cocks, and some hens picking up crumbs upon

my bed. The mules were loaded in the living-room.
The mercury was only 26° at 9 A.M., and under cloudless sunshine the powdery snow glittered and crackled.
There were difficulties ahead, we heard. The road
heavily blocked with snow was only just open, and the
Persian post, which should have passed forty-eight hours
before, had not been heard of, showing that the snow is
very deep farther on.

It was beautiful, that uplifted, silent world of snow
and mountains, on whose skirts for some miles grew small
apple and pear trees, oak, ash, and hawthorn, each twig a
coral spray. In the deepest depression, among great
rocks, now masses of snow, tumbles a now partially
arrested stream, gleaming with icicles, one of the head-
waters of the Holwan. After getting through this
picturesque forest of scrub, the road emerges on the
plateau of the Kirrind valley, the greatest altitude of
which is about 5800 feet. It is said to be irrigated and
fertile. It is now, as I describe it, a wide valley, without a tree or bush, a rolling plain of snow from two to
three feet deep, marked only by lines made by birds' feet
and the beating of the tips of birds' wings, the track across
it a corrugated trench, wide enough for one mule, the sun
brilliant, the sky blue, the surface of the snow flashing
light from millions of crystals with a glitter not to be
borne, all dazzling, " glistering," silent,—a white world
and a blue heaven, with a sun " shining in his strength,"
—light without heat.

It has been a tremendous day's march, only fourteen
miles in seven and a half hours of severe toil! The
katirgis asked us to keep together in case of difficulties
with caravans. Difficulties indeed! A mild term! I
was nearly smashed. I little knew what meeting a
caravan in these circumstances meant till we met the
first sixty animals, each laden with two heavy packing-

cases. The question arises who is to give way, and who
is to drive his heavily-laden beasts off the track, to
struggle, flounder, and fall in three feet of snow, not to
get up again without being unloaded, and even then
with difficulty.

The rub came on a bank near a stream where there
was a deep drift. I decided to give way, but nothing
would induce my mule to face the snow. An orderly
was in front and Hadji behind. Down the track came
sixty animals, loaded with their great packing-cases.
They could not and would not give way, and the two
caravans came into collision. There were mules
struggling and falling, loads overturned, muleteers yell-
ing and roaring, Hadji groaning " God help us ! " my mule,
a new one, a big strong animal, unused to a bit, plunging
and kicking, in the middle of a " free fight." I was
struck hard on my ankle by a packing-case and nearly
knocked off. Still, down they came, in apparently
endless hordes ; my mule plunged her bridle off, and
kicked most violently ; there were yells all round. My
snow spectacles were knocked off and lost, then came
another smash, in which I thought a bone was broken.
Fearing that I should be laid up with a broken limb for
weeks in some horrible caravanserai, and really desperate
with the danger and confusion, I called over and over
again to Hadji to get off and pull my mule into the snow
or I should be killed ! He did not stir, but sat dazed on
his pack moaning " God help us ! " till he, the mule, and
the load were rolled over in the drift. The orderly con-
trived to get the bridle on my mule, and to back his
own in front of me, and as each irrepressible animal
rolled down the bank he gave its load a push, which, nicely
balanced as these loads are, made it swerve, and saved
me from further damage. Hadji had rolled off four times
previously, and the last I saw of him at that time and

of the caravan was a man, five mules, and their loads buried in the snow. The personal results to me of what is euphemistically called a "difficulty," are my blue glasses gone, a number of bruises, a badly-torn riding-skirt, and a bad cut, which bled profusely, and then the blood froze.

A number of caravans snowed up for several days were *en route*, and there were many similar encounters, and donkeys and mules falling with their loads and rolling into the deep snow, and *katirgis* coming to blows over the right-of-way. If a donkey is forced off the track it goes down at once. I unfortunately caught my foot in the pack of one and rolled it over, and as it disappeared in the snow its pack and saddle fell over its head and displayed the naked vertebræ of its poor back.

This Kirrind valley must be fully twenty miles long by from two to five broad, but there was only one village inhabited and two in ruins. As we floundered along in the snow with our jaded animals, two well-armed men on fine horses met and joined us, sent by the *Agha* Abdul Rahim, son of the British agent at Kirmanshah, whose guests we are to be. Following them was a *taktrawan* or litter for me, a wooden box with two side doors, four feet high, six feet long, and three feet wide. At each end are long shafts, and between each pair of shafts a superb mule, and each mule has a man to lead him. I could never use such a thing except in case of a broken limb, but I am very grateful to Abdul Rahim for sending it fifty-six miles.

The temperature fell with the sun; the snowy hills took on every shade of rose and pink, and in a universal blush of tender colouring we reached Kirrind. All of a sudden the colour died out, the rose-flushed sky changed to blue-gray, and pallid wastes of unbroken snow stretching into the gray distance made a glorious winter landscape. We are now fairly in for the rigours of a Persian winter.

Kirrind, the capital of the Kirrind Kurds, is either grotesquely or picturesquely situated in and around a narrow gap in a range of lofty hills, through which the Ab-i-Kirrind rushes, after rising in a spring immediately behind. The gap suggests the word jaws, and in these open jaws rise one above another flat-roofed houses straggling down upon the plain among vineyards, poplars, willows, fruit-trees, and immense walnuts and gardens. There are said to be 900 houses, but many of them are ruinous. The stream which bursts from the hills is divided into innumerable streamlets, which must clothe these gardens with beauty.

A *farāsh* riding on ahead had engaged a house, so we avoided the horrors of the immense caravanserai, crammed to-night with storm-bound caravans. The house is rough, but has three adjoining rooms, and the servants are comfortable. A fire, with its usual accompaniment of stinging smoke, fails to raise the temperature of my room to the freezing-point, yet it is quite possible to be comfortable and employ oneself.

Mahidasht, Jan. 24.—My room at Kirrind was very cold. The ink froze. The mercury fell to 2° below zero in it, and outside in the sun was only 14° at 8.30. There was a great Babel at starting. Some men had sold four chickens for the high price of 2s. each, the current price being 6d., and had robbed the servants of two, and they took one of the mules, which was sent after us by an official. Slipping, floundering, and falling in the deep snow, and getting entangled among caravans, we rode all day over rolling levels. The distance seemed interminable over the glittering plains, and the pain and stiffness produced by the intense cold were hard to bear, and it was not possible to change the cramped position by walking. The mercury fell to 4°, as with tired animals we toiled up the slope on which Harunabad stands.

A very large caravanserai and a village of sixty houses occupy the site of a town built by Harun-al-Raschid on the upper waters of the Kerkhah. It has the reputation of being one of the coldest places in Persia, so cold that its Ilyat inhabitants desert it in winter, leaving two or three men who make a business of supplying caravans. Usually people come out of the villages in numbers as we arrive, but we passed group after group of ruinous hovels without seeing a creature. We obtained awfully cold rooms at a great height above a bazar, now deserted. I write "awfully" advisedly, for the mercury in them at sunset was 2° below zero, the floors were plaster, slippery with frozen moisture, the walls were partly wood, with great apertures between the planks; where they were mud the blistered plaster was fringed with icicles. Later the mercury sank to 12°, and before morning to 16° below zero, and the hot water froze in my basin before I could use it!

We were to have started at eight, as there was no possible way of dividing the nine hours' march, but when the time came the *katirgis* said it was too cold to rope the loads, a little later that we could only get half-way, and later that there was no accommodation for mules half-way and that we must go the whole way! At nine the mercury was at 4° below zero, and the slipperiness was fearful. The poor animals could scarcely keep on their feet. We have crossed two high passes, Nal Shikan (the Horse-Shoe breaking pass) and the Charzabar Pass, in tremendous snow, riding nine hours, only dismounting to walk down one hill. At the half-way hamlet I decided to go on, having still a lingering prejudice against sharing a den with a quantity of human beings, mules, asses, poultry, and dogs.

On one long ascent we encountered a "blizzard," when the mercury was only 3° above zero. It was awful. The men covered their heads with their *abbas* and turned their backs to the wind. I got my heavy mackintosh over everything, but in taking off three pairs of gloves for one minute to button it the pain of my hand was literally excruciating. At the summit the snow was four feet deep, and a number of mules were down, but after getting over the crest of the Nal Shikan Pass and into the Zobeideh valley it became better. But after every descent there was another ascent to face till we reached the pass above the Cheshmeh-i-Charzabar torrent, in a picturesque glen, with a village and some primitive flour mills.

Below this height lies the vast and fertile plain of Mahidasht, one expanse of snow, broken by mud villages looking like brown islands, and the truncated cone of Goree, a seat of the ancient fire-worship. In the centre of the plain is an immense caravanserai with some houses about it. When this came into sight it was only five miles off, but we were nearly three hours in reaching it ! The view was wonderful. Every speck on the vast plain was seen distinctly ; then came a heavy snow blink, above which hovered ghosts of snow mountains rising into a pale green sky, a dead and lonely wilderness, looking as if all things which lived and moved had long ago vanished from it. Those hours after first sighting the village were very severe. It seemed to grow no nearer. I was half-dead with the journey of twenty-two miles at a slow foot's pace, and was aching and cramped from the intense cold, for as twilight fell the mercury sank to 3° below zero. The Indian servants, I believe, suffered more than I did, and some of the *katirgis* even more than they.

At last by a pointed brick bridge we crossed the

little river of Mahidasht, and rode into the house of
the headman, who is a sort of steward of Abdul
Rahim, our future host, the owner of many villages on
this plain.   The house is of the better class of
Kurdish houses, with a broad passage, and a room on
each side, at the end a great, low, dark room, half living-
room, half stable, which accommodates to-night some of the
mules, the muleteers, the servants, and the men of the
family.   Beyond this again is a large stable, and below-
ground, reached by a sloping tunnel, is the sheep-fold.
One room has neither door nor window, mine has an
outer and inner door, and a fire of live embers in a hole
in the floor.

The family in vacating the room have left their goods
behind,—two plank beds at one end heaped with carpets
and felts, a sacking cradle hanging from the roof, two
clay jars five feet high for storing grain, and in the
takchahs, or recesses of the walls, *samovars* or tea-urns,
pots, metal vases, cartridge belts, and odds and ends.
Two old guns, an old sword, and a coarse coloured print
of the Russian Imperial family are on the wall.

I was lifted from the mule to my bed, covered
with all available wraps, a pot of hot embers put by
the bed, my hands and feet rubbed, hot syrup coloured
with tea produced in Russian glasses, and in two
hours I was able to move.   The caravan, which we
thought could not get through the snow, came in three
hours later, men and mules thoroughly knocked up, and
not till nine could we get a scanty dinner.   It has been
a hard day all round.   The *farāshes* in the kitchen are
cursing the English sahibs, who will travel in the winter,
wishing our fathers may be burned, etc., two of the
muleteers have been howling with pain for the last two
hours, and I went into the kitchen to see the poor
fellows.

In a corner of the big room, among the rough trunks of trees which support the sooty roof, the muleteers were lying in a heap in their big-sleeved felt coats round a big fire, about another the servants were cooking their food, the *farāshes* were lying round another, and some of the house people about a fourth, and through smoke and flame a background of mules and wolf-like dogs was dimly seen, a gleam now and then falling into the dark stable beyond, where the jaded baggage animals were lying in heaps.

Mahidasht is said to be one of the finest and most fertile plains in Persia, seventy-two miles long by fifteen broad, and is irrigated throughout by a small stream swarming with turtles. Its population, scattered over it in small villages, is estimated — over-estimated probably — at 4000. At a height of 5050 feet the winters are severe. The snow is nearly three feet deep already, and more is impending.

The mercury in my room fell to 5° below zero before midnight, but rose for a gray cloudy day. The men and animals were so done up that we could not start till nearly eleven. The march, though not more than sixteen miles, was severe, owing to the deep snow and cold wind. Five miles over the snowy billows of the Mahidasht plain, a long ascent, on which the strong north wind was scarcely bearable, a succession of steep and tiresome ridges, many "difficulties" in passing caravans, and then a gradual descent down a long wide valley, opened upon the high plateau, on which Kirmanshah, one of the most important cities in Persia, is situated.

Trees, bare and gaunt, chiefly poplars, rising out of unsullied snow, for two hours before we reached it, denoted the whereabouts of the city, which after many disappointments bursts upon one suddenly. The view from the hill above the town was the most glorious snow view I ever saw. All around, rolled to a great height, smooth as the icing of a cake, hills, billowy like the swell of the Pacific after a storm—an ocean of snow ; below them a plateau equally unsullied, on the east side of which rises the magnificently precipitous Besitun range, sublime in its wintry grandeur, while on the distant side of the plateau pink peaks raised by an atmospheric illusion to a colossal height hovered above the snow blink, and walled in the picture. Snow was in the air, snow clouds were darkening over the Besitun range ; except for those pink peaks there were no atmospheric effects ; the white was very pallid, and the gray was very black ; no illusions were possible, the aspect was grim, desolate, and ominous, and even before we reached the foot of the descent the huge peaks and rock masses of Besitun were blotted out by swirls of snow.

Kirmanshah, approached from the south-west, added no elements of picturesqueness to the effect. A ruinous wall much too large for the shrunken city it encloses, parts of it lying in the moat, some ruinous loopholed towers, lines of small domes denoting bazars below, a few good-look-ing houses rising above the insignificant mass, gardens, orchards, vineyards, and poplars stretching up the southerly hollow behind, and gardens, now under frozen water, to the north, made up a not very interesting contrast with the magnificence of nature.

We circled much of the ruinous wall on thin ice, turned in between high walls and up an alley cumbered with snow, dismounted at a low door, were received by a number of servants, and were conducted through a frozen courtyard into a handsomely-carpeted room with divans beside a blazing fire, a table in the centre covered with apples, oranges, and sweetmeats, and the large Jubilee photograph of Queen Victoria hanging over the fire-place.

                                                    I. L. B.

LETTER V

KIRMANSHAH, *Jan. 31.*

THIS hospitable house is the residence of the British Agent or *Vakil* for Kirmanshah, in whose absence at Tihran, his son, Abdul Rahim, performs the duties of hospitality in a most charming manner, as if though a very busy man he had nothing else to do but carry out the wishes of his guests. His hospitality is most unobtrusive also, and considerate. If such a wish is expressed as to visit the sculptures of the Takt-i-Bostan, or anything else, everything is quietly and beautifully arranged ; a landau-and-four with outriders, superb led saddle-horses, and arrangements for coffee are ready outside the walls, with the host as *cicerone*, ready to drive or ride at the pleasure of his guests. The rooms in which he receives Europeans are on the opposite side of the courtyard from the house, and have been arranged according to European ideas.

The family history, as usually told, is an interesting one. They are Arabs, and the grandfather of our host, Hadji Khalil, was a trusted *katirgi* in the employment of Sir Henry Rawlinson, and saved his life when he fell from a scaffolding while copying the Besitun inscriptions. His good qualities, and an honesty of character and purpose rare among Orientals, eventually placed him in the important position of British *Vakil* here, and he became a British subject, and was succeeded in his position by his son, Agha Hassan, who is now by virtue of singular business capacities the wealthiest man in this province and possibly in Persia, and bears the very highest character for trustworthiness and honour.[1]

Abdul Rahim is a very fine-looking man, with noticeable eyes, very large and prominent. He has a strong sense of humour, which flits over his face in an amused smile. He and his father are very large landowners, and are always adding land to land, and are now the owners of the magnificent sculptures and pleasure-grounds of the Takt-i-Bostan. They are bankers likewise, and money-lenders, merchants on a large scale, and have built a very fine caravanserai, with great brick warehouses for the use of traders. Agha Hassan travels *en prince*, driving to Tihran and back in an English landau with four horses and a number of outriders and attendants, and his son entertains visitors in the same way, mounting even the outriders and pipe-bearers on well-bred Arabs. When he walks in the city it is like a royal progress. Everybody bows low, nearly to the ground, and his purse-bearer follows, distributing alms among the poor.

I mention all this because it is a marvel in Persia, where a reputation for wealth is the last thing a rich man desires. To elevate a gateway or to give any external sign of affluence is to make himself a mark for the official rapacity which spares none. The policy is to let a man grow quietly rich, to "let the sheep's wool grow," but as soon as he shows any enjoyment of wealth

[1] I had the pleasure of seeing Agha Hassan at the British Legation at Tihran. He is charming, both in appearance and manner, a specimen of the highest type of Arab good breeding, with a courteous kindliness and grace of manner, and is said to have made a very favourable impression when he went to England lately to be made a C.M.G. Both father and son wear the Arab dress, in plain colours but rich materials, with very large white turbans of Damascus embroidery in gold silk, and speak only Arabic and Persian.

to deprive him of his gains, according to a common Persian expression, "He is ripe, he must be squeezed." The *Vakil* and his son are the only men here who are not afraid to show their wealth, and for the simple reason that it cannot be touched, because they are British subjects. They can neither be robbed, squeezed, nor mulcted beyond the legitimate taxation by Persian officials, and are able to protect the property of others when it is entrusted to their keeping. British protection has been in fact the making of these men.

The *ménage* is simple. The dining-room is across the frozen courtyard. The meals are served in European fashion, the *major-domo* being an ancient man, "born in the house," who occasionally inserts a remark into the conversation or helps his master's memory. The interpreter sits on the floor during meals. I breakfast in my room, but lunch and dine with our host, who spends the evening in the *salon*; sherbet is provided instead of wine. Abdul Rahim places me at the head of the table, and I am served first! The interpreting is from Persian into Hindustani, and *vice versâ*. Our host expresses almost daily regret that he cannot talk with me on politics!

Kirmanshah, which is said to be a favourable specimen of a Persian town, is absolutely hideous and uninteresting. It is really half in ruins. It has suffered terribly from "plague, pestilence, and famine," and from the awful rapacity of governors. It once had 12,000 houses, but the highest estimate of its present population is 25,000. So severely have the town and province been oppressed that some years ago three-quarters of the inhabitants migrated, the peasants into Turkey, and the townspeople into the northern province of Azerbijan. If a governor pays 30,000 *tumans* (£10,000) to the Shah for an appointment, of which he may be deprived any day, it can scarcely be expected of Oriental, or indeed of any human nature, that he will not make a good thing of it while he has it, and squeeze all he can out of the people.

The streets are very narrow, and look narrower just now, because the snow is heaped almost to the top of the mud walls, which are not broken up as in Turkish towns by projecting lattice windows, but are absolutely blank, with the exception of low-arched entrances to the court-yards within, closed by heavy, unpainted wooden doors, studded with wooden nails. The causeways, on which, but for the heaps of slippery snow two men might walk abreast, have a ditch two or three feet wide between them, which is the roadway for animals. There are some open spaces, abounding in ruinous heaps, others where goods are unloaded, surrounded with warehouses, immense brick bazars with domed roofs, a citadel or *ark*, where the Governor lives, a large parade ground and barracks for 2000 men, mosques of no pretensions, public baths, caravanserais, brick warehouses behind the bazars, public gardens, with fountains and avenues of poplars, a prison, and some good houses like this one, hidden behind high mud walls. Although the snow kindly veils a good deal of deformity, the city impresses one as ruinous and decayed; yet it has a large trade, and is regarded as one of the most prosperous places in the Empire.[1]

The bazars are spacious and well stocked with European goods, especially with Manchester cottons of colours and patterns suited to Oriental taste, which loves carnation red. There are many Jews, otherwise the people are Shiah Moslems, with an increasing admixture of the secret sect of the *Bābis*. In some

[1] A journey of nine months in Persia, chiefly in the west and north-west, convinced me that this aspect of ruin and decay is universal.

respects the Shiahs are more fanatical than the Sunnis, as, for instance, it is quite possible to visit a mosque in Turkey, but here a Christian is not allowed to cross the threshold of the outer gate. Certain customs are also more rigidly observed. A Persian woman would be in danger of death from the mob if she appeared unveiled in the streets. When I walked through the town, though attended by a number of men, the *major-domo* begged me to exchange my gauze veil for a mask, and even when I showed this deference to custom the passing through the bazars was very unpleasant, the men being decidedly rude, and inclined to hoot and use bad language. Even the touch of a Christian is regarded as polluting, and I nearly got into trouble by handling a " flap-jack," mistaking it for a piece of felt. The bazars are not magnificent. No rich carpets or other goods are exposed to view for fear of exactions. A buyer wanting such things must send word privately, and have them brought to his house.

Justice seems to be here, much as in Turkey, a marketable commodity, which the working classes are too poor to buy. A man may be kept in prison because he is too poor to get out, but justice is usually summary, and men are not imprisoned for long terms. If prisoners have friends, the friends feed them, if not they depend on charity, and charity is a Moslem virtue. There is no prison here for women. They are punished by having their heads shaved, and by being taken through the town on asses. Various forms of torture are practised, such as burning with hot irons, the bastinado, and squeezing the fingers in a vice. The bastinado is also most extensively used as a punishment.

Yesterday by appointment we were received by the Governor of the Province. Riding through the slippery snow-heaped alleys is not what Europeans would think

of, and our host with his usual courtesy humoured the
caprice by walking with us himself, preceded by six
farāshes (lit. carpet-spreaders) and followed by his purse-
bearer casting money to the poor, and a train of servants.
The Citadel, or Governor's residence, like all else, is
forlorn, dirty, and ruinous in its approaches, which are
long vaulted corridors capable of much adornment.
Crowds of soldiers, *mollahs*, dervishes, and others were
there to see the visit, which was one of ceremony. The
Palace and Government offices are many-windowed, well-
built brick-and-tile buildings, arranged round a large
place with trees and fountains.

Two little fellows in scarlet uniform were at the
entrance, and the lobby upstairs was crowded with
Persian and Negro servants, all in high, black lambskin
caps, tight black trousers, and tight coats with full
skirts. The Governor received us in a very large, lofty,
vacant-looking room, and shook hands. I never saw a
human being more nearly like an ape in appearance, and
a loud giggle added to the resemblance. This giggle and
a fatuous manner are possibly assumed, for he has the
widespread reputation of being a very able man, shrewd
in business and officially rapacious, as was his father
before him. The grotesque figure, not more than five
feet high, was dressed in a black Astrakan cap, a coat of
fine buff Russian kerseymere with full skirts, and tight
trousers of the same, and an under-coat of rich, Kerman
silk brocade, edged with costly fur. He made a few
curt remarks to his foreign guests, and then turned to
Abdul Rahim, and discussed local affairs for the
remainder of a very long visit.

A table covered with exquisite-looking sweetmeats
was produced, and we were regaled with tea *à la
Russe* in Russian glasses, ice-cream, and *gaz*. Then
young, diminutive, raw-looking soldiers in scarlet coats

and scarlet trousers with blue stripes marched into the courtyard, and stood disconsolately in the snow, and two bands brayed and shrieked for an hour. Then *kalians* were smoked, and coffee was handed round, the cups being in gold filigree holders incrusted with turquoises. This was the welcome signal for the termination of a very tedious visit. The reception-room is a dismal combination of Persian and European taste, invariably a failure. The carpets are magnificent, but the curtains are common serge bordered with white cotton lace, and the tea-table with its costly equipments was covered with a tawdry cretonne cover, edged with some inferior black cotton lace. The lofty walls of plain plaster of Paris have their simplicity destroyed by some French girandoles with wax grapes hanging from them.

The Governor returned the visit to-day, arriving on horseback with fully forty mounted attendants, and was received in a glass room on the roof, furnished with divans, tables covered with beautiful confectionery, and tea and coffee equipages. The conversation was as local as yesterday, in spite of our host's courteous efforts to include the strangers in it. The Governor asked if I were going to Tihran to be *Hakīm* to the Shah's *haram*, which our host says is the rumour in Kirmanshah! During such visits there are crowds of attendants in the room all the time pouring out tea, filling *kalians*, and washing cups on the floor, and as any guest may be a spy and an enemy, the conversation is restricted to exaggerated compliments and superficial remarks.

Everything is regulated by an elaborate code of etiquette, even the compliments are meted out by rule, and to give a man more than he is entitled to is understood to be intended as sarcasm. The number of bows made by the entertainer, the distance he advances to meet his guest, and the position in which he seats him are matters of careful calculation, and the slightest mistake in any particular is liable to be greatly resented by a superior.

The Persian is a most ceremonious being. Like the Japanese he is trained from infancy to the etiquette of his class, and besides the etiquette of class there is here the etiquette of religion, which is far more strict than in Turkey, and yields only when there is daily contact, as in the capital, between Moslems and Christians. Thus, a Moslem will not accept refreshments from a Christian, and he will not smoke a pipe after a Christian even if he is his guest, and of equal or higher rank.

The custom is for a visitor, as in the case of the Governor, to announce his visit previously, and he and his train are met, when he is the superior, by a mounted servant of the recipient of the honour, who precedes him to the door, where the servants are arranged according to their rank, and the host waits to take his hand and lead him to a seat. On entering the room a well-bred Persian knows at once what place he ought to take, and it is rare for such a *fiasco* as that referred to in Luke xiv. 9 to occur. Refreshments and pipes are served at regulated intervals, and the introduction of a third cup of tea or coffee and a third *kalian* is the signal for the guest to retire. But it is necessary to ask and receive permission to do so, and elaborate forms of speech regulated by the rank of the visitor are used on the occasion. If he is of equal or superior rank, the host, bowing profoundly, replies that he can have no other wish than that of his guest, that the house has been purified by his presence, that the announcement of the visit brought good luck to the house, that his headache or toothache has been cured by his arrival, and these flowery compliments escort the ordinary guest to the door, but if he be of superior rank the host walks in advance to

the foot of the stairs, and repeats the compliments
there.

The etiquette concerning pipes is most elaborate.[1]
Kalians are invariably used among the rich. The great
man brings his own, and his own pipe-bearer. The
kalian is a water pipe, and whatever its form the
principle is the same, the smoke being conducted to
the bottom of a liberal supply of water, to be sucked up
in bubbles through it with a gurgling noise, as in the
Indian "hubble-bubble." This water-holder is decanter-
shaped, of plain or cut glass, with a wide mouth; the
fire-holder, as in the case of the Governor's pipe, is often
a work of high art, in thin gold, chased, engraved,
decorated with *repoussé* work, or incrusted with turquoises, or ornamented with rich enamel, very costly,
£40 or even £50 being paid by rich men for the decoration of a single pipe-head. Between this and the water-
holder is a wooden tube about fourteen inches long, from
one end of which an inner tube passes to the bottom of
the water. A hole in the side of the tube admits the
flexible smoking tube, more used in Turkey than in
Persia, or the wooden stem, about eighteen inches long.
The fire-holder is lined with clay and plaster of Paris.
Besides these there is the wind-guard, to prevent the
fire from falling or becoming too hot, usually of silver,
with dependent silver chains, and four or six silver or
gold chains terminating in flat balls hang from the fire-
holder.

The *kalian* is one of the greatest institutions of
Persia. No man stirs without it, and as its decoration
gives an idea of a man's social position, immense sums
are lavished upon it, and the pipe-bearer is a most
important person. The lighting is troublesome, and

[1] The reader curious as to this and other customs of modern Persia
should read Dr. Wills's book, *The Land of the Lion and the Sun.*

after all there seems "much ado about nothing," for a
few whiffs exhaust its capacities.

The tobacco, called *tumbaku*, which is smoked in
kalians is exceptionally poisonous. It cannot be used
the first year, and improves with age, being preserved
in bags sewn up in raw hide. Unless it is moistened it
produces alarming vertigo. When the *kalian* is required,
about three-quarters of an ounce is moistened, squeezed
like a sponge, and packed in the fire-holder, and morsels
of live charcoal, if possible made from the root of the
vine, are laid upon it and blown into a strong flame.
The pipe-bearer takes two or three draws, and with an
obeisance hands it with much solemnity to his master.
Abdul Rahim smokes three or four pipes every evening,
and coffee served with the last is the signal for his
departure.

A guest, if he does not bring his own pipe and pipe-
bearer, has a *kalian* offered to him, but if the host be
of higher rank any one but an ignoramus refuses it till
he has smoked first. If under such circumstances a
guest incautiously accepts it, he is invariably mortified by
seeing it sent into the ante-room to be cleaned and refilled
before his superior will smoke. If it be proper for him to
take it, he offers it in order of rank to all present, but
takes good care that none accept it till he has enjoyed
it, after which the attendant passes it round according to
rank. In cases of only one *kalian* and several guests,
they smoke in order of position, but each one must pay
the compliment of suggesting that some one else should
smoke before himself. The etiquette of smoking is most
rigid. I heard of a case here in which a *mollah*, who
objected to smoke after a European, offered it to one
after he had smoked it himself—so gross a piece of
impertinence that the other called the pipe-bearer,
saying, "You can break that pipe to pieces, and burn

the stick, I do not care to smoke it," upon which the *mollah*, knowing that his violation of etiquette merited this sharp rebuke, turned pale and replied, " You say truly, I have eaten dirt."

The lower classes smoke a coarse Turkish tobacco, or a Persian mild sort looking like whitish sawdust, which is merely the pounded leaf, stalk, and stem. The pipe they use and carry in their girdles has a small iron, brass, or clay head, and a straight cherry-wood stick, with a very wide bore and no mouthpiece, and it is not placed in the teeth but is merely held between the lips. Smoking seems a necessity rather than a luxury in Persia, and is one of the great features of social life.

Kirmanshah is famous for its " rugs," as carpets are called in this country. There are from twenty-five to thirty kinds with their specific names. Aniline dyes have gone far to ruin this manufacture, but their import is now prohibited. A Persian would not look at the carpets loosely woven and with long pile, which are made for the European market, and are bought just now from the weavers at 13s. the square yard. A carpet, according to Persian notions, must be of fast colours, fine pile, scarcely longer than Utrecht velvet, and ready to last at least a century. A rug can scarcely be said to have reached its prime or artistic mellowness of tint till it has been " down" for ten years. The permanence of the dyes is tested by rubbing the rug with a wet cloth, when the worthless colours at once come off.

Among the real, good old Persian carpets there are very few patterns, though colouring and borders vary considerably. A good carpet, if new, is always stiff; the ends when doubled should meet evenly. There must be no creases, or any signs on the wrong side of darning or " fine-drawing" having been resorted to for taking out creases, and there must be no blue in the white

cotton finish at the ends.   Carpets with much white are
prized, as the white becomes primrose, a colour which
wears well.   Our host has given me a rug of the oldest
Persian pattern, on a white ground, very thin and fine.
Large patterns and thick wool are comparatively cheap.
It is nearly impossible to say what carpets sell at, for if
one has been made by a family and poverty presses, it
may be sold much under value, or if it is a good one and
they can hold on they may force a carpet fancier to give
a very high price.   From what Abdul Rahim says, the price
varies from 13s. to 50s. a square yard, the larger carpets,
about fourteen feet by eight feet, selling for £40.[1]

Abdul Rahim took me to see carpet-weaving, a process carried on in houses, hovels, and tents by women
and children.   The "machinery" is portable and marvellously simple, merely two upright beams fixed in the
floor, with a cross-beam near the top and bottom, round
which the stout cotton or woollen threads which are the
basis of the carpet are stretched.   The wools are cut in
short lengths and are knotted round two threads, according to the pattern, which, however elaborate, the weaver
usually carries in her head. After a few inches have been
woven in this simple way the right side is combed and the
superfluous length cut off with rough scissors.   Nothing
can be more simple than the process or more beautiful
than the result.   The vegetable dyes used are soft and
artistic, specially a madder red and the various shades of
indigo.   A soft turquoise blue is much used, and an
"olive green," supposed to be saffron and indigo.   The
dull, rich tints, even when new, are quite beautiful.
The women pursue this work chiefly in odds and ends of

[1] A rug only eight feet by five feet was given me by a Persian in Tihran,
which was valued for duty at Erzerum at £3 the square yard, with the
option of selling it to the Custom-house at that price, which implies that
its value is from 70s. to 80s. per yard.   It has a very close pile, nearly as
short and fine as velvet

time, and in some cases make it much of a pastime. Men being present they were very closely veiled, and found great difficulty in holding on the *chadars* and knotting the wool at the same time.

After taking tea in the pleasant upper room of the carpet-weaver's house, we visited the large barracks and parade ground. The appearance of the soldiers could not possibly impress a stranger favourably. They looked nothing better than " dirty, slouching ragamuffins," slip-shod, in tattered and cast-off clothes of all sorts, on the verge of actual mendicancy, bits of rusty uniform appearing here and there amongst their cotton rags. The quarters are not bad. The rank and file get one and a half pounds of bread daily and five rupees a month nominally, but their pay is in arrears, and they eke it out by working at different trades. These men had not been drilled for two months, and were slovenly and unsoldierly to a degree, as men must be who have no proper pay, rations, instruction, clothing, or equipments.

The courtesy of the host leaves nothing unthought of. In returning from a long stroll round the city a wet place had to be crossed, and when we reached it there were saddle-horses ready. On arriving at dusk in the bazar several servants met us with lanterns. The lantern is an important matter, as its size is supposed to indicate the position of the wearer. The Persian lantern has a tin or iron top and bottom, between which is a collapsible wired cylinder of waxed muslin. The light from the candle burning inside is diffused and soft. Three feet long and two feet wide is not an uncommon size. They are carried close to the ground, illustrating " Thy Word is a lamp unto my path," and none but the poor stir out after dark without a lantern-bearer in front. Our lanterns, as befits the *Vakil's* position, are very large.

There is something Biblical in the progress of Abdul

Rahim through the streets, always reminding me of "greetings in the market-place," and "doing alms to be seen of men,"—not that I think our kind host sins in either direction. "Peace be with you," say the people, bending low. "To you be peace," replies the Agha.

A wish having been expressed to visit the rock-sculptures of the Takt-i-Bostan, a winter picnic was quietly arranged for the purpose. There was a great snowstorm on the night we arrived, succeeded by intense frost and clear blue skies,—glorious Canadian winter weather. Outside the wall an English landau, brought in pieces from Baghdad, awaited us, with four Arab horses, two of them ridden. There were eleven outriders and some led horses, and a Turki pipe-bearer rode alongside the carriage with two cylinders of leather containing *kalians* in place of holsters, on one side, behind a leather water-bottle, and on the other a brazier of lighted charcoal hanging by chains much below the horse's body. Another pipe-bearer lighted the *kalian* at intervals and handed it into the carriage to his master. Some of the horsemen carried rifles and wore cartridge-belts.

Reaching the Karasu river we got out into deep mud, were ferried over in a muddy box hauling on a rope, and drove to the Takt-i-Bostan, where several tanks of clear water, a house built into the rock, a number of Kurds on fine horses, the arched recesses in the rock which contain the sculptures, and the magnificent range of the Jabali-Besitun formed a very striking scene.

Sir H. Rawlinson considers these sculptures the finest in Persia, and regards them as the work of Greek artists The lower of the two bas-reliefs at the back of the main recess is a colossal figure of a king on horseback, "the staff of whose spear is as a weaver's beam." On the sides of the recess, and, like the equestrian figure, in very high relief and very much undercut, are scenes from the chase of a most spirited description, representing a king and court mounted on elephants, horses, and camels, hunting boars, stags, and other animals, their enthusiasm in the pursuit being successfully conveyed by the art of the sculptor. In the spandrels of the archway of the main recess are carved, winged female figures. In the smaller arch, also containing a bas-relief, is a Pehlevi inscription.[1]

There is a broad stone platform in front of the arch, below which flows direct from the mountain a great volume of water, which replenishes the tanks. The house, which also contains a tank fed by the same living water, the mountain and its treasures, the tanks, and some miles of avenues of willows, have been bought by the *Vakil*, and his son laughingly says that he hopes to live to see a time when Cook will give " tourist excursion tickets " by rail to the Takt-i-Bostan !

Coffee and *kalians* were served to the Kurds in the arch, and mounting the horses we rode to a country house belonging to our host in the midst of large rose gardens, and with a wonderful view of the magnificent Besitun range, of the rolling snowy hills on which Kirmanshah and its plantations lay like a black splotch, and of this noble plain, six miles long from north to south, and thirty from east to west, its absolutely unbroken snow gleaming like satin, and shadows lying upon it in pure blue. Many servants and a large fire awaited us in that pleasant bungalow, as well as coffee and sweetmeats, and we stayed there till the sinking sun flushed all the surrounding hills with pink, and the gray twilight came on.

I rode a splendid Arab, with a neck " clothed with

---

[1] For the Sasanian inscriptions, vide *Early Sasanian Inscriptions*, by E. Thomas. The great work published by the French Government, *Voyage en Perse*, Paris, 1851, by Messieurs Flandin et Coste, contains elaborate and finely-executed representations of these rock sculptures, which are mostly of the time of the later Sasanian monarchs.

thunder," a horse to make one feel young again, with his elastic stride and pride of bearing, but indeed I "snatched a fearful joy," for the snow was extremely slippery, and thirteen Arab horses in high condition restrained to a foot's pace had belligerent views of their own, tending to disconcert an unwary rider. We crossed the Karasu by a deep and devious ford up to the girths, and had an exhilarating six miles' ride by moonlight in keen frost, the powdery snow crackling under the horses' feet. It was too slippery to enter the town on horse-back, but servants with lanterns awaited us at the gates and roaring fires and dinner were ready here, after a delightful expedition.

I dined alone with our host, Hadji, who understands and speaks English fairly well, acting as interpreter. Abdul Rahim at once plunged into politics, and asked very many intelligent questions about English politics and parties, the condition and housing of our working classes, and then about my own family and occupations. He is a zealous Moslem, and the pious phrases which sit so oddly on Hadji come very naturally from his lips. In reply to a sketch of character which I gave him he said: "What God does is good. He knows, we submit. He of whom you speak laid up great treasure for another life. Whoso loves and befriends the poor is acceptable to God. One day we shall know all. God is good." He said he had been too busy to learn English, but that he understands a great deal, and added, with a roguish gleam lighting up his whole face, and a very funny laugh, "And I hear what M—— says." He has seen but very few English ladies, and it shows great quickness of apprehension that he should never fail in the respectfulness and quiet courteous attentions which would be shown to a lady by an English host.

Even after India, the quantity of servants employed in

such a household as this is very impressive.   Besides
a number who are with the *Vakil* in Tihran, there are
the *nazr* or steward, who under the master is supreme,
cooks and their assistant s, table servants, *farāshes*, who
are sweepers and message-runners, in any number, pipe-
bearers, coffee and ice-makers, plate-cleaners, washermen,
lamp-cleaners, who are also lantern-bearers, a head groom,
with a groom for each horse under him, and a number
more, over forty in all, receiving, if paid at the usual
rate of wages in Kirmanshah, which is a cheap place,
from sixty *krans* a month down to twenty, the *kran* being
now about 8d.   These wages do not represent the actual
gains of a servant, for he is entitled to perquisites, which
are chiefly in the form of commissions on things bought
and sold by his master, and which are regarded as legitimate if they do not exceed 10 per cent.   It is of no use
to fight again this "*modakel*," or to vex one's soul in any
way about it.   Persians have to submit to it as well
as Europeans.   Hadji has endeavoured to extract from
50 to 80 per cent on purchases made by him for me,
but this is thought an outrage.

This *modakel* applies to all bargains.   If a *charvadar*
(no longer a *katirgi*) is hired, he has to pay one's servant
10 per cent on the contract price.   If I sell a horse, my
servant holds out for a good price, and takes his 10 per
cent, and the same thing applies to a pair of shoes, or
a pound of tea, or a chicken, or a bottle of milk.   The
system comes down from the highest quarters.   The
price paid by the governor of a province to the Shah is
but the Shah's *modakel*, and when a governor farms the
taxes for 60,000 *tumans* and sells them for 80,000, the
difference is his *modakel*, and so it goes on through all
official transactions and appointments, and is a fruitful
source of grinding oppression, and of inefficiency in the
army and other departments.   The servant, poor fellow,

may stop at 10 per cent, but the Shah's servant may think himself generous if he hesitates at 50 per cent. I have heard it said that when the late Shah was dying he said to the present sovereign: "If you would sit long upon the throne, see that there is only one spoon among ten men," and that the system represented by this speech is faithfully carried out.   I. L. B.

LETTER VI

KIRMANSHAH, *Feb. 2.*

ON January 28 there was a tremendous snowfall, and even before that the road to Hamadan, which was our possible route, had been blocked for some days. The temperature has now risen to 31°, with a bitter wind, and much snow in the sky. The journey does not promise well. Two of the servants have been ill. I am not at all well, and the reports of the difficulties farther on are rather serious. These things are certain,—that the marches are very long, and without any possibility of resting *en route* owing to mud or snow, and that the food and accommodation will be horrible.

Hadji is turning out very badly. He has fever now, poor fellow, and is even more useless than usual. Abdul Rahim does not like him to interpret, and calls him " the savage." He does no work, and is both dirty and dishonest. The constant use of pious phrases is not a good sign either of Moslem or Christian. I told him this morning that I could not eat from so dirty a plate. " God is great," he quietly answered. He broke my trestle bed by not attending to directions, and when I pointed out what he had done, he answered, " God knows all, God ordains all things." It is really exasperating.

It is necessary to procure an additional outfit for the journey—a slow process—masks lined with flannel, sheepskin bags for the feet, the thick felt coats of the country for all the servants, additional blankets, *kajawehs* for me, and saddle-horses. The marches will frequently be from twenty to thirty miles in length, and the fatigue of riding them at a foot's pace when one cannot exchange riding for walking will be so great that I have had a pair of *kajawehs* made in which to travel when I am tired of the mule. These panniers are oblong wooden boxes, eighteen inches high, with hoops over them for curtains. One hangs on each side of the mule on a level with his back, and they are mounted, *i.e.* they are scrambled into from the front by a ladder, which is carried between them. Most women and some men travel in them. They are filled up with quilts and cushions. The mule which is to carry them is a big and powerful animal, and double price is charged for him.

Horses are very good and cheap here. A pure Arab can be bought for £14, and a cross between an Arab and a Kurdish horse—a breed noted for endurance—for even less. But to our thinking they are small, never exceeding fifteen hands. The horses of the Kirmanshah province are esteemed everywhere, and there is a steady drain upon them for the Indian market. The stud of three horses requires a groom, and Abdul Rahim is sending a *sowar*, who looks a character, to attend us to Tihran. A muleteer, remarkable in appearance and beauty, and twelve fine mules have been engaged. The *sowar* and several other men have applied to me for medicine, having fearful coughs, etc., but I have not been fortunate enough to cure them, as their maladies chiefly require good feeding, warm bedding, and poultices, which are unattainable. It is pitiable to see the poor shivering in their thin cotton clothes in such weather. The men make shift with the seamless felt coats—more cloaks than coats, with long bag-like sleeves tapering to the size of a glove but with a slit midway, through which the hands can be protruded when need arises. The women have no outer garment but the thin cotton *chadar*.

I have tried to get a bed made, but there is no wood strong enough for the purpose, and the bazars cannot produce any canvas.

Sannah, Feb. 5.—Yesterday we were to have started at nine, but the usual quarrelling about loads detained us till 10.30, so that it was nearly dark when we reached the end of the first stage of a three weeks' journey. From the house roof the prospect was most dismal. It was partly thawing, and through the whiteness of the plain ran a brown trail with sodden edges, indicating mud. The great mass of the Jabali-Besitun, or Behistun, or Behishtan, though on the other side of the plain, seemed actually impending over the city, with its great black rock masses, too steep to hold the snow, and the Besitun mountain itself, said to be twenty-four miles away, looming darkly through gray snow clouds, looked hardly ten. Our host had sent men on to see if the landau could take me part of the way at least; but their verdict was that the road was impassable.

After much noise the caravan got under way, but it was soon evident that the fine mules we had engaged had been changed for a poor, sore-backed set, and that the fine saddle-mule I was to have had was metamorphosed into a poor weak creature, which began to drop his leg from the shoulder almost as soon as we were outside the walls, and on a steep bridge came down on his nose with a violent fall, giving me a sharp strain, and fell several times afterwards; indeed, the poor animal could scarcely keep on his legs during the eight hours' march.

Hadji rode in a *kajaweh*, balanced by some luggage, and was to keep close to me, but when I wanted to change my broken-down beast for a pannier he was not to be seen, then or afterwards, and came in late. The big mule had fallen, he was bruised, the *kajawehs* were

smashed to pieces, and were broken up for firewood, and
I am now without any means of getting any rest from
riding! "It's the pace that kills." In snow and mud
gallops are impossible, and three miles an hour is good
going.

An hour from Kirmanshah the road crosses the Karasu
by a good brick bridge, and proceeds over the plain for
many miles, keeping the Besitun range about two miles
on the left, and then passes over undulating ground to the
Besitun village. Two or three large villages occur at a
distance from the road, now shut in, and about eight miles
from Besitun there are marble columns lying on the
ground among some remains of marble walls, now only
hummocks in the snow.

The road was churned into deep mud by the passage
of animals, and the snow was too deep to ride in. My
mule lost no opportunity of tumbling down, and I felt
myself a barbarian for urging him on. Hills and mountains glistened in all directions. The only exception to
the general whiteness was Piru, the great rock mass of
Besitun, which ever loomed blackly overhead through
clouds and darkness, and never seemed any nearer. It
was very solitary. I met only a caravan of carpets, and
a few men struggling along with laden asses.

It was the most artistic day of the whole journey,
much cloud flying about, mountains in indigo gloom, or in
gray, with storm clouds round their heads, or pure white,
with shadows touched in with cobalt, while peaks and
ridges, sun-kissed, gleamed here and there above indigo
and gray. Not a tree or even bush, on them or on the
plain, broke the monotony after a summer palace of the
Shah, surrounded by poplars, was passed. There is
plenty of water everywhere.

As the sun was stormily tinging with pink the
rolling snow-clouds here and there, I halted on the brow

of a slope under the imposing rock front of Besitun to wait for orders. It was wildly magnificent: the huge precipice of Piru, rising 1700 feet from the level, the mountains on both sides of the valley approaching each other, and behind Piru a craggy ravine, glorified here and there by touches of amber and pink upon the clouds which boiled furiously out of its depths. In the foreground were a huge caravanserai with a noble portal, a solitary thing upon the snow, not a dwelling, but offering its frigid hospitality to all comers; a river with many windings, and the ruinous hovels of Besitun huddled in the mud behind. An appalling view in the wild twilight of a winter evening; and as the pink died out, a desolate ghastliness fell upon it. As I waited, all but worn out by the long march, the tumbling mule, and the icy wind, I thought I should like never to hear the deep chimes of a Persian caravan, or see the huge portal of a Persian caravanserai any more. These are cowardly emotions which are dispelled by warmth and food, but at that moment there was not much prospect of either.

Through seas of mud and by mounds of filth we entered Besitun, a most wretched village of eighteen hovels, chiefly ruinous, where we dismounted in the mixed snow and mud of a yard at a hovel of three rooms vacated by a family. It was a better shelter than could have been hoped for, though after a fire was made, which filled the room with smoke, I had to move from place to place to avoid the drip from the roof.

Hadji said he was ill of fever, and seemed like an idiot; but the orderly said that the illness was shammed and the stupidity assumed in order not to work. I told him to put the mattress on the bed; "Pour water on the mattress," he replied. I repeated, "Put—the—mattress —on—the—bed," to which he replied, "Put the mattress into water!" I said if he felt too ill for his work he might go to bed. "God knows," he answered. "Yes, knows that you are a lazy, good-for-nothing, humbugging brute"—a well-timed objurgation from M——, which elicited a prolonged " *Ya Allah* !" but produced no effect, as the tea and *chapatties* were not relatively but absolutely cold the next morning.

The next day dawned miserably, and the daylight when it came was only a few removes from darkness, yet it was enough to bring out the horrors of that wretched place, and the dirt and poverty of the people, who were a prey to skin diseases. Many readers will remember that Sir H. Rawlinson considers that there are good geographical and etymological reasons for identifying Besitun with the Baghistan, or Place of Gardens of the Greeks, and with the famous pleasure-grounds which tradition ascribes to Semiramis. But of these gardens not a trace remains. A precipitous rock, smoothed at its lower part, a vigorous spring gushing out at the foot of the precipice, two tablets, one of which, at a height of over 300 feet, visible from the road but inaccessible, is an Achæmenian sculpture portraying the majesty of Darius, with about a thousand lines of cuneiform writing, are all that survive of the ancient splendours of Besitun, with the exception of some buttresses opposite the rock, belonging to a vanished Sasanian bridge over the Gamasiab, and some fragments of other buildings of the Sasanian epoch. These deeply interesting antiquities have been described and illustrated by Sir H. Rawlinson, Flandin and Coste, and others.

It has been a severe day. It was so unpromising that a start was only decided on after many pros and cons. Through dark air small flakes of snow fell sparsely at intervals from a sky from which all light had died out. Gusts of icy wind swept down every gorge. Huge ragged masses of cloud drifted wildly round the frowning mass

of Piru.   Now and then the gusts ceased, and there was
an inauspicious calm.

I rode a big mule not used to the bit, very troublesome and mulish at first, but broken in an hour.   A
clear blink revealed the tablets, but from their great altitude the tallest of the figures only looked two feet high.
There is little to see on this march even under favourable circumstances.   A few villages, the ruined fort of
Hassan Khan, now used as a caravanserai, on a height,
the windings of the Gamasiab, and a few canals crossed
by brick bridges, represent its chief features.   Impressions of a country received in a storm are likely to be
incorrect, but they were pleasurable.   Everything seemed
on a grand scale : here desolate plateaus pure white, there
high mountains and tremendous gorges, from which white
mists were boiling up—everything was shrouded in
mystery—plain prose ceased to be for some hours.

The others had to make several halts, so I left the
"light division" and rode on alone.   It became dark and
wild, and presently the surface of the snow began to
move and to drift furiously for about a foot above the
ground.   The wind rose to a gale.   I held my hat on
with one half-frozen hand.   My mackintosh cape blew
inside out, and struck me such a heavy blow on the eyes
that for some time I could not see and had to trust to
the mule.   The wind rose higher; it was furious, and the
drift, not only from the valley but from the mountain
sides, was higher than my head, stinging and hissing as
it raced by.   It was a "blizzard," a brutal snow-laden
north - easter, carrying fine, sharp, hard - frozen snow
crystals, which beat on my eyes and blinded them.

After a short experience of it my mule "turned tail"
and needed spurring to make him face it.   I fought on
for an hour, crossed what appeared to be a bridge, where
there were a few mud hovels, and pressed on down a

narrower valley. The blizzard became frightful; from every ravine gusts of storm came down, sweeping the powdery snow from the hillsides into the valley; the mountains were blotted out, the depression in the snow which erewhile had marked the path was gone, I could not even see the mule's neck, and he was floundering in deep snow up to the girths; the hiss of the drift had increased to a roar, the violence of the storm produced breathlessness and the intense cold numbness. It was dangerous for a solitary traveller, and thinking that M—— would be bothered by missing one of the party under such circumstances, I turned and waited under the lee of a ruinous mud hovel for a long, long time till the others came up—two of the men having been unhorsed in a drift.

In those hovels there were neither accommodation nor supplies, and we decided to push on. It was never so bad again. The wind moderated, wet snow fell heavily, but cleared off, and there was a brilliant blue heaven with heavy sunlit cloud-wreaths, among which colossal mountain forms displayed themselves, two peaks in glorious sunlight, high, high above a whirling snow-cloud, which was itself far above a great mountain range below. There were rifts, valleys, gorges, naked, nearly perpendicular rocks, the faces of mountains, half of which had fallen down in the opposite direction, a snow-filled valley, a winding river with brief blue stretches, a ruined fort on an eminence, a sharp turn, a sudden twilight, and then another blizzard far colder than the last, raging down a lateral ravine, up which, even through the blinding drift, were to be seen, to all seeming higher than mountains of this earth, the twin peaks of Shamran lighted by the sun. I faced the blizzard for some time, and then knowing that Hadji and the cook, who were behind me, would turn off to a distant village, all trace of a track

having disappeared, I rode fully a mile back and waited
half an hour for them.   They were half-frozen, and had
hardly been able to urge their mules, which were lightly
laden, through the snow, and Hadji was groaning " *Ya
Allah* ! "

The blizzard was over and the sky almost cloudless,
but the mercury had fallen to 18°, and a keen wind was
still blowing the powdery snow to the height of a foot.
I sent the two men on in front, and by dint of calling to
them constantly, kept them from getting into drifts of
unknown depth.   We rode up a rising plateau for two
hours—a plateau of deep, glittering, blinding, trackless
snow, giving back the sunshine in millions of diamond
flashings.   Through all this region thistles grow to a
height of four feet, and the only way of finding the track
was to look out for a space on which no withered thistle-
blooms appeared above the snow.

This village of Sannah lies at an altitude of about 5500
feet, among poplar plantations and beautiful gardens, in
which fine walnut trees are conspicuous.   Though partly
ruinous it is a flourishing little place, its lands being
abundantly watered by streams which run into the
Gamasiab.   It is buried now in snow, and the only mode
of reaching it is up the bed of a broad sparkling stream
among the gardens.   The *sowar* met us here, the navigation being difficult, and the "light division" having
come up, we were taken to the best house in the village,
where the family have vacated two rooms, below the
level of a yard full of snow.   The plateau and its adjacent mountains were flushed with rose as we entered
Sannah, and as soon as the change to the pallor of death
came on the mercury raced down to zero outside, and it
is only 6° in the room in which I am writing.

There is a large caravanserai at the entrance to Sannah,
and I suspect that the *sowar* in choosing private quarters

bullies the *ketchuda* (headman) and throws the village into confusion, turning the women and children out of the rooms, the owners, though they get a handsome sum for the accommodation, having to give him an equally handsome *modakel*.

After nearly nine hours of a crawling pace and exposure to violent weather, I suffered from intense pain in my joints, and was dragged and lifted in and put into a chair. I write "put," for I was nearly helpless, and had to take a teaspoonful of whisky in warm milk. While the fire was being made two women, with a gentle kindliness which won my heart, chafed my trembling, nearly frozen hands with their own, with kindly, womanly looks, which supplied the place of speech.

I lay down under a heap of good blankets, sorry to see them in thin cotton clothes, and when I was less frozen observed my room and its grotesquely miserable aspect, " the Savage " never taking any trouble to arrange it. There are no windows, and the divided door does not shut by three inches. A low hole leads into the granary, which is also the fowl-house, but the fowls have no idea of keeping to their own apartment. Two sheep with injured legs lie in a corner with some fodder beside them. A heap of faggots, the bed placed diagonally to avoid the firehole in the floor, a splashed tarpaulin on which Hadji threw down the saddle and bridle plastered with mud, and all my travelling gear, a puddle of frozen water, a plough, and some ox yokes, an occasional gust of ashes covering everything, and clouds of smoke from wood which refuses to do anything but smoke, are the luxuries of the halt. The house is full of people, and the women come in and out without scruple, and I am really glad to see them, though it is difficult to rouse Hadji from his opium pipe and coffee, and his comfortable lounge by a good fire, to interpret for them.

The day's experiences remind me of the lines—

> " Bare all he could endure,
>   And bare not always well."

But tired and benumbed as I am I much prefer a march
with excitements and difficulties to the monotony of
splashing through mud in warm rain.

Hamilabad, Feb. 7.—The next morning opened cloudless, with the mercury at 18°, which was hardly an excuse
for tea and *chapatties* being quite cold.   I was ready much
too early, and the servants having given out that I am
a *Hakīm*, my room was crowded with women and children, all suffering from eye diseases and scrofula, five
women not nearly in middle life with cataract advanced
in both eyes, and many with incurved eyelids, the
result of wood smoke.   It was most painful to see their
disappointment when I told them that it would need
time to cure some of them, and that for others I could
do nothing.   Could I not stay ? they pleaded.   I could
have that room and milk and eggs—the best they had.
" And they lifted up their voices and wept."   I felt like
a brute for leaving them.   The people there showed much
interest in our movements, crowding on the roofs to see
our gear, and the start.

The order of march now is — light division, three
mules with an orderly, Hadji, and the cook upon them,
the two last carrying what is absolutely necessary for the
night in case the heavy division cannot get on.   M——
and an orderly, the *sowar*, Abbas Khan, another who is
changed daily, the light division and I, sometimes start
together ; but as the others are detained by work on the
road, I usually ride on ahead with the two servants.

To write that we all survived the march of that day
is strange, when the same pitiless blast or " demon wind,"
blowing from " the roof of the world "—the Pamir desert,

made corpses of five men who started with a caravan ahead of us that morning. We had to climb a long ascending plateau for 1500 feet, to surmount a pass. The snow was at times three feet deep, and the tracks even of a heavy caravan which crossed before us were effaced by the drift in a few minutes.

A sun without heat glared and scintillated like an electric light, white and unsympathetic, out of a pitiless sky without a cloud. As soon as we emerged from Sannah the " demon wind " seized on us—a steady, blighting, searching, merciless blast, no rise or fall, no lull, no hope. Steadily and strongly it swept, at a temperature of 9°, across the glittering ascent—swept mountain-sides bare; enveloped us at times in glittering swirls of powdery snow, which after biting and stinging careered over the slopes in twisted columns; screeched down gorges and whistled like the demon it was, as it drifted the light frozen snow in layers, in ripples, in waves, a cruel, benumbing, blinding, withering invisibility !

The six woollen layers of my mask, my three pairs of gloves, my sheepskin coat, fur cloak, and mackintosh piled on over a swaddling mass of woollen clothing, were as nothing before that awful blast. It was not a question of comfort or discomfort, or of suffering more or less severe, but of life or death, as the corpses a few miles ahead of us show. I am certain that if it had lasted another half-hour I too should have perished. The torture of my limbs down to my feet, of my temples and cheek-bones, the anguish and uselessness of my hands, from which the reins had dropped, were of small consequence compared with a chill which crept round my heart, threatening a cessation of work.

There were groans behind me; the cook and Hadji had rolled off into the snow, where Hadji was calling on Him " who is not far from every one of us." M—— was on foot. His mask was frozen hard. He was using a scientific instrument, and told his orderly, an Afghan, a smart little " *duffadar* " of a crack Indian *corps*, to fasten a strap. The man replied sadly, " I can't, Sahib." His arms and hands were useless. My mask was frozen to my lips. The tears extorted from my eyes were frozen. I was so helpless, and in such torture, that I would gladly have lain down to die in the snow. The mercury fell to 4°.

After fighting the elements for three hours and a half, we crossed the crest of the pass at an altitude of 7000 feet, to look down upon a snow world stretched out everywhere, pure, glistering, awful ; mountains rolling in snowy ranges, valleys without a trace of man, a world of horror, glittering under a mocking sun.

Hadji, with many pious ejaculations, gasped out that he was dying (in fact, for some time all speech had been reduced to a gasp) ; but when we got over the crest there was no more wind, and all the benumbed limbs resumed sensation, through an experience of anguish.

The road to Kangawar lies through a broad valley, which has many streams. Among the mountains which encompass it are the Kuh-i-Hassan, Boka, the Kuh-i-Paran, and the Kuh-i-Bozah. I rode on with the two servants, indulging in no higher thoughts than of the comfort I should have in lying down, when just in front of me Hadji turned a somersault, my alpenstock flying in one direction and the medicine chest in another, while he lay motionless, flat on his back with all his limbs stretched out, just as soldiers who have been shot lie in pictures. In getting to him my mule went down in a snow-drift, out of which I extricated him with difficulty. I induced Hadji, who said his back was broken, and was groaning and calling on Allah, to get up, and went on to secure his mule, which had the great pack-saddle under its body, and was kicking with all its might at my bed and "hold-all," which were between its hind legs, and succeeded in catching and holding it till Hadji came up. I told him to unfasten the surcingle, for the animal was wild with the things among its legs, and he wrung his hands and beat his breast, exclaiming, "God is great! God knows I shall never see Bushire again!" and was quite helpless. Seeing a caravan of asses approaching, I rode on as fast as I could to the well-situated little town of Kangawar, expecting him to follow shortly. At present the entrance into Kangawar is up the bed of a stream.

We had been promised good accommodation there, and the town could evidently afford it, but Abbas Khan had chosen something very wretched, though it was up-stairs, and had an extensive snow view. Crumbling, difficult stairs at each end of a crumbling mud house led to rooms which barely afforded a shelter, with a ruinous barn between, where the servants, regardless of conse-quences, kept up a bonfire. A man shovelled most of the snow out of my room, and tried to make a fire but failed, as neither he nor I could stand the smoke produced by the attempt. This imperfect shelter had a window-frame, with three out of its four wooden panes gone, and a cracked door, which could only ensure partial privacy by being laid against the posts from the outer landing, which was a flat roof. The wall was full of cracks big enough for a finger, through which the night wind rioted in a temperature 5° below zero.

There was nothing to sit upon, and I walked up and down for two hours, half-frozen, watching the straggling line of the caravan as it crawled along the valley, till the sunset flush changed into the chill blue-gray of twilight. Hadji arrived with it, having broken his girth after I left him. There was not much comfort after the severe march, owing to the draughts and the smoke, but one is always hungry and sleepy, and the hybernation of the insects makes up for any minor discomforts. It was so cold that some water in a cup froze before I could drink it, and the blanket over my face was hard frozen.

Kangawar was full of mourning. The bodies of two men and a boy, who had perished on the plain while we were struggling up the pass, had been brought in. This boy of twelve was "the only son of his mother and she was a widow." He had started from Kangawar in the morning with five asses laden with chopped straw to sell for her, and had miserably perished. The two men were married, and had left families.

Kangawar is a town of a thousand people built below a high hill, on some natural and artificial mounds. Some traditions regarding Semiramis are localised there, and it is supposed to be on the site of Pancobar, where she erected a temple to Anaitis or Artemis. Ruins of a fortress, now snow-buried, occupy the crest of a hill above the town, and there are other ruins, regarded by antiquaries as Grecian, representing a temple or palace, "a vast building constructed of enormous blocks of dressed stone." Of these remains I saw nothing but some columns and a pilaster, which are built into the miserable mud walls of a house near the bazar.

At night the muleteers were beseeching on their knees. They said that they could not go on, that the caravan which had attempted to leave Kangawar in the morning had put back with three corpses, and that they and their mules would perish. In the morning it was for some time doubtful whether they could be induced or bribed to proceed. The day was fine and still, but they said that the snow was not broken. At last they agreed to start if we would promise to return at the first breath of wind!

Every resource against cold was brought out and put

on.   One eye was all that was visible of the servants'
faces.   The *charvadars* relied on their felt coats and raw
sheepskins, with the fur inside, roped round their legs.
There is danger of frost-bite even with all precautions.
In addition to double woollen underclothing I put on a
pair of thick Chitral socks over two pairs of woollen
stockings, and over these a pair of long, loose Afghan
boots, made of sheepskin with the fur inside.   Over my
riding dress, which is of flannel lined with heavy homespun,
I had a long homespun jacket, an Afghan sheepskin coat, a
heavy fur cloak over my knees, and a stout " regulation "
waterproof to keep out the wind.   Add to this a cork
helmet, a fisherman's hood, a " six-ply " mask, two pairs of
woollen gloves with mittens and double gauntlets, and
the difficulty of mounting and dismounting for a person
thus *swaddled* may be imagined !   The Persians are all in
cotton clothes.

However, though they have no " firesides," and no
cheerful crackle and blaze of wood, they have an arrangement by which they can keep themselves warm
for hours by the expenditure of a few handfuls of animal
fuel.   The fire hole or *tāndūr* in the middle of the
floor is an institution.   It is circular, narrows somewhat at the top and bottom, has a flue leading to the
bottom from the outside, and is about three feet deep
and two in diameter.   It is smoothly lined with clay
inside.

Over this is the *karsi* or platform, a skeleton wooden
frame like an inverted table, from two to five feet square,
covered with blankets or a thickly-wadded cotton quilt,
which extends four or five feet beyond it.   Cushions are
placed under this, and the women huddle under it all
day, and the whole family at night, and in this weather
all day—the firepot in the hole giving them comfortable
warmth both for sleeping and waking.   They very rarely

wash, and the *karsi* is so favourable for the development of vermin that I always hurry it out of the room when I enter.   So excellent and economical is the contrivance, that a *tāndūr* in which the fire has not been replenished for eighteen hours has still a genial heat.

It was a serious start, so terribly slippery in the heaped-up alleys and uncovered bazars of Kangawar that several of the mules and men fell.   Outside the town was a level expanse of deep, wrinkled, drifted, wavy, scintillating snow, unbroken except for a rut about a foot wide, a deep long "mule ladder," produced by heavily-laden mules and asses each stepping in its predecessor's footsteps, forming short, deep corrugations, in which it is painful and tedious for horses or lightly-laden animals to walk.   For nine hours we marched through this corrugated rut.

Leaving on the left the summer route to Tihran *via* Hamadan, which is said to have been blocked for twenty days, we embarked upon a glittering plain covered with pure snow, varying in depth from two feet on the level to ten and fifteen in the drifts, crossed by a narrow and only slightly beaten track.

Ere long we came on solemn traces of the struggle and defeat of the day before: every now and then a load of chopped straw thrown away, then the deep snow much trampled, then the snow dug away and piled round a small space, in which the *charvadars* had tried to shelter themselves from the wind as the shadows of death fell, then more straw, and a grave under a high mound of snow; farther on some men busy burying one of the bodies.   The air was still, and the sun shone as it had shone the day before on baffled struggles, exhaustion, and death.   The trampling of the snow near the track marked the place where the caravan had turned, taking three out of the five bodies back to Kangawar. The fury with which the wind had swept over the plain was shown by the absolute level to which it had reduced the snow, the deep watercourses being filled up with the drifts.

After crossing a brick bridge, and passing the nearly buried village of Hussenabad, we rode hour after hour along a rolling track among featureless hills, till in the last twilight we reached the village of Pharipah, a low-lying place ("low-lying" must never be understood to mean anything lower than 5000 feet) among some frozen irrigated lands and watered gardens. I arrived nearly dead from cold, fatigue, and the severe pains in the joints which are produced by riding nine hours at a foot's pace in a temperature of 20°. My mule could only be urged on by spurring, and all the men and animals were in a state of great fatigue. My room was very cold, as much of one side was open to the air, and a fire was an impossibility.

Except for the crossing of a pass with an altitude of 7500 feet, the next day's route was monotonous, across plains, among mountains, all pure white, the only incidents being that my chair was broken by the fall of a mule, and that my mule and I went over our heads in a snow-drift. The track was very little broken, and I was four hours in doing ten miles.

Hamilabad is a village of about sixty mud hovels, and in common with all these mountain hamlets has sloping covered ways leading to pens under the house, where cattle, sheep, and goats spend much of the winter in darkness and warmth.

I have a house, i.e. a mud room, to myself. These two days I have had rather a severe chill, after getting in, including a shivering lasting about two hours, perhaps owing to the severe fatigue; and I was lying

down with the blankets over my face and was just
getting warm when I heard much buzzing about me,
and looking up saw the room thronged with men, women,
and children, just such a crowd as constantly besieged
our blessed Lord when the toilsome day full of "the
contradiction of sinners against Himself" was done,
most of them ill of "divers diseases and torments,"
smallpox, rheumatism, ulcers on the cornea, abortive and
shortened limbs, decay of the bones of the nose, palate,
and cheek, tumours, cancers, skin maladies, ophthalmia,
opaque films over the eyes, wounds, and many ailments
too obscure for my elementary knowledge. Nothing is
more painful than to be obliged to say that one cannot
do anything for them.

I had to get up, and for nearly two hours was hearing their tales of suffering, interpreted by Hadji with
brutal frankness; and they crowded my room again this
morning. All I could do was to make various ointments,
taking tallow as the basis, drop lotion into some eyes,
give a few simple medicines, and send the majority sadly
away. The *sowar*, Abbas Khan, is responsible for spread-
ing my fame as a *Hakīm*. He is being cured of a severe
cough, and comes to my room for medicine (in which I
have no faith) every evening, a lean man with a lean
face, lighted with a rapacious astuteness, with a *kaftan*
streaming from his brow, except where it is roped
round his shaven skull, a zouave jacket, a skirt something
like a kilt, but which stands out like a ballet dancer's
dress, all sorts of wrappings round his legs, a coarse
striped red shirt, a double cartridge-belt, and a perfect
armoury in his girdle of pistols and knives. He is a wit
and a rogue. Dogs, deprived of their usual shelter, shook
my loose door at intervals all night. This morning is
gray, and looks like change.

Nanej, Feb. 9.—It was thawing, and the march here

was very soft and splashy.   The people are barbarous in
their looks, speech, manners, and ways of living, and have
a total disregard of cleanliness of person, clothing, and
dwellings.   Whether they are actually too poor to have
anything warmer than cotton clothing, or whether they
have buried hoards I do not know; but even in this
severe weather the women of this region have nothing on
their feet, and their short blue cotton trousers, short, loose,
open jackets, short open chemises, and the thin blue sheet
or *chadar* over their heads, are a mere apology for clothing.

The journey yesterday was through rolling hills, enclosing level plains much cultivated, with villages upon
them mostly at a considerable distance from the road.   I
passed through two, one larger and less decayed than
usual, but fearfully filthy, and bisected by a foul stream,
from which people were drinking and drawing water.
Near this is a lofty mound, a truncated cone, with some
" Cyclopean" masonry on its summit, the relics of a fire
temple of the Magi.   Another poorer and yet filthier
village was passed through, where a man was being
buried; and as I left Hamilabad in the morning, a long
procession was escorting a corpse to its icy grave, laid on
its bedding on a bier, both these deaths being from smallpox, which, though very prevalent, is not usually fatal,
and seldom attacks adults.   Indeed, it is regarded as a
childish malady, and is cured by a diet of melons and by
profuse perspirations.

A higher temperature had turned the path to slush,
and made the crossing of the last plain very tedious.
This is an abominable village, and the thaw is revealing
a state of matters which the snow would have concealed;
but it has been a severe week's journey, and I am glad
of Sunday's rest even here.   It is a disheartening place.
I dismounted in one yard, in slush up to my knees,
and from this splashed into another, round which are

stables, cowsheds, and rooms which were vacated by the *ketchuda* and his family, but only partially, as the women not only left all their "things" in my room, but had a *godown* or storehouse through it, to which they resorted continually. I felt ill yesterday, and put on a blister, which rendered complete rest desirable; but it is not to be got. The room filled with women as soon as I settled myself in it.

They told me at once that I could not have a fire unless I had it under the *karsi*, that the smoke would be unbearable. When I asked them to leave me to rest, they said, "There's no shame in having women in the house." M—— came an hour later and cleared the room, but as soon as he went away it filled again, and with men as well as women, and others unscrupulously tore out the paper panes from the windows. This afternoon I stayed in bed feeling rather ill, and about three o'clock a number of women in blue sheets, with a very definite leader, came in, arranged the *karsi*, filling the room with smoke, as a preliminary, gathered themselves under the quilt, and sat there talking loudly to each other. I felt myself the object of a focused stare, and covered my head with a blanket in despair. Then more women came in with tea-trays, and they all took tea and sat for another hour or two talking and tittering, Hadji assuring me that they were doing it out of kindness, because I was not well, and they thought it dull for me alone! The room was again cleared, and I got up at dark, and hearing a great deal of whispering and giggling, saw that they had opened the door windows, and that a crowd was outside. When I woke this morning a man was examining my clothes, which were hanging up. They feel and pull my hair, finger all my things, and have broken all the fine teeth out of my comb. They have the curiosity without the gracefulness of the Japanese.

This is a house of the better sort, though the walls are not plastered. A carpet loom is fixed into the floor with a half-woven carpet upon it. Some handsome rugs are laid down. There are two much-decorated marriage chests, some guns and swords, a quantity of glass tea-cups and ornaments in the recesses, and coloured wood-cuts of the Russian Imperial family, here, as in almost every house, are on the walls.

There is great rejoicing to-night "for joy that a man is born into the world," the first-born of the *ketchuda's* eldest son. In their extreme felicity they took me to see the mother and babe. The room was very hot, and crowded with relations and friends. The young mother was sitting up on her bed on the floor and the infant lay beside her dressed in swaddling clothes. She looked very happy and the young father very proud. I added a small offering to the many which were brought in for luck, and it was not rejected.

A sword was brought from my room, and with it the *mamaché* traced a line upon the four walls, repeating a formula which I understood to be, " I am making this tower for Miriam and her child."[1] I was warned by Hadji not to look on the child or to admire him without saying " Mashallah," lest I should bring on him the woe of the evil eye. So greatly is it feared, that precautions are invariably taken against it from the hour of birth, by bestowing amulets and charms upon the child. A paragraph of the Koran, placed in a silk bag, had already been tied round the infant's neck. Later, he will wear another bag round his arm, and turquoise or blue beads will be sewn upon his cap.

If a visitor admires a child without uttering the word *Mashallah*, and the child afterwards falls sick, the visitor

[1] This custom, supposed to be an allusion to our Lord and His mother, is described by Morier in his *Second Journey in Persia*.

at once is regarded as answerable for the calamity, and the relations take a shred of his garment, and burn it in a brazier with cress seed, walking round and round the child as it burns.

Persian mothers are regarded as convalescent on the third day, when they go to the *hammam* to perform the ceremonies required by Moslem law. A boy is weaned at the end of twenty-six months and a girl at the end of twenty-four. If possible, on the weaning day the child is carried to the mosque, and certain devotions are performed. The weaning feast is an important function, and the relations and friends assemble, bringing presents, and the child in spite of his reluctance is forced to partake of the food.

At the earliest possible period the *mamaché* pronounces in the infant's ear the Shiah profession of faith : " God is God, there is but one God, and Mohammed is the Prophet of God, and Ali is the Lieutenant of God." A child becomes a Moslem as soon as this *Kelemah Islam* has been spoken into his ear; but a ceremony attends the bestowal of his name, which resembles that in use among the Buddhists of Tibet on similar occasions.

Unless the father be very poor indeed, he makes a feast for his friends on an auspicious day, and invites the village *mollahs*. Sweatmeats are solemnly eaten after the guests have assembled. Then the infant, stiffened and mummied in its swaddling clothes, is brought in, and is laid on the floor by one of the *mollahs*. Five names are written on five slips of paper, which are placed between the leaves of the Koran, or under the edge of the carpet. The first chapter of the Koran is then read. One of the slips is then drawn at random, and a *mollah* takes up the child, and pronounces in its ear the name found upon it, after which he places the paper on its clothes.

The relations and friends give it presents according to

their means, answering to our christening gifts, and
thereafter it is called by the name it has received.
Among men's names there is a preponderance of those
taken from the Old Testament, among which Ibrahim,
Ismail, Suleiman, Yusuf, and Moussa are prominent.
Abdullah, Mahmoud, Hassan, Raouf, Baba Houssein, Imam
are also common, and many names have the suffix of Ali
among the Shiahs. Fatmeh is a woman's name, but girl-
children usually receive the name of some flower or bird,
or fascinating quality of disposition or person.

The journey is beginning to tell on men and animals.
One of the Arab horses has had a violent attack of pain
from the cold, and several of the men are ailing and depressed.

Dizabad, Feb. 11.—Nanej is the last village laid down
on any map on the route we are taking for over a hundred
miles, *i.e.* until we reach Kum, though it is a caravan
route, and it does not appear that any Europeans have published any account of it. Just now it is a buried country,
for the snow is lying from one to four feet deep. It is
not even possible to pronounce any verdict on the roads,
for they are simply deep ruts in the snow, with "mule
ladders." The people say that the plains are irrigated
and productive, and that the hills pasture their sheep and
cattle; and they all complain of the exactions of local
officials. There is no variety in costume, and very little
in dwellings, except as to size, for they are all built of
mud or sun-dried bricks, within cattle yards, and have
subterranean pens for cattle and goats. The people abound
in diseases, specially of the eyes and bones.

The salient features of the hills, if they have any, are
rounded off by snow, and though many of them rise to
a great height, none are really impressive but Mount
Elwand, close to Hamadan. The route is altogether
hilly, but the track pursues valleys and low passes as
much as possible, and is never really steep.

Yesterday we marched twenty-four miles in eight hours without any incident, and the "heavy division" took thirteen hours, and did not come in till ten at night! There are round hills, agglomerated into ranges, with easy passes, the highest 7026 feet in altitude, higher summits here and there in view, the hills encircling level plains, sprinkled sparsely with villages at a distance from the road, denoted by scrubby poplars and willows; sometimes there is a *kanaat* or underground irrigation channel with a line of pits or shafts, but whatever there was, or was not, it was always lonely, grim, and desolate. The strong winds have blown some of the hillsides bare, and they appear in all their deformity of shapeless mounds of black gravel, or black mud, with relics of last year's thistles and euphorbias upon them. So great is the destitution of fuel that even now people are out cutting the stalks of thistles which appear above the snow.

As the hours went by, I did rather wish for the smashed *kajawehs*, especially when we met the ladies of a governor's *haram*, to the number of thirty, reclining snugly in pairs, among blankets and cushions, in panniers with tilts, and curtains of a thick material, dyed Turkey red. The cold became very severe towards evening.

The geographical interest of the day was that we crossed the watershed of the region, and have left behind the streams which eventually reach the sea, all future rivers, however great their volume, or impetuous their flow, disappearing at last in what the Americans call "sinks," but which are known in Persia as *kavirs*, usually salt swamps. Near sunset we crossed a bridge of seven pointed arches with abutments against a rapid stream, and passing a great gaunt caravanserai on an eminence, and a valley to the east of the bridge with a few villages giving an impression of fertility, hemmed in by some shapely mountains, we embarked on a level plain, bounded on all sides by hills so snowy that not a brown patch or outbreak of rock spotted their whiteness, and with villages and caravanserais scattered thinly over it. On the left, there are the extensive ruins of old Dizabad, and a great tract of forlorn graves clustering round a crumbling *imamzada*.

As the sun sank the distant hills became rose-flushed, and then one by one the flush died off into the paleness of death, and in the gathering blue-grayness, in desolation without sublimity, in ghastliness, impressive but only by force of ghastliness, and in benumbing cold, we rode into this village, and into a yard encumbered with mighty piles of snow, on one side of which I have a wretched room, though the best, with two doors, which do not shut, but when they are closed make it quite dark—a deep, damp, cobwebby, dusty, musty lair like a miserable eastern cowshed.

I was really half-frozen and quite benumbed, and though I had plenty of blankets and furs, had a long and severe chill, and another to-day. M—— also has had bad chills, and the Afghan orderly is ill, and moaning with pain in the next room. Hadji has fallen into a state of chronic invalidism, and is shaking with chills, his teeth chattering, and he is calling on Allah whenever I am within hearing.

The chilly dampness and the rise in temperature again may have something to do with the ailments, but I think that we Europeans are suffering from the want of nourishing food. Meat has not been attainable for some days, the fowls are dry and skinny, and milk is very scarce and poor. I cannot eat the sour wafers which pass for bread, and as Hadji cannot boil rice or make flour porridge, I often start in the morning having only had a cup of tea. I lunch in the saddle on dates, the milk in the holsters having been frozen lately ; then is the time for finding the value of a double peppermint lozenge!

Snow fell heavily last night, and as the track has not been broken, and the *charvadars* dared not face it, we are detained in this miserable place, four other caravans sharing our fate. The pros and cons about starting were many, and Abbas Khan was sent on horseback to reconnoitre, but he came back like Noah's dove, reporting that it was a trackless waste of snow outside. It is a day of rest, but as the door has to be open on the snow to let in light, my hands are benumbed with the damp cold. Still, a bowl of Edwards' desiccated soup— the best of all travelling soups—has been very reviving, and though I have had a severe chill again, I do not mean to succumb. I do not dwell on the hardships, but they are awful. The soldiers and servants all have bad coughs, and dwindle daily. The little orderly is so ill to-day that we could not have gone on even had the track been broken.

Saruk, Feb. 12.—Unladen asses, followed by unladen mules, were driven along to break the track this morning, and as two caravans started before us, it was tolerable, though very deep. The solitude and desolation were awful. At first the snow was somewhat thawed, but soon it became immensely deep, and we had to plunge through hollows from which the beasts extricated themselves with great difficulty and occasionally had to be unloaded and reloaded.

As I mentioned in writing of an earlier march, it is difficult and even dangerous to pass caravans when the only road is a deep rut a foot wide, and we had most tedious experience of it to-day, when some of our men, weakened by illness, were not so patient as usual. Abbas Khan and the orderly could hardly sit on their horses, and Hadji rolled off his mule at intervals. As the *charvadars* who give way have their beasts floundering in the deep snow and losing their loads, both attempt to keep the road, the result of which is a violent collision.   The two animals which " collide " usually go down, and some of the others come on the top of them, and to-day at one time there were eight, struggling heels uppermost in the deep snow, all to be reloaded.

This led to a serious *mêlée*.   The rival *charvadar*, aggravated by Hadji, struck him on the head, and down he went into the snow, with his mule apparently on the top of him, and his load at some distance.   The same *charvadar* seized the halters of several of our mules, and drove them into the snow, where they all came to grief.   Our *charvadar*, whose blue eyes, auburn hair and beard, and exceeding beauty, always bring to mind a sacred picture, became furious at this, and there was a fierce fight among the men (M—— being ahead) and much bad language, such epithets as " son of a dog " and " sons of burnt fathers " being freely bandied about. The fray at last died out, leaving as its result only the loss of an hour, some broken surcingles, and some bleeding faces.   Even Hadji rose from his " gory bed " not much worse, though he had been hit hard.

There was no more quarrelling though we passed several caravans, but even when the men were reasonable and good nature prevailed some of the mules on both sides fell in the snow and had to be reloaded.   When the matter is not settled as this was by violence, a good deal of shouting and roaring culminates in an understanding that one caravan shall draw off into a place where the snow is shallowest, and stand still till the other has gone past; but to-day scarcely a shallow place could be found.   I always give place to asses, rather to avoid a painful spectacle than from humanity.   One step off the track and down they go, and they never get up without being unloaded.

When we left Dizabad the mist was thick, and as it

cleared it froze in crystallised buttons, which covered
the surface of the snow, but lifting only partially it
revealed snowy summits, sun-lit above heavy white
clouds; then when we reached a broad plateau, the
highest plain of the journey, 7800 feet in altitude, gray
mists drifted very near us, and opening in rifts divulged
blackness, darkness, and tempest, and ragged peaks
exposed to the fury of a snowstorm. Snow fell in
showers on the plain, and it was an anxious time, for
had the storm which seemed impending burst on that
wild, awful, shelterless expanse, with tired animals, and
every landmark obliterated, some of us must have
perished. I have done a great deal of snow travelling,
and know how soon every trace of even the widest and
deepest path is effaced by drift, much more the narrow
rut by which we were crossing this most exposed
plateau. There was not a village in sight the whole
march, no birds, no animals. There was not a sound
but the venomous hiss of snow-laden squalls. It was
" the dead of winter."

My admirable mule was ill of cold from having my
small saddle on him instead of his great stuffed pack-
saddle, the *charvadar* said, and he gave me instead a
horse that I could not ride. Such a gait I never felt;
less than half a mile was unbearable. I felt as if my
eyes would be shaken out of their sockets! The bit
was changed, but in vain. I was obliged to get off, and
M——— kindly put my saddle on a powerful Kirmanshah
Arab. I soon found that my intense fatigue on this
journey had been caused by riding mules, which have
no elasticity of movement. I rode twenty miles to-day
with ease, and could have ridden twenty more, and had
several canters on the few places where the snow was
well trodden.

I was off the track trying to get past a caravan

and overtake the others, when down came the horse and
I in a drift fully ten feet deep. Somehow I was not
quite detached from the saddle, and in the scrimmage
got into it again, and a few desperate plunges brought us
out, with the horse's breastplate broken.

When we reached the great plateau above this village,
a great blank sheet of snow, surrounded by mountains,
now buried in white mists, now revealed, with snow
flurries drifting wildly round their ghastly heads, I found
that the Arab, the same horse which was so ill at Nanej,
was "dead beat," and as it only looked a mile to the
village I got off, and walked in the deep snow along the
rungs of the "mule ladders," which are so fatiguing for
horses. But the distance was fully three miles, with a
stream to wade through, half a mile of deep wet soil to
plunge through, and the thawed mud of a large village to
splash through; and as I dared not mount again for fear
of catching cold, I trailed forlornly into Saruk, following
the men who were riding.

Can it be said that they rode? They sat feebly on
animals, swaddled in felts and furs, the *pagri* concealing
each face with the exception of one eye in a blue
goggle; rolling from side to side, clutching at ropes and
halters, moaning "*Ya Allah*!"—a deplorable cavalcade.

Saruk has some poplars, and is surrounded by a
ruinous mud wall. It is a village of 150 houses, and is
famous for very fine velvety carpets, of small patterns,
in vivid vegetable dyes. At an altitude of 7500 feet, it
has a severe climate, and only grows wheat and barley,
sown in April and reaped in September. All this
mountainous region that we are toiling through is blank
on the maps, and may be a dead level so far as anything
there is represented, though even its passes are in several
cases over 7000 feet high.

Saruk, Feb. 13.—The circumstances generally are

unfavourable, and we are again detained. The Afghan orderly, who is also interpreter, is very ill, and though he is very plucky it is impossible for him to move; the cook seems " all to pieces," and is overcome by cough and lassitude; Abbas Khan is ill, and his face has lost its comicality; and in the same room Hadji lies, groaning and moaning that he will not live through the night. Even M——'s herculean strength is not what it was. I have chills, but in spite of them and the fatigue am really much better than when I left Baghdad, so that though I exercise the privilege of grumbling at the hardships, I ought not to complain of them, though they are enough to break down the strongest men. I really like the journey, except when I am completely knocked up, or the smoke is exceptionally blinding.

The snow in this yard is lying in masses twelve feet high, rising out of slush I do not know how many feet deep. It looks as if we had seen the last of the winter. The mercury is at 32° now. It is very damp and cold sitting in a room with one side open to the snow, and the mud floor all slush from the drip from the roof. The fuel is wet, and though a man has attempted four times to light a fire, he has only succeeded in making an overpowering smoke, which prefers hanging heavily over the floor and me to making its exit through the hole in the roof provided for it. The door must be kept open to let in light, and it also lets in fowls and many cats. My *dhurrie* has been trampled into the slush, and a deadly cold strikes up through it. Last night a man (for Hadji was *hors de combat*) brought in some live embers, and heaped some gum tragacanth thorns and animal fuel upon them; there was no chimney, and the hole in the roof was stopped by a clod. The result was unbearable. I covered my head with blankets, but it was still blinding and stifling, and I had to extinguish

the fire with water and bear the cold, which then was
about 20°.   Later, there was a tempest of snow and
rain, with a sudden thaw, and water dripped with an
irksome sound on my well-protected bed, no light would
burn, and I had the mortification of knowing that the
same drip was spoiling writing paper and stores which
had been left open to dry!   But a traveller rarely lies
awake, and to-day by keeping my feet on a box, and
living in a mackintosh, I am out of both drip and mud.
Such a room as I am now in is the ordinary room of a
Persian homestead.   It is a cell of mud, not brick, either
sun or kiln dried.   Its sides are cracked and let in air.
Its roof is mud, under which is some brushwood lying
over the rafters.   It has no light holes, but as the door
has shrunk considerably from the door posts, it is not
absolutely dark.   It may be about twelve feet square.
Every part of it is blackened by years of smoke.
The best of it is that it is raised two feet from the
ground to admit of a fowl-house below, and opens on a
rough platform which runs in front of all the dwelling-
rooms.   With the misfitting door and cracked sides it is
much like a sieve.

I have waited to describe a Persian peasant's house
till I had seen more of them.   The yard is an almost
unvarying feature, whether a small enclosure with a low
wall and a gateway closed at night by a screen of reeds,
or a great farmyard like this, with an arched entrance
and dwelling-rooms for two or three generations along
one or more of the sides.

The house walls are built of mud, not sun-dried brick,
and are only one story high.   The soil near villages is
mostly mud, and by leading water to a given spot, a pit of
mortar for building material is at once made.   This being
dug up, and worked to a proper consistency by the feet
of men, is then made into a wall, piece after piece being

laid on by hand, till it reaches a height of four feet and a thickness of three—the imperative tradition of the Persian builder. This is allowed a few days for hardening, when another layer of similar height but somewhat narrower is laid upon it, *takchahs* or recesses a foot deep or more being worked into the thickness of the wall, and the process is repeated till the desired height is attained. When the wall is thoroughly dry it is plastered inside and outside with a mixture of mud and chopped straw, and if this plastering is repeated at intervals, the style of construction is very durable.

The oven or *tāndūr* is placed in the floor of one room, at least, and answers for cooking and heating. A peasant's house has no windows, and the roof does not project beyond the wall.

All roofs are flat. Rude rafters of poplar are laid across the walls about two feet apart. In a *ketchuda's* or a wealthier peasant's house, above these are laid in rows peeled poplar rods, two inches apart, then a rush mat, and then the resinous thorns of the tragacanth bush, which are not liable to decay; but in the poorer houses the owner contents himself with a coarse reed mat or a layer of brushwood above the rafters. On this is spread a well-trodden-down layer of mud, then eight or ten inches of dry earth, and the whole is thickly plastered with mixed straw and mud. A slight slope at the back with a long wooden spout carries off the water. Such a roof is impervious to rain except in very severe storms if kept in order, that is, if it be plastered once a year, and well rolled after rain. Few people are so poor as not to have a neatly-made stone roller on their roofs. If this is lacking, the roof must be well tramped after rain by bare feet, and in all cases the snow must be shovelled off.

These roofs, among the peasantry, have no parapets. They are the paradise of dogs, and in hot weather the people take up their beds and sleep there, partly for coolness and partly because the night breeze gives freedom from mosquitos. In simple country life, though the premises of the peasants for the sake of security are contiguous, there are seldom even balustrades to the roofs, though in summer most domestic operations are carried on there. Fifty years ago Persian law sanctioned the stoning without trial or mercy of any one caught in the act of gazing into the premises of another, unless the gazer were the king.

Upon the courtyard stables, barns, and store-rooms open, but so far I notice that the granary is in the house, and that the six-feet-high clay receptacles for grain are in the living-room.

Looking from above upon a plain, the poplars which surround villages where there is a sufficiency of water attract the eye. At this season they are nothing but a brown patch on the snow. The villages themselves are of light brown mud, and are surrounded usually by square walls with towers at the corners, and all have a great gate. Within the houses or hovels the families are huddled irregularly, with all their appurtenances, and in winter the flocks and herds are in subterranean pens beneath. In summer the animals go forth at sunrise and return at sunset. The walls, which give most of the villages a fortified aspect, used to afford the villagers a degree of protection against the predatory Turkomans, and now give security to the flocks against Lur and other robbers.

Every village has its *ketchuda* or headman, who is answerable for the taxes, the safety of travellers, and other matters.

Siashan, Feb. 16.—The men being a little better, we left Saruk at nine on the 14th, I on a bright little Baghdadi horse, in such good case that he frequently

threw up his heels in happy playfulness. The temperature
had fallen considerably, there had been a fresh snowfall,
and the day was very bright. The Arab horses are
suffering badly in their eyes from the glare of the snow.

If I had not had such a lively little horse I should
have found the march a tedious one, for we were six
hours in doing eleven and a half miles on a level! The
head *charvadar* had gone on early to make some arrangements, and the others loaded the animals so badly that
Hadji and the cook rolled off their mules into the deep
semi-frozen slush from the packs turning just outside
the gates. We had three mules with us with worn-out
tackle, and the loads rolled over many times, the riders,
who were too weak to help themselves, getting bad falls.
As each load, owing to the broken tackle, took fifteen
minutes to put on again, and the men could do little,
a great deal of hard, exasperating work fell on M——.
After one bad fall in a snowdrift myself, I rode on alone
with one mule with a valuable burden. This, turning for the fourth time, was soon under his body, and he
began to kick violently, quite dismaying me by the bang
of his hoofs against cases containing scientific instruments.
It was a droll comedy in the snow. I wanted to get
hold of his halter, but every time I went near him he
whisked round and flung up his heels, till I managed to
cut the ragged surcingle and set him free, when I caught
him in deep snow, in which my horse was very unwilling
to risk himself.

Soon after leaving Saruk, which, as I mentioned before,
is famous for very fine carpets, we descended gently upon
the great plain of Feraghan, perhaps the largest carpet-
producing district of Persia. These carpets are very fine
and their patterns are unique, bringing a very high price.
This plain has an altitude of about 7000 feet, is 45 miles
in length by from 8 to 15 in breadth, is officially stated

to have 650 villages upon it, all agricultural and carpet
producing, and is considerably irrigated by streams, which
eventually lose themselves in a salt lake at its eastern
extremity.   It is surrounded by hills, with mountain
ranges behind them, and must be, both as to productive-
ness and population, one of the most flourishing districts
in Persia.

We were to have marched to Kashgird, but on reaching the hamlet of Ahang Garang I found that Abbas
Khan had taken quarters there, saying that Kashgird was
in ruins.

Hadji, who had allowed himself to roll off several
times, was moaning and weeping on the floor of my
room, groaning out, with many cries of *Ya Allah*, "Let
me stay here till I'm better; I don't want any wages; I
shall be killed, oh, killed!   Oh, my family!   I shall
never see Bushire any more!"   Though there was much
reason to think he was shamming, I did the little that he
calls his "work," and left him to smoke his opium pipe
and sleep by the fire in peace.

I was threatened with snow-blindness in one eye; in
fact I saw nothing with it, and had to keep it covered
up.   One of the *charvadars* lay moaning outside my
room, poor fellow, taking chlorodyne every half-hour, and
another had got a bad foot from frost-bite.   They have
been terribly exposed, and the soft snow at a higher
temperature has been worse for them than the dry
powdery snow at a low temperature, as it soaks their
socks, shoes, and leggings, and then freezes.   Making
Liebig's beef tea warms one, and they like it even from
a Christian hand.   The Afghan orderly bore up bravely,
but was very weak.   Indeed the prospect of getting
these men to Tihran is darkening daily.

My room, though open to the snow at one end, was
comfortable.   The oven had been lighted twelve hours

before, and it was delightful to hang one's feet into the warm hole. There were holes for light in the roof, and cold though it was, so long as daylight lasted these were never free from veiled faces looking down.

In order to become thoroughly warm it was necessary to walk long and briskly on the roof, and this brought all the villagers below it to stare the stare of vacuity rather than of curiosity. A snow scene is always beautiful at sunset, and this was exceptionally so, as the long indigo shadows on the plain threw into greater definiteness the gleaming, glittering hills, at one time dazzling in the sunshine, at another flushed in the sunset. The plain of Feraghan as seen from the roof was one smooth expanse of pure deep snow, broken only by brown splashes, where mud villages were emphasised by brown poplars, the unbroken, unsullied snow, two feet deep on the level and any number in the drifts, looking like a picture of the Arctic Ocean, magnificent in its solitude, one difficult track, a foot wide, the solitary link with the larger world which then seemed so very far away.

Things went better yesterday on the whole, though the mercury fell to zero in the night, and I was awakened several times by the cold of my open room, and when a number of people came at daylight for medicines my fingers were so benumbed that I could scarcely measure them. What a splendid field for a medical missionary loving his profession this plain with its 650 villages would be, where there are curable diseases by the hundred! Many of the suffering people have told me that they would give lodging and the best of their food to any English doctor who would travel among them.

The loads were well balanced yesterday, and Hadji only pulled his over once and only rolled off once, when Abbas Khan exclaimed, "He's not a man; why did

Allah make such a creature ?" We got off at nine, the roofs being crowded to see us start. Fuel is very scarce at Ahang Garang. For the cooking and "parlour" fire, the charge was forty-five *krans*, or about twenty-eight shillings! Probably this included a large *modakel*. For a room from two to four *krans* is expected.

Through M——'s kindness I now have a good horse to ride, and the difference in fatigue is incredible. We embarked again on the vast plain of snow. It was a grim day, and most ghastly and desolate this end of the plain looked, where the waters having done their fertilising work are lost in a salt lake, the absolutely white hills round the plain being emphasised by the blue neutral tint of the sky. For the first ten miles there was little more than a breeze, for the last ten a pitiless, ruthless, riotous north-easterly gale, blowing up the snow in hissing drifts, as it swept across the plain with a desolate screech.

The coverings with which we were swaddled were soon penetrated. The cold seemed to enter the bones, and to strike the head and face like a red-hot hammer, stunning as it struck, the tears wrung from the eyes were frozen, at times even the eyelids were frozen together. The frozen snow hit one hard. Hands and feet were by turns benumbed and in anguish, terrific blasts loaded with hard lumps of snow came down from the hills, snow was drifting from all the white ranges above us; on the more exposed part of the track the gusts burst with such violence as to force some of the mules off it to flounder in the deep snow; my Arab was struck so mercilessly on his sore swollen eyes that at times I could scarcely, with my own useless hands, induce him to face the swirls of frozen snow. Swifter and more resistless were the ice-laden squalls, more and more obliterated became the track, till after a fight of over three hours, and the ceaseless crossing of rolling hills and deep hollows, we reached the top of a wind-bared slope 7700 feet in altitude and saw this village, looking from that distance quite imposing, on a hill on the other side of a stream crossed by a brick bridge, with a ruined fort on a height above it. It promised shelter—that was all. Below the village there was an expanse of snow, sloping up to pure white hills outlined against an indigo depth of ominous-looking clouds.

While M—— went up a hill for some scientific work, I followed the orderly, who could scarcely sit on his horse from pain and weakness, into the most wretchedly ruinous, deserted-looking village I have yet seen, epitomising the disenchantment which a near view of an Eastern city brings, and up a steep alley to a ruinous yard heaped with snow-covered ruins, on one side of which were some ruinous rooms, their backs opening on a precipice above the river, and on the north-east wind. I tumbled off my horse, Abbas Khan, the least sick of the men, with benumbed hands breaking my fall. The severe cold had stiffened all my joints. We could scarcely speak; the bones of my face were in intense pain, and I felt as if the cold were congealing my heart.

With Abbas Khan's help I chose the rooms, the worst we have ever had. The one I took for myself has an open-work door facing the wind, and it is impossible to have a fire, for the draught blows sticks, ashes, and embers over the room. The others are worse. It is an awful night, blowing and snowing; all the men but two are *hors de combat*. The poor orderly, using an Afghan phrase, said, "The wind has played the demon with me." He has a fearful cough, and hæmorrhage from the lungs or throat. The cook is threatened with pleurisy. It may truly be called "Hospital Sunday." The day has been chiefly spent in making mustard poultices, which M——

is constantly crossing the yard in three feet of snow to put on, and protectors for the chests and backs, preparing beef tea, making up medicines, etc.

Surely things must have reached their worst. Out of seven men only one servant, and he an Indian lad with a fearful squint and eyes so badly inflamed that he can hardly see where he puts things down, is able to do anything. Two of the *charvadars* are lying ill in the stable. Mustard plasters, Dover's powders, salicylate of soda, emetics, poultices, clinical thermometers, chlorodyne, and beef tea have been in requisition all day. The cook, the Afghan orderly, and Hadji seem really ill. At eight this morning groans at my door took me out, and one of the muleteers was lying there in severe pain, with the hard fine snow beating on him. Later I heard fresh moaning on my threshold, and found Hadji fallen there with my breakfast. I got him in and he fell again, upsetting the tea, and while I attended to him the big dogs ate up the *chapatties*! He had a good deal of fever, and severe rheumatism, and on looking at his eyes I saw that he was nearly blind. He lost his blue glasses some 'days ago. I sent him to bed in the " kitchen" for the whole day, where he lay groaning in comfort by the fire with his opium pipe and his tea. He thinks he will not survive the night, and has just given me his dying directions !

Afterwards M—— came for the thermometer and chlorodyne, and remarked that my room was " unfit for a beast." The truth is I share it with several very big dogs. It did look grotesquely miserable last night— black, fireless, wet, dirty, with all my things lying on the dirty floor, having been tumbled about by these dogs in their search for my last box of Brand's meat lozenges, which they got out of a strong, tightly-tied-up bag, which they tore into strips. On going for my fur cloak to-day, these three dogs, who, I believe, would take on civilisation more quickly than their masters, were all found rolled up under it, and lying on my bed.

The mercury in the "parlour" with a large fire cannot be raised above 36°. In my room to-night the wet floor is frozen hard and the mercury is 20°. This is nothing after 12° and 16° below zero, but the furious east wind and a singular dampness in the air make it very severe. Yesterday, before the sky clouded over, there was a most remarkable ring or halo of prismatic colours round the sun, ominous of the storm which has followed.

This place standing high without shelter is fearfully exposed; there is no milk and no comfort of any kind for the sick men. We have decided to wrap them up and move them to Kûm, where there is a Persian doctor with a European education; but it is a great risk, though the lesser of two. I have just finished four protectors for the back and chest, three-quarters of a yard long by sixteen inches wide, buttoning on the shoulders, of a very soft felt *namad* nearly half an inch thick—a precaution much to be commended.

I think that Hadji, though in great pain, poor fellow, is partly shamming. He professed this evening to have violent fever, and the thermometer shows that he has none. Even the few things which I thought he had done for me, such as making *chapatties*, I find have been done by others. It is a pity for himself as well as for me that he should be so incorrigibly lazy.

Taj Khatan, Feb. 18.—Yesterday we had a severe march, and owing first to the depth of the snow, and then to the depth of the mud, we were seven hours in doing twenty-one miles. The wind was still intensely cold—bitter indeed. There are few remarks to be made about a country buried in snow. The early miles were across the fag end of the dazzling plain of Feraghan, which instead of being covered with villages is an uninhabited desert with a salt lake. Then the road winds among mountains of an altitude of 8000 and 9000 feet and more, its highest point being 8350 feet, where we began a descent which will land us at Tihran at a level under 4000 feet. Snowy mountains and snowy plains were behind—bare brown earth was to come all too soon.

Winding wearily round low hills, meeting caravans of camels to which we had to give way, and of asses floundering in the snow, we came in the evening to a broad slope with villages, poplars, walnuts, and irrigated lands, then to the large and picturesquely situated village of Givr on a steep bank above a rapid stream, and just at dusk to the important village of Jairud, also on high ground above the same river, and surrounded by gardens and an extraordinary number of fruit trees. The altitude is 6900 feet.[1] I had a *balakhana*, very. cold, and was fairly benumbed for some time after the long cold march.

A great many people applied for medicine, and some of the maladies, specially when they affect children, make one sick at heart. Hadji is affecting to be stone deaf, so he no longer interprets for sick people, which creates an additional difficulty. We left this morning at ten, descended 2000 feet, and suddenly left the snow behind. Vast, gray, and grim the snow-covered mountains looked as they receded into indigo gloom, with snow clouds drifting round their ghastly heads and across the dazzling snow plains in which we had been floundering for thirty days. It is strange to see mother earth once more— rocky, or rather stony hills, mud hills, mud plains, mud

[1] Jairud exports fruit to Kûm and even to Tihran, and in the autumn I was interested to find that the best pears and peaches in the Hamadan market came from its luxuriant orchards.

slopes, a brown world, with a snow world above. Two pink hills rise above the brown plain, and some toothed peaks, but the rest of the view is simply hills and slopes of mud and gravel, bearing thorns, and the relics of last year's thistles and wormwood. The atmospheric colouring is, however, very fine.

This is a large village with beehive roofs in, and of, mud. A quagmire surrounds it and is in the centre

PERSIAN BREAD-MAKING.

of it, and the crumbling houses are thrown promiscuously down upon it. It is nearly the roughest place I have seen, and the worst accommodation, though Abbas Khan says it is the best house in the village. My room has an oven in the floor, neatly lined with clay, and as I write the women are making bread by a very simple process. The oven is well heated by the live embers of animal fuel. They work the flour and water dough, to which a piece of leaven from the last baking has been added, into a flat round cake, about eighteen inches in diameter and half an inch thick, place

it quickly on a very dirty cushion, and clap it against
the concave interior of the oven, withdrawing the cushion.
In one minute it is baked and removed.

A sloping hole in the floor leads to the fowl-house.
The skin of a newly-killed sheep hangs up. A pack
saddle and gear take up one corner, my bed another, and
the owner's miscellaneous property fills up the rest of the
blackened, cracked mud hovel, thick with the sooty
cobwebs and dust of generations. The door, which can
only be shut by means of a wooden bolt outside, is six
inches from the ground, so that fowls and cats run in
and out with impunity. Behind my bed there is a doorless entrance to a dark den, full of goat's hair, bones, and
other stores. In front there is a round hole for letting
in light, which I persistently fill up with a blanket which
is as persistently withdrawn. There is no privacy, for
though the people are glad to let their rooms, they only
partially vacate them, and are in and out all the time.
Outside there is mud a foot deep, then a steep slope, and
a disgusting green pool, and the drinking water is
nauseous and brackish. The village people here and
everywhere seem of a very harmless sort.

Kûm, Ash Wednesday, 1896.—It was really very
difficult to get away from Taj Khatan. The *charvadar*
came on here, leaving only two men to load twelve
mules. M—— practically had to load them himself,
and to reload them when the tackle broke and the loads
turned. Hadji and the cook were quite incapable, the
Afghan orderly, who seemed like a dying man, was left
behind ; in fact there were no servants and no interpreters,
and the groom was so ill he could hardly sit on a horse.

The march of twenty-five miles took fully eight hours,
but on the Arab horse, and with an occasional gallop, I
got through quite comfortably, and have nothing to
complain of. The road lies through a country of mud

hills, brown usually, drab sometimes, streaked with deep madder red, and occasionally pale green clay—stones, thistles, and thorns their only crop. [I passed over much of this country in the spring, and though there were a few flowers, chiefly bulbs, and the thorns were clothed with a scanty leafage, and the thistles and artemisia were green-gray instead of buff, the general aspect of the region was the same.] There was not a village on the route, only two or three heaps of deserted ruins and two or three ruinous mud *imamzadas*, no cultivation, streams, or springs, the scanty pools brackish, here and there the glittering whiteness of saline efflorescence, not a tree or even bush, nothing living except a few goats, picking up, who knows how, a scanty living,—a blighted, blasted region, a land without a *raison d'être*.

Then came low mud ranges, somewhat glorified by atmosphere, higher hills on the left, ghastly with snow which was even then falling, glimpses far away to the northward of snowy mountains among heavy masses of sunlit clouds, an ascent, a gap in the mud hills, some low peaks of white, green, and red clay, a great plain partly green with springing wheat, and in the centre, in the glow of sunset, the golden dome and graceful minarets of the shrine of Fatima, the sister of Reza, groups of trees, and the mud houses, mud walls, and many domes and minarets of the sacred city of Kûm.

Descending, we trotted for some miles through irrigated wheat, passed a walled garden or two, rode along the bank of the Abi Khonsar or Abi Kûm, which we had followed down from Givr, admired the gleaming domes and tiled minarets of the religious buildings on its bank, and the nine-arched brick bridge which spans it, and reached a sort of hotel outside the gates, a superior caravanserai with good, though terribly draughty guest-rooms upstairs, furnished with beds, chairs, and tables, suited for the upper class of pilgrims who resort to this famous shrine.

To have arrived here in good health, and well able for the remaining journey of nearly a hundred miles, is nothing else than a triumph of race, of good feeding through successive generations, of fog - born *physique*, nurtured on damp east winds!

There is an air of civilisation about this place. The rooms have windows with glass panes and doors which shut, a fountain in front, beyond that a garden, and then the river, and the golden shrine of Fatima and its exquisite minarets. My door opens on a stone-flagged roof with a fine view of the city and hills—an excellent place for taking exercise. So strong is Mohammedan fanaticism here that much as I should like to see the city, it would be a very great risk to walk through it except in disguise.

M—— borrowed a *taktrawan* from the telegraph clerk and sent it back with two horses to Taj Khatan for the orderly, who was left there very ill yesterday morning, under Abbas Khan's charge, the Khan feeling so ill that he lay down inside it instead of riding. Hadji gave up work altogether, so I unpacked and pitched my bed, glad to be warmed by exercise. Near 8 P.M. Abbas Khan burst into the "parlour" saying that the *taktrawan* horses were stuck in the mud. He evidently desired to avoid the march back, but two mules have been sent to replace the horses, and two more are to go to-morrow. The orderly was so ill that I expect his corpse rather than himself.

This morning Hadji, looking fearful, told me that he should die to-day, and he and the cook are now in bed in opposite corners of a room below, with a good fire, feverish and moaning. It is really a singular disaster, and shows what the severity of the journey has been. The Persian doctor, with a European medical education, on whom our hopes were built, when asked to come and see these poor men, readily promised to do so; but the Princess, the Shah's daughter, whose physician he is, absolutely refuses permission, on the ground that we have come through a region in which there is supposed to be cholera!

I. L. B.

LETTER VII

KÛM, *Feb. 21.*

AT five yesterday afternoon Abbas Khan rode in saying that the *taktrawan*, with the orderly much better, was only three miles off. This was good news; a mattress was put down for him next the fire and all preparations for his comfort were made. Snow showers had been falling much of the day, there was a pitiless east wind, and as darkness came on snow fell persistently. Two hours passed, but no *taktrawan* arrived. At 7.30 Abbas Khan was ordered to go in search of it with a good lantern; 8, 9, 10 o'clock came without any news. At 10.30, the man whose corpse I had feared to see came in much exhausted, having crawled for two miles through the mire and snow. The *sowar*, who pretended to start with the lantern, never went farther than the coffee-room at the gate, where he had spent an unconscientious but cheery evening!

In the pitch darkness the *taktrawan* and mules had fallen off the road into a gap, the *takrawan* was smashed, and a good white mule, one of the "light division," was killed, her back being broken. This was not the only disaster. Hadji had lain down on the borrowed mattress and it had taken fire from the live ashes of his pipe and was burned, and he was a little scorched.

The telegraphist was to have started for Isfahan the next morning with his wife and child in the litter, in

order to vacate the house for the new official and his
family, and their baggage had actually started, but now
they are detained till this *taktrawan* can be repaired.   In
the meantime another official has arrived with his goods
and a large family, a most uncomfortable situation for
both parties, but they bear it with the utmost cheerfulness
and good nature.

Last night I made Hadji drink a mug of hot milk
with two tablespoonfuls of brandy in it, and it worked
wonders.   This morning, instead of a nearly blind man
groping his way about with difficulty, I beheld a man
with nothing the matter but a small speck on one eye.
It must have been snow-blindness.   He looks quite
" spry."   It is not only the alcohol which has cured him,
but that we are parting by mutual consent ; and feeling
sorry for the man, I have given him more than his wages,
and his full demand for his journey back to Bushire, with
additional warm clothing.   M—— has also given him a
handsome present.

I fear he has deceived me, and that the stone deafness, feebleness, idiocy, and the shaking, palsied gait of
a man of ninety—all but the snow-blindness—have been
assumed in order to get his return journey paid, when
he found that the opportunities for making money were
not what he expected.   It is better to be deceived
twenty times than to be hard on these poor fellows
once, but he has been exasperating, and I feel somewhat
aggrieved at having worked so hard to help a man who
was " malingering."   The last seen of him was an active,
erect man walking at a good pace by the side of his
mule, at least forty years thrown off.   [He did not
then leave Kûm, but being seized with pleurisy was
treated with great kindness by Mr. Lyne the electrician,
and afterwards by the Amin-es-Sultan (the Prime
Minister), who was visiting Kûm, and who, thinking to

oblige me, brought him up to Tihran in his train !]
Those who had known him for years gave a very bad
account of him, but said that if he liked he could be a
good servant. It is the first time that I have been
unfortunate in my travelling servant.

The English telegraph line, and a post-office, open
once a week, are the tokens of civilisation in Kûm.
A telegraphic invitation from the British Minister in
Tihran, congratulatory telegrams on our safety from
Tihran, Bushire, and India, and an opportunity for
posting letters, make one feel once more in the world.
The weather is grim, bitterly cold, with a strong north-
east wind, raw and damp, but while snow is whitening
the hills only rain and sleet fall here. The sun has
not shone since we came, but the strong cold air is
invigorating like our own climate.

Taking advantage of it being Friday, the Mohammedan
day of rest, when most of the shops are closed and the
bazars are deserted, we rode through a portion of them
preceded by the wild figure of Abbas Khan, and took
tea at the telegraph office, where they were most kind
and pleasant regarding the accident which had put them
to so much inconvenience.

Kûm is on the beaten track, and has a made road
to Tihran. Almost every book of travels in Persia has
something to say upon it, but except that it is the
second city in Persia in point of sanctity, and that it
thrives as much by the bodies of the dead which are
brought in thousands for burial as by the tens of
thousands of pilgrims who annually visit the shrine of
Fatima, and that it is renowned for fanaticism, there is
not much to say about it.

Situated in a great plain, the gleam of its golden
dome and its slender minarets is seen from afar, and
the deep green of its orchards, and the bright green of

the irrigated and cultivated lands which surround it,
are a splash of welcome fertility on the great brown
waste. Singular toothy peaks of striated marl of brilliant
colouring—red, blue, green, orange, and salt peaks
very white—give a curious brilliancy to its environment, but this salt, which might be a source of wealth
to the city, is not worked, only an ass-load or two at
a time being brought in to supply the necessities of the
market.

The shrine of Fatima, the sister of Reza the eighth

THE SHRINE OF FATIMA.

Imam, who sleeps at Meshed, is better to Kûm than
salt mines or aught else. Moslems, though they regard
women with unspeakable contempt, agree to reverence
Fatima as a very holy and almost worshipful person,
and her dust renders Kûm a holy place, attracting tens
of thousands of pilgrims every year, although, unlike
pilgrimages to Meshed and Kerbela, Kûm confers no
lifelong designation on those by whom it exists. Its
estimated population is 10,000 souls, and at times this
number is nearly doubled. Pilgrimage consists in a
visit to the tomb of Fatima, paying a fee, and in some
cases adding a votive offering. Vows of abstinence

from some special sin are frequently made at the shrine and are carefully registered.

The dead, however, who are annually brought in thousands to be buried in the sacred soil which surrounds the shrine, are the great source of the wealth of Kûm. These corpses travel, as to Kerbela, on mules, four being lashed on one animal occasionally, some fresh, some decomposing, others only bags of exhumed bones. The graves occupy an enormous area, of which the shrine is the centre. The kings of the Kajar dynasty, members of royal families, and 450 saints are actually buried within the precincts of the shrine. The price of interments varies with the proximity to the dust of Fatima from six *krans* to one hundred *tumans*. The population may be said to be a population of undertakers. Death meets one everywhere. The Ab-i-Khonsar, which supplies the drinking water, percolates through "dead men's bones and all uncleanness." Vestments for the dead are found in the bazars. Biers full and empty traverse the streets in numbers. Stone-cutting for gravestones is a most lucrative business. The *charvadars* of Kûm prosper on caravans of the dead. There is a legion of gravediggers. Kûm is a gruesome city, a vast charnel-house, yet its golden dome and minarets brighten the place of death.

The dome of Fatima is covered with sheets of copper plated with gold an eighth of an inch in thickness, and the ornament at the top of the dome, which is of pure gold, is said to weigh 140 lbs. The slender minarets which front this *imamzada* are covered with a mosaic of highly-glazed tiles of exquisite tints, in which an azure blue, a canary yellow, and an iridescent green predominate, and over all there is a sheen of a golden hue. The shrine is inaccessible to Christians. I asked a Persian doctor if I might look in for one moment at the threshold of the outer court, and he replied in French, "Are you then weary of life?"[1]

My Indian servant, an educated man on whose faithful though meagre descriptions I can rely, visited the shrine and describes the dome as enriched with arabesques in mosaic and as hung with *ex votos*, consisting chiefly of strips of silk and cotton. The tomb itself, he says, is covered with a wooden ark, with certain sacred sentences cut upon it, and this is covered by a large brown shawl. Round this ark, which is under the dome, Kerman, Kashmir, and Indian shawls are laid down as carpets. This open space is surrounded with steel railings inlaid with gold after the fashion of the *niello* work of Japan, and the whole is enclosed with a solid silver fence, the rails of which are "as thick as two thumbs, and as high as a tall man's head." This *imamzada* itself is regarded as of great antiquity.

Two Persian kings, who reigned in the latter part of the seventeenth century, are buried near the beautiful minarets, which are supposed to be of the same date. There are many mosques and minarets in Kûm, besides a quantity of conical *imamzadas*, the cones of which have formerly been covered with glazed blue tiles of a turquoise tint, some of which still remain. It was taken by the Afghans in 1772, and though partially rebuilt is very ruinous. It has a mud wall, disintegrating from neglect, surrounded occasionally by a ditch, and at other times by foul and stagnant ponds. The ruinousness of Kûm can scarcely be exaggerated.

The bazars are large and very busy, and are considerably more picturesque than those of Kirmanshah. The town lives by pilgrims and corpses, and the wares

---

[1] I spent two days at Kûm five weeks later, and saw the whole of it in disguise, and in order to attain some continuity of description I put my two letters together.

displayed to attract the former are more attractive than usual.   There are nearly 450 shops, of which forty-three sell Manchester goods almost exclusively.   Coarse china, and 'pottery often of graceful shapes with a sky-blue glaze, and water-coolers are among the industries of this city, which also makes shoes, and tans leather with pomegranate bark.

The Ab-i-Khonsar is now full and rapid, but is a mere thread in summer.   The nine-arched bridge, with its infamously paved roadway eighteen feet wide, is an interesting object from all points of view, for while its central arch has a span of forty-five feet, the others have only spans of twenty.   The gateway beyond the bridge is tawdrily ornamented with blue and green glazed tiles. After seeing several of the cities of Persia, I am quite inclined to give Kûm the palm for interest and beauty of aspect, when seen from any distant point of view.

That it is a "holy" city, and that a pilgrimage to its shrine is supposed to atone for sin, are its great interests. Its population is composed in large proportion of *mollahs* and *Seyyids*, or descendants of Mohammed, and as a whole is devoted to the reigning Shiah creed.   It has a theological college of much repute, established by Fath' Ali Shah, which now has 100 students.   The women are said to be very devout, and crowd the mosques on Friday evenings, when their devotions are led by an *imam*.   The men are fanatically religious, though the fanaticism is somewhat modified.   No wine may be sold in Kûm, and no Jew or Armenian is allowed to keep a shop.

Kûm, being a trading city, manufactures a certain amount of public opinion in its business circles, which differs not very considerably from that which prevails at Kirmanshah.   The traders accept it as a foregone conclusion that Russia will occupy Persia as far as Isfahan on the death of the present Shah, and regard such a destiny as " fate." If only their religion is not interfered with, it matters little, they say, whether they pay their taxes to the Shah or the Czar. To judge from their speech, Islam is everything to them, and their country very little, and the strong bond of the faith which rules life and thought from the Pillars of Hercules to the Chinese frontier far outweighs the paltry considerations of patriotism. But my impression is that all Orientals prefer the tyrannies and exactions, and the swiftness of injustice or justice of men of their own creed and race to good government on the part of unintelligible aliens, and that though Persians seem pretty comfortable in the prospect of a double occupation of Persia, its actual accomplishment might strike out a flash of patriotism.

Probably this ruinous, thinly-peopled country, with little water and less fuel, and only two roads which deserve the name, has possibilities of resurrection under greatly changed circumstances. Of the two occupations which are regarded as certain, I think that most men, at least in Central and Southern Persia, would prefer an English occupation, but every one says, " England talks and does not act," and that " Russia will pour 100,000 troops into Persia while England is talking in London."   I. L. B.

LETTER VIII

CARAVANSERAI OF ALIABAD, *Feb. 23.*

TWELVE hours and a half of hard riding have brought us here in two days. No doctor could be obtained in Kûm, and it was necessary to bring the sick men on as quickly as possible for medical treatment. It was bitterly cold on the last day, though the altitude is only 3400 feet, and it was a tiresome day, for I had not only to look over and repack, but to clean the cooking utensils and other things, which had not been touched apparently since we left Baghdad!

This is a tedious part of the journey, a " beaten track " with few features of interest, the great highway from Isfahan to Tihran, a road of dreary width; where it is a made road running usually perfectly straight, with a bank and a ditch on each side. The thaw is now complete, and travelling consists of an attempt to get on by the road till it becomes an abyss which threatens to prove bottomless, then there is a plunge and a struggle to the top of the bank, or over the bank to the trodden waste, but any move can be only temporary, the all-powerful mire regulates the march. The snow is nothing to the mud. Frequently carcasses of camels, mules, and asses, which have lain down to die under their loads, were passed, then caravans with most of the beasts entangled in the miry clay, unable to rise till they were unloaded by men up to their knees in the quagmire, and, worst of all, mules loaded with the dead, so loosely tied up in planks that in some cases when the mule flounders and falls, the miserable relics of humanity tumble out upon the swamp; and these scenes of falling, struggling, and even perishing animals are repeated continually along the level parts of this scarcely passable highroad.

Our loads, owing to bad tackle, were always coming off, the groom's mule fell badly, the packs came off another, and half an hour was spent in catching the animal, then I was thrown from my horse into soft mud.

Cultivation ceases a short distance from Kûm, giving place to a brown waste, with patches of saline efflorescence upon it, on which high hills covered partially with snow send down low spurs of brown mud. The water nearly everywhere is brackish, and only just drinkable. After crossing a rapid muddy river, nearly dry in summer, by a much decayed bridge of seven or eight low arches, we reached *terra firma*, and a long gradual ascent and a series of gallops brought us to the large caravanserai of Shashgird, an immense place with imposing pretensions which are fully realised within. In the outer court camels were lying in rows. A fine tiled archway leads to an immense quadrangle, with a fine stone *abambar* or covered receptacle for water in the middle. All round the quadrangle are arched recesses or mangers, each with a room at the back, to the number of eighty. At two of the corners there are enclosed courtyards with fountains, several superior rooms with beds (much to be avoided), chairs, mirrors, and tables fairly clean—somewhat dreary luxury, but fortunately at this season free from vermin. That caravanserai can accommodate 1000 men in rooms, and 1500 mules.

To-day's long march, which, however, has had more road suitable for galloping, has been over wild, weird, desolate, God-forsaken country, interesting from its desolation and its great wastes, forming part of the Kavir or Great Salt Desert of Persia, absolutely solitary, with scarcely a hamlet—miles of the great highway of Persia without a living creature, no house, no bush, nothing.   Later, there were some vultures feasting on a dead camel, and a mule-load of two bodies down in the mud.

Some miles from Shashgird, far from the road, there is a large salt lake over which some stationary mists were brooding.   Beyond this an ascent among snow clouds along some trenched land where a few vines and saplings have been planted leads to a caravanserai built for the accommodation of state officials on their journeys, where in falling snow we vindicated our origin in the triumphant West by taking lunch on a windy verandah outside rather than in the forlorn dampness of the inside, and brought a look of surprise even over the impassive face of the *seraidar*.

When we left the snow was falling in large wet flakes, and the snow clouds were drifting wildly among the peaks of a range which we skirted for a few miles and then crossed at a considerable height among wonderful volcanic formations, mounds of scoriæ, and outcrops of volcanic rock, hills of all shapes fantastically tumbled about, chiefly black, looking as if their fires had only just died out, streaked and splotched with brilliant ash—orange, carmine, and green—a remarkable volcanic scene, backed by higher hills looking ghastly in the snow.

After passing over an absolutely solitary region of camel-brown plains and slopes at a gallop, M—— a little in front always, and Abbas Khan, the wildest figure imaginable, always half a length behind, the *thud* of the thundering hoofs mingling with the screech of the cutting north wind which, coming over the snowy Elburz range, benumbed every joint, on the slope of a black volcanic hill we came upon the lofty towers and gaudy tiled front of this great caravanserai, imposing at a distance in the solitude and snow clouds, but shabby on a nearer view, and tending to disintegrate from the presence of saltpetre in the bricks and mortar.

There are successions of terraces and tanks of water with ducks and geese upon them, and buildings round the topmost terrace intended to be imposing. The *seraidar* is expecting the Amin-es-Sultan (the Prime Minister) and his train, who will occupy rather a fine though tawdry "suite of apartments"; but though they were at our service, I prefer the comparative cosiness of a small, dark, damp room, though with a very smoky chimney, as I find to my cost.

British Legation, Tihran, Feb. 26.—The night was very cold, and the reveille specially unwelcome in the morning. The people were more than usually vague about the length of the march, some giving the distance at twenty-five miles, and others making it as high as thirty-eight. As we did a good deal of galloping and yet took more than seven hours, I suppose it may be about twenty-eight. Fortunately we could desert the caravan, as the caravanserais are furnished and supply tea and bread. The baggage mules took ten hours for the march.

The day was dry and sunny, and the scenery, if such a tract of hideousness can be called scenery, was at its best. Its one charm lies in the solitude and freedom of a vast unpeopled waste.

The "made road" degenerates for the most part into a track "made" truly, but rather by the passage of thousands of animals during a long course of ages than by men's hands. This track winds among low ranges of sand and mud hills, through the "Pass of the Angel of Death," crosses salt and muddy streams, gravelly stretches, and quagmires of mud and tenacious clay, passing through a country on the whole inconceivably hideous, unfinished, frothy, and saturated with salt—the great brown desert which extends from Tihran to Quetta in Beloochistan, a distance of 2000 miles.

On a sunny slope we met the Prime Minister with a considerable train of horsemen. He stopped and spoke with extreme courtesy, through an interpreter, for, unlike most Persians of the higher class, he does not speak French. He said we had been for some time expected at Tihran, and that great fears were entertained for our safety, which we had heard at Kûm. He is a pleasant-looking man with a rather European expression, not more than thirty-two or thirty-three, and in spite of intrigues and detractors has managed to keep his hazardous position for some years. His mother was lately buried at Kûm, and he was going thither on pilgrimage. After the usual compliments he bowed his farewells, and the gay procession with its brilliant trappings and prancing horses flashed by. The social standing of a Persian is evidenced by the size of his retinue, and the first of the Shah's subjects must have been attended by fully forty well-mounted men, besides a number of servants who were riding with his baggage animals.

Shortly after passing him a turn among the hills brought the revelation through snow clouds of the magnificent snow-covered chain of the Elburz mountains, with the huge cone of Demavend, their monarch, 18,600 feet [1] in height, towering high above them, gleaming sunlit above the lower cloud-masses. Swampy water-courses, a fordable river crossed by a broad bridge of five arches, more low hills, more rolling desert, then a plain of mud irrigated for cultivation, difficult ground for the horses, the ruins of a deserted village important enough to have possessed two *imamzadas*, and then we reached the Husseinabad, which has very good guest-rooms, with mirrors on the walls.

[1] The altitude of Demavend is variously stated.

This caravanserai is only one march from Tihran, and it seemed as if all difficulties were over. Abbas Khan and the sick orderly were sent on early, with a baggage mule loaded with evening dress and other necessities of civilisation; the caravan was to follow at leisure, and M—— and I started at ten, without attendants, expecting to reach Tihran early in the afternoon.

It is six days since that terrible ride of ten hours and a half, and my bones ache as I recall it. I never wish to mount a horse again. It had been a very cold night, and for some time after we started it was doubtful whether snow or rain would gain the day, but after an hour of wet snow it decided on rain, and there was a steady downpour all day. The Elburz range, which the day before had looked so magnificent when fifty miles off, was blotted out. This was a great disappointment.

An ascent of low, blackish volcanic hills is made by a broad road of gray gravel, which a torrent has at some time frequented. Thorns and thistles grow there, and skeletons of animals abound. Everything is grim and gray. From these hills we descended into the Kavir, a rolling expanse of friable soil, stoneless, strongly impregnated with salt, but only needing sufficient water to wash the salt out of it and to irrigate it to become as prolific as it is now barren.

It is now a sea of mud crossed by a broad road indicated by dykes, that never-to-be-forgotten mud growing deeper as the day wore on. Hour after hour we plunged through it, sometimes trying the road, and on finding it impassable scrambling through the ditches and over the dykes to the plain, which after offering firmer foothold for a time became such a " slough of despond " that we had to scramble back to the road, and so on, hour after hour, meeting nothing but one ghastly caravan of corpses, and wretched asses falling in the mud.

At mid-day, scrambling up a gravel hill with a little wormwood upon it, and turning my back to the heavy rain, I ate a lunch of dates and ginger, insufficient sustenance for such fatigue. On again!—the rain pouring, the mud deepening, my spine in severe pain. We turned off to a caravanserai, mostly a heap of ruins, the roofs having given way under the weight of the snow, and there I sought some relief from pain by lying down for the short thirty minutes which could be spared in the *seraidar's* damp room. It was then growing late in the afternoon, all landmarks had disappeared in a brooding mist, there were no habitations, and no human beings of whom to ask the way.

The pain returned severely as soon as I mounted, and increased till it became hardly bearable. Ceaseless mud, ceaseless heavy rain, a plain of mud, no refuge from mud and water, attempts to gallop were made with the risk of the horses falling into holes and even *kanaats*. M—— rode in front. Not a word was spoken. A gleaming dome, with minarets and wood, appeared below the Shimran hills. Unluckily, where two roads met one looked impassable and we took the other, which, though it eventually took us to Tihran, was a *détour* of some miles.

In the evening, when I was hoping that Tihran was at hand, we reached the town of Shah Abdul Azim, built among the ruins of an ancient city, either Rhages or Rhei. The gilded dome is the shrine of Abdul Azim, and is a great place of pilgrimage of the picnic order from Tihran. The one railroad of Persia runs from the capital to this town. As we floundered in darkness along wide roads planted with trees, there was the incongruity of a railway whistle, and with deep breathing and much glare an engine with some carriages passed near the road, taking away with its harsh Western noises that glorious freedom of the desert which outweighs all the hardship even of a winter journey.

It was several miles from thence to the gate of Tihran. It was nearly pitch dark when we got out of Abdul Azim and the rain still fell heavily. In that thick rainy darkness no houses were visible, even if they exist, there were no passengers on foot or on horseback, it was a " darkness which might be felt."

There was a causeway which gave foothold below the mud, but it was full of holes and broken culverts, deep in slime, and seemed to have water on each side not particular in keeping within bounds. It was necessary to get on, lest the city gates should be shut, and by lifting and spurring the jaded horses they were induced to trot and canter along that road of pitfalls. I have had many a severe ride in travelling, but never anything equal to that last two hours. The severe pain and want of food made me so faint that I was obliged to hold on to the saddle. I kept my tired horse up, but each flounder I thought would be his last. There was no guidance but an occasional flash from the hoofs of the horse in front, and the word " spur " ringing through the darkness.

After an hour of riding in this desperate fashion we got into water, and among such dangerous holes that from that point we were obliged to walk our horses, who though they were half dead still feebly responded to bit and spur. We reached the dimly-lighted city gate just as half of it was shut, and found Abbas Khan waiting there. The caravan with the other sick men never reached Tihran till late the next morning.

At the gate we learned that it was two miles farther to the British Legation, and that there was no way for me to get there but on horseback. One lives through a good deal, but I all but succumbed to the pain and faintness. Inside the gate there was an open sea of liquid mud,

across which, for a time, certain lights shed their broken
reflections.   There was a railway shriek, and then the
appearance of a station with shunting operations vaguely
seen in a vague glare.

Then a tramway track buried under several inches of
slush came down a slope, and crowded tramway cars with
great single lamps came down the narrow road on
horses too tired to be frightened, and almost too tired to
get out of the way.   Then came a street of mean houses
and meaner shops lighted with kerosene lamps, a region
like the slums of a new American city, with *cafés* and
saloons, barbers' shops, and European enormities such as
gazogenes and effervescing waters in several windows.
Later, there were frequent foot passengers preceded by
servants carrying huge waxed cambric lanterns of a
Chinese shape, then a square with barracks and artillery,
a causewayed road dimly lit, then darkness and heavier
rain and worse mud, through which the strange spectacle
of a carriage and pair incongruously flashed.

By that time even the courage and stamina of an
Arab horse could hardly keep mine on his legs, and with
a swimming head and dazed brain I could hardly guide
him, as I had done from the gate chiefly by the wan
gleam of Abbas Khan's pale horse ; and expecting to fall
off every minute, I responded more and more feebly and
dubiously to the question frequently repeated out of the
darkness, " Are you surviving ? "

Just as endurance was on the point of giving way, we
turned from the road through a large gateway into the
extensive grounds which surround the British Legation,
a large building forming three sides of a quadrangle,
with a fine stone staircase leading up to the central door.
Every window was lighted, light streamed from the open
door, splashed carriages were dashing up and setting
down people in evening dress, there were crowds of

servants about, and it flashed on my dazed senses that it must be after eight, and that there was a dinner party !

Arriving from the mud of the Kavir and the slush of the streets, after riding ten hours in ceaseless rain on a worn-out horse ; caked with mud from head to foot, dripping, exhausted, nearly blind from fatigue, fresh from mud hovels and the congenial barbarism of the desert, and with the rags and travel-stains of a winter journey of forty-six days upon me, light and festivity were overwhelming.

Alighting at a side door, scarcely able to stand, I sat down in a long corridor, and heard from an English steward that "dinner is waiting." His voice sounded very far off, and the once familiar announcement came like a memory out of the remote past. Presently a gentleman appeared in evening dress, wearing a star, which conveyed to my fast-failing senses that it was Sir H. Drummond Wolff. It was true that there was a large dinner party, and among the guests the Minister with thoughtful kindness had invited all to whom I had letters of introduction. But it was no longer possible to make any effort, and I was taken up to a room in which the comforts of English civilisation at first made no impression upon me, and removing only the mackintosh cloak, weighted with mud, which had served me so well, I lay down on the hearthrug before a great coal fire till four o'clock the next morning. And "so the tale ended," and the winter journey with its tremendous hardships and unbounded mercies was safely accomplished.[1]   I. L. B.

[1] I remained for three weeks as Sir H. Drummond Wolff's guest at the British Legation, receiving from him that courtesy and considerate kindness which all who have been under his roof delight to recall. I saw much of what is worth seeing in Tihran, including the Shah and several of the Persian statesmen, and left the Legation with every help that could be given for a long and difficult journey into the mountains of Luristan.

NOTES ON TIHRAN [1]

IT is a matter of individual taste, but few cities in the
East interest me in which national characteristics in
architecture, costume, customs, and ways generally are
either being obliterated or are undergoing a partial
remodelling on Western lines. An Eastern city pure and
simple, such as Canton, Niigata, or Baghdad, even with
certain drawbacks, forms a harmonious whole gratifying
to the eye and to a certain sense of fitness; while Cairo,
Tokio, Lahore, and I will now add Tihran, produce the
effect of a series of concussions.

Tihran—set down on a plain, a scorched desert, the
sublimity of which is interfered with by *kanaats* or underground watercourses with their gravel mounds and ruinous shafts—has few elements of beauty or grandeur
in its situation, even though " the triumphant barbarism
of the desert " sweeps up to its gates, and the scored and
channelled Shimran range, backed by the magnificent
peak, or rather cone, of Demavend, runs to the north-east
of the city within only ten miles of its walls.

The winter with its snow and slush disappeared
abruptly two days after I reached Tihran, and as abruptly
came the spring—a too transient enjoyment—and in a few
days to brownness and barrenness succeeded a tender

[1] A volume of travels in Persia would scarcely be complete without some
slight notice of the northern capital ; but for detailed modern accounts of
it the reader should consult various other books, especially Dr. Wills' and
Mr. Benjamin's, if he has not already done so.

mist of green over the trees in the watered gardens, rapidly thickening into dark leafage in which the *bulbul* sang, and nature helped by art spread a carpet of violets and irises over the brown earth. But all of verdure and greenery that there is lies within the city walls. Outside is the unconquerable desert, rolling in endless shades of buff and brown up to the Elburz range, and elsewhere to the far horizon.

Situated in the most depressed part of an uninteresting waste in Lat. 35° 40′ N. and Long. 51° 25′ E., and at an altitude of 3800 feet, the climate is one of extremes, the summer extreme being the most severe. For some weeks the heat is nearly insupportable, and the Legations, and all of the four hundred Europeans who are not bound to the city by a fate which they execrate, betake themselves to " yailaks," or summer quarters on the slopes of the adjacent mountains.

Entering Tihran in the darkness, it was not till I saw it coming back from Gulahek, the " yailak " of the British Legation, when the mud was drying up and the willows were in their first young green, that I formed any definite idea of its aspect, which is undeniably mean, and presents no evidences of antiquity ; indeed, it has no right to present any, for as a capital it only came into existence a century ago, with the first king of the present Kajar dynasty. The walls are said to be eleven miles in circuit, and give the impression of being much too large, so many are the vacant spaces within them. They consist chiefly of a broad ditch, and a high sloping rampart without guns. Twelve well-built domed gateways give access to the city. These are decorated with glazed tiles of bright colours and somewhat gaudy patterns and designs, representing genii, lions, and combats of mythical heroes.

Above the wall are seen tree-tops, some tile-covered minarets, the domes of two mosques, and the iron ribs of a roofless theatre in the Shah's garden, in which under a temporary awning the *Tazieh* or Passion Play (elsewhere referred to) is acted once a year in presence of the Shah and several thousand spectators.

Entering by a gateway over which is depicted a scene in the life of Rustem, the Achilles of Persia, or by the Sheikh Abdul Azim gate, where the custom-house is established and through which all caravans of goods must reach Tihran, the magnitude of the untidy vacant spaces, and the shabby mud hovels which fringe them, create an unfavourable impression. Then there are the inevitable ruinousness, the alleys with broken gutters in the centre, the pools of slime or the heaps of dust according to the weather, and the general shabbiness of blank walls of sun-dried bricks which give one the impression, I believe an unjust one, of decay and retrogression. I never went through those mean outskirts of Tihran which are within the city walls without being reminded of a man in shabby clothes preposterously too big for him.

The population is variously estimated at from 60,000 to 160,000 souls. It varies considerably with the presence or absence of the Court. The streets and bazars are usually well filled with people, and I did not see many beggars or evidences of extreme poverty, even in the Jewish quarter. On the whole it impressed me as a bustling place, but the bustle is not picturesque. It is framed in mean surroundings, and there is little variety in costume, and much sober if not sad colouring.

In " old " Tihran the alleys are crooked, dirty, and narrow, and the bazars chiefly frequented by the poor are very mean and untidy; but the better bazars, whether built as some are, round small domed open spaces, or in alleys roofed with low brick domes, are decidedly handsome, and are light, wide, clean, and in every way adapted for the purposes of buying and selling. European women, even though unattended, can walk through them quite freely without being mobbed or stared at.

The best bazars are piled with foreign merchandise, to the *apparent* exclusion of native goods, which, if they are of the better quality, must be searched for in out-of-the-way corners. Indeed, if people want fine carpets, *curios*, rich embroideries, inlaid arms, and Kerman stuffs, they must resort to the itinerant dealers, who gauge the tastes and purchasing powers of every European resident and visitor, and who may be seen at all hours gliding in a sort of surreptitious fashion round the Legation compounds, conveying their beautiful temptations on donkeys' backs.

It is chiefly in the fine lofty saddlery bazar and some small bazars that native manufactures are *en évidence.* All travelling is on horseback, and the Persian, though sober in the colours of his costly clothing, loves crimson and gold in leather and cloth, embroidered housings and headstalls, and gorgeous saddle-covers for his horse. The usual saddle is of plain wood, very high before and behind, and without stuffing. A thick soft *namad* or piece of felt covers the horse's back, and over this are placed two or more saddle-cloths covered with a very showy and often highly ornamental cover, with tasselled ends, embroidered in gold and silks and occasionally with real gems. The saddle itself is smoothly covered with a soft ornamental cover made to fit it, and the crupper, breast-plate, and headstall are frequently of crimson leather embroidered in gold, or stitched ingeniously with turquoise beads.

The mule, whether the pacing saddle-mule worth from £60 to £80, much affected by rich Persians in Tihran, or the humbler beast of burden, is not forgotten by the traders in the great saddlery bazar. Rich *charvadars* take great pride in the "outfit" of their mules, and do not grudge twenty *tumans* upon it. Hence are to be seen elaborate headstalls, breastplates, and straps for bells, of showy embroidery, and leather stitched completely over with turquoise beads and cowries—the latter a favourite adornment—while cowried headstalls are also ornamented with rows of woollen tassels dyed with beautiful vegetable dyes. In this bazar too are found *khurjins*—the great leather or carpet saddle-bags without which it is inconvenient to travel—small leather portmanteaus for strapping behind the saddles of those who travel *chapar, i.e.* post, —cylindrical cases over two feet long which are attached in front of the saddle—decorated holsters, the multifarious gear required for the travelling pipe-bearers, the deep leather belts which are worn by *chapar* riders, the leathern water-bottles which are slung on the saddles, the courier bags, and a number of other articles of necessity or luxury which are regarded as essential by the Persian traveller.

In most of the bazars the shops are packed to the ceiling with foreign goods. It looks as if there were cottons and woollen cloth for the clothing of all Persia. I saw scarcely any rough woollen goods or shoddy. The Persian wears superfine, smooth, costly cloth, chiefly black and fawn, stiff in texture, and with a dull shine upon it. The best comes exclusively from Austria, a slightly inferior quality from Germany, and such cloth fabrics as are worn by Europeans from England and Russia.

The European cottons, which are slowly but surely displacing the heavy durable native goods, either undyed, or dyed at Isfahan with madder, saffron, and indigo, are of colours and patterns suited to native taste, white and canary yellow designs on a red ground predominating, and are both of Russian and English make, and the rivalry which extends from the Indian frontier, through Central Asia, is at fever-heat in the cotton bazars of Tihran. It does not appear that at present either side can claim the advantage.

In a search for writing paper, thread, tapes, and what are known as " small wares," I never saw anything that was not Russian. The cheap things, such as oil lamps, *samovars*, coarse coloured prints of the Russian Imperial family in tawdry frames, lacquered tin boxes, fitted work-boxes, glass teacups, china tea-pots, tawdry lacquered trays, glass brooches, bead necklaces, looking-glasses, and a number of other things which are coming into use at least in the south-west and the western portions of the Empire, are almost exclusively Russian, as is natural, for the low price at which they are sold would leave no margin of profit on such imports from a more distant country.

A stroll through the Tihran bazars shows the observer something of the extent and rapidity with which Europe is ruining the artistic taste of Asia. Masses of rubbish, atrocious in colouring and hideous in form, the principle of shoddy carried into all articles along with the quintessence of vulgarity which is pretence, goods of nominal utility which will not stand a week's wear, the refuse of European markets—in art Philistinism, in most else " Brummagem," without a quality of beauty or solidity to recommend them—are training the tastes and changing the habits of the people.

One squarish bazar, much resorted to for glass and hardware and what the Americans call " assorted notions," is crammed with Austrian glass, kerosene lamps of all sizes in hundreds, chandeliers, etc. The amount of glass exhibited there for sale is extraordinary, and not less remarkable is the glut of cheap hardware and worthless *bijouterie*. It is the Lowther Arcade put down in Tihran.

Kerosene and candles may be called a Russian monopoly, and Russia has completely driven French sugar from the markets. In the foreign town, as it may be called, there are two or three French shops, an American shop for " notions," and a German chemist.

The European quarter is in the northern part of Tihran, and is close to vacant and airy spaces. There are the Turkish Embassy, and the Legations of England, France, Germany, Russia, Italy, Belgium, Austria, and America, and a Dutch Consulate-General, each with its Persian *gholams* who perform escort duty. Their large and shady compounds, brightened by their national flags, and the stir and circumstance which surround them, are among the features of the city. The finest of all the Legation enclosures is that of England, which is beautifully wooded and watered. The reception-rooms and hall of the Minister's residence are very handsome, and a Byzantine clock tower gives the building a striking air of distinction. The grounds contain several detached houses, occupied by the secretaries and others.

A very distinct part of the foreign quarter is that occupied by the large and handsome buildings of the American Presbyterian Mission, which consist of a church occupied at stated hours by a congregation of the Reformed Armenian Church, and in which in the afternoons of Sundays Dr. Potter, the senior missionary, reads the English Liturgy and preaches an English sermon for the benefit of the English-speaking residents, very fine boarding-schools for Armenian girls and boys, and the houses of the missionaries—three clerical, one medical, and several ladies, one of whom is an M.D.

Outside this fine enclosure is a Medical Missionary Dispensary, and last year, in a good situation at a considerable distance, a very fine medical missionary hospital was completed. The boys' and girls' schools are of a very high class. To my thinking the pupils are too much Europeanised in dress and habits; but I understand that this is at the desire of the Armenian parents. The missionaries are not allowed to receive Moslem pupils; but besides Armenians they educate Jewish youths, some of whom have become Christians, and a few Guebres or Zoroastrians.

I do not think that the capital is a hopeful place for missionary work.   The presence of Europeans of various creeds and nationalities complicates matters, and the fine, perhaps too fine, mission buildings in proximity to the houses of wealthy foreigners are at so great a distance from the Moslem and Jewish quarters, that persons who might desire to make inquiries concerning the Christian faith must be deterred both by the space to be traversed and the conspicuousness of visiting a mission compound in such a position.   The members of the mission church last year were altogether Armenians.   The education and training given in the schools are admirable.

Indications of the changes which we consider improvements abound in Tihran.   There are many roads accessible to wheeled vehicles.   There are hackney carriages.   A tramway carrying thousands of passengers weekly has been laid down from the *Maidan* or central square to one of the southern gates.   There are real streets paved with cobble stones, and bordered with definite sidewalks, young trees, and shops.   There is a railroad about four miles long, from the city to the village of Sheikh Abdul Azim. There are lamp-posts and fittings, though the light is somewhat of a failure.   There is an organised city police, in smart black uniforms with violet facings, under the command of Count Monteforte, an Italian.   Soldiers in Europeanised uniforms abound, some of them, the " Persian Cossacks," in full Russian uniforms ; and military bands instructed by a French bandmaster play European airs, not always easily recognisable, for the pleasure of the polyglot public.

All ordinary business can be transacted at the Imperial Bank, which, having acquired the branches and business of the New Oriental Bank, bids fair to reign supreme in the commercial world of Persia, the Shah, who has hitherto kept his hoards under his own eye, having set an example of confidence by becoming a depositor.

European tailors, dressmakers, and milliners render a resort to Europe unnecessary. There are at least two hotels where a European may exist. About five hundred European carriages, many of them Russian, with showy Russian horses harnessed *à la Russe*, dash about the streets with little regard to pedestrians, though an accident, if a European were the offender, might lead to a riot. The carriages of the many Legations are recognisable by their outriders, handsomely-dressed *gholams*.

But even the European quarter and its newish road, on which are many of the Legations, some of the foreign shops, and the fine compound and handsome buildings of the Imperial Bank, has a Persian admixture. Some of the stately houses of official and rich Persians are there, easily recognisable by their low closed gateways and general air of seclusion. Many of these possess exquisite gardens, with fountains and tanks, and all the arrangements for the out-of-doors life which Persians love. In the early spring afternoons the great sight of the road outside the British Legation is the crowd of equestrians, or rather of the horses they ride. However much the style of street, furniture, tastes, art, and costume have been influenced by Europe, fortunately for picturesque effect the Persian, even in the capital, retains the Persian saddle and equipments.

From later observation I am inclined to think very highly of the hardiness and stamina of the Persian horse, though at the time of my visit to Tihran I doubted both. Such showy, magnificent-looking animals, broken to a carriage which shows them to the best advantage, fine-legged, though not at the expense of strength, small-eared, small-mouthed, with flowing wavy manes, " necks clothed with thunder," dilated nostrils showing the carmine interior, and a look of scorn and high breeding, I never saw elsewhere. The tail, which in obedience to fashion we mutilate and abridge, is allowed in Persia its full development, and except in the case of the Shah's white horses, when it is dyed magenta, is perfectly beautiful, held far from the body like a flag. The arched neck, haughty bearing, and easy handling which Easterns love are given by very sharp bits; and a crowd of these beautiful animals pawing the ground, prancing, caracoling, walking with a gait as though the earth were too vulgar for their touch, or flashing past at a gallop, all groomed to perfection and superbly caparisoned, ridden by men who know how to ride, and who are in sympathy with their animals, is one of the fascinations of Tihran.

Creeping along by the side-walk is often seen a handsome pacing saddle-mule, or large white ass, nearly always led, carrying a Persian lady attended by servants— a shapeless black bundle, with what one supposes to be the outline of a hand clutching the enshrouding black silk sheet tightly over her latticed white mask: so completely enveloped that only a yellow shoe without a heel, and a glimpse of a violet trouser can be seen above the short stirrups.

Another piece of Orientalism unaffected by Western influence is the music performed daily at sunset in the upper stories of some of the highly-decorated tiled gateways which lead into and out of the principal squares. This is evoked from drums, fifes, cymbals, and huge horns, and as the latter overpower all the former, the effect is much like that of the braying of the colossal silver horns from the roofs of the Tibetan *lamaserais*. Many people suppose that this daily homage to the setting sun is a relic of the ancient fire or sun worship.

Two great squares, one of them with a tank in the middle with a big gun at each corner, artillery barracks on three sides, and a number of smooth-bore twenty-four-pounder guns on the fourth, are among the features of Tihran. In this great *Maidan* there are always soldiers in multifarious uniforms lounging, people waiting for the tram-cars, and Royal footmen, whose grotesque costumes border on the ridiculous. They are indeed a fitting accompaniment to the Royal horses with their magenta tails and spots, for they wear red coats with ballet-dancer skirts and green facings, green knee-breeches, white stockings, and tall stiff erections resembling a fool's cap on the head, topped by crests suggestive of nothing but a cock's comb.

A gateway much ornamented leads from the artillery square, or *Maidan Topkhaneh*, by a short road shaded with trees to the Citadel or Ark, which is an immense enclosure, rather mangy and unprepossessing in its exterior, which contains the palace of the Shah, the arsenal, certain public offices, the royal colleges, etc. Over the gateway floats rather grandly the Royal standard, bearing the Lion and the Sun in yellow on a green ground.

The Shah's palace is very magnificent, and the shady gardens, beautifully kept, with their fountains and tanks of pale blue tiles, through which clear water constantly moves, are worthy of a Royal residence. From the outside above the high wall the chief feature is a very lofty pavilion, brilliantly and elaborately painted, with walls inclining inwards, and culminating in two high towers. This striking structure contains the *andarun* or *haram* of the sovereign and his private apartments.

This hasty sketch exhausts those features of Tihran which naturally arrest the stranger's attention. There is no splendour about it externally, but there is splendour within it, and possibly few European residences can exceed in taste and magnificence the palaces of the Minister of Justice (the *Muschir-u-Dowleh*), the *Naib-es-Sultan*, the *Zil-es-Sultan*, and a few others, though I regret that much of the furniture has been imported from Europe, as it vexes the eye more or less with its incongruity of form and colouring. The current of European influence, which is affecting externals in Tihran, is not likely now to be stemmed. Eastern civilisation is doomed, and the transition period is not beautiful, whatever the outcome may be.

So much for what is within the walls. That which is outside deserves a passing notice as the environment of the capital. The sole grandeur of the situation lies in the near neighbourhood of the Shimran mountains—a huge wall, white or brown according to the season, with some irrigated planting near its base, which is spotted with villages and the *yailaks* not only of the numerous Legations but of rich Europeans and Persians. Otherwise the tameless barbarism of a desert, which man has slashed, tunnelled, delved, and heaped, lies outside the city walls, deformed by the long lines of *kanaats*—some choked, others still serviceable—by which the city is supplied with water from the mountains, their shafts illustrating the Scriptural expression "ruinous heaps." In the glare of the summer sun, with the mercury ranging from 95° to 110° in the shade, and with the heated atmosphere quivering over the burning earth, these wastes are abandoned to carcasses and the vultures which fatten on them, and travelling is done at night, when a breeze from the Shimran range sends the thermometer down from 10° to 15°.

Curving to the south-west of Tihran, the mountains end in a bare ridge, around the base of which, according to many archæologists, lie vestiges of the ancient city of

Rhages, known in later days as Rhei. A tomb of
brick with angular surfaces, sacred to the memory
of an ancient and romantic attachment, remains of fortifications, and the Parsee cemetery on a ledge overlooking these remains, break the monotony of the waste in
that direction.

This cemetery, or "Tower of Silence," a white splash
on the brown hillside, is visible from afar. The
truncated cones which in many places mark seats of the
ancient Zoroastrian worship have been mentioned here
and there, but it is only in Tihran and Yezd that the
descendants of the ancient fire-worshippers are found in
such numbers as to be able to give prominence to their
ancient rites of sepulture. Probably throughout Persia
their number does not exceed 8000. Their head resides
in Tihran. They bear a good character for uprightness,
and except in Yezd, where they weave rich stuffs, they
are chiefly agriculturists. They worship firelight and the
sun on the principles symbolised by both, they never use
tobacco, and it is impolite to smoke in their presence
because of the sacredness of fire.

Their belief has been, and is, that to bury the dead in
the earth is to pollute it; and one among the reasons of
the persecution of the early Christians by the Zoroastrians
was their abhorrence of the desecration of the ground
produced by the modes of Christian burial.

This "Tower of Silence" near Tihran is a large round
edifice of whitewashed mud and stone. On the top of it,
a few feet below the circular parapet, the dead are laid
to be devoured by birds and consumed by exposure to
the elements. The destiny of the spirit is supposed to
be indicated by the eye which is first devoured by the
fowls of the air, the right eye signifying bliss.

In a northern direction, to which the eye always
turns to be refreshed by the purity of the icy cone of

Demavend, or to watch the rosy light deepening into purple on the heights of Shimran, are palaces and country seats in numbers, with a mass of irrigated plantations extending for twenty miles, from Vanēk on the east to Kamaraniēh on the west. These are reached by passing through the Shimran gate, the most beautiful of the outer gates, tiled all over with yellow, black, blue, and green tiles in conventional designs, and with an immense coloured mosaic over the gateway representing Rustēm, Persia's great mythical hero, conquering some of his enemies.

On the slopes of the hills are palaces and hunting seats of the Shah, beginning with the imposing mass of the Kasr-i-Kajār, on a low height, surrounded by majestic groves, in which are enormous tanks. Palaces and hunting seats of ministers and wealthy men succeed each other rapidly, a perfect seclusion having been obtained for each by the rapid growth of poplars and planes, each dwelling carrying out in its very marked individuality a deference to Persian custom, and each if possible using running water as a means of decoration. Many of these palaces are princely, and realise some of the descriptions in the *Arabian Nights*, with the beauty of their decorated architecture, the deep shade of their large demesnes, the cool plash of falling water, the songs of nightingales, and the scent of roses—sensuous Paradises in which the Persian finds the summer all too short.

Beyond this enchanting region, and much higher up on the mountain slopes, are the hunting grounds of the Shah and his sons, well stocked with game and rigidly preserved; for the Shah is a keen sportsman, and is said to prefer a free life under canvas and the pleasures of the chase to the splendid conventionalities of the Court of Tihran.

The two roads and the many tracks which centre in the

capital after scoring the desert for many miles around it, are a feature of the landscape not to be overlooked, the Meshed, Resht, Bushire, and Tabriz roads being the most important, except the route from Baghdad by Kirmanshah and Hamadan, which in summer can be travelled by caravans in twenty-eight days, and by which many bulky articles of value, such as pianos, carriages, and valuable furniture, find their way to Tihran.[1]

These are some of the features of the environments of Tihran. A traveller writing ten years hence may probably have to tell that the city has extended to its walls, that Western influence is nearly dominant in externals, and possibly that the *concessionaires* who for years have been hanging about the Palace in alternations of hope and despondency have made something of their concessions, and that goods reach the capital in another way than on the backs of animals.

---

[1] There are *only* two roads, properly so called, in Persia, though in the summer wheeled carriages with some assistance can get from place to place over several of the tracks. These two are the road from Kûm to the capital, formerly described, and one from Kasvin to the capital, both under 100 miles in length. Goods are everywhere carried on the backs of animals.

The distance between Bushire and Tihran is 698 miles.

The summer freight per ton is	.	.	.	.	.	£14 1 8
The winter do.	.	.	.	.	.	20 2 0

The distance between Tihran and Resht on the Caspian is 211 miles.

The summer freight per ton is	.	.	.	.	.	£4 0 5½
The winter do.	.	.	.	.	.	8 0 11¾

From the Caspian to the Persian Gulf the summer freight per ton is

	.	.	.	.	.	£18 2 3
The winter do.	.	.	.	.	.	28 3 4

inclusive of some insignificant charges.

The time taken for the transit of goods between Bushire and Tihran is forty-two days, and between Resht and Tihran twelve days.

The cost per ton by rail, if taken at Indian rates, between the Gulf and the Caspian, would be £3 : 11 : 10.

On these figures the promoters of railway enterprise in Persia build their hopes.

LETTER IX

THREE weeks have passed quickly by since that terrible ride from Husseinabad. The snow is vanishing from the Shimran hills, the spring has come, and I am about to leave the unbounded kindness and hospitality of this house on a long and difficult journey. It is very pleasant to go away carrying no memories but those of kindness, received not only from Europeans and Americans, but from Persians, including the Amin-es-Sultan and the Muschir-u-Dowleh.

It is impossible to bear away other than pleasant impressions of Tihran society. Kindness received personally always sways one's impressions of the people among whom one is thrown, and even if I had any unfavourable criticisms to make I should not make them.

Society, or rather I should say the European population, is divided into classes and knots. There are the eleven American missionaries, whose duties and interests lie apart from those of the rest of the community, the diplomatic body, which has a monopoly of political interests, the large staff of the Indo-European telegraph, married and single, with Colonel Wells at its head, and the mercantile class, in which the manager and *employés* of the Imperial Bank may be included. Outside of these recognised classes there is a shifting body of passing travellers, civil and military, and would-be *concessionaires* and adventurers, besides a few Europeans in Persian employment.

From four to five hundred Europeans is a large foreign settlement, and it is a motley one, very various in its elements, "and in their idiosyncrasies, combinations, rivalries, and projects is to be found an inexhaustible fund of local gossip," writes Mr. Curzon in one of his recent brilliant letters to the *Times*, "as well as almost the sole source of non-political interest."

Outside of the diplomatic circle the relations of England and Russia with each other and with the Shah afford a topic of ceaseless interest. England is just now considered to be in the ascendant, so far as her diplomacy is concerned, but few people doubt that Russian policy will eventually triumph, and that North Persia at least will be " absorbed."

One or two specially pleasant things I must mention. Sir H. Drummond Wolff kindly wrote asking permission from the Shah for me to see his Museum, *i.e.* his treasure-house, and we, that is the Minister, the whole party from the Legation, and Dr. Odling of the telegraph staff and Mrs. Odling, went there yesterday. There was a great crowd outside the Palace gates, where we were received by many men in scarlet. The private gardens are immense, and beautifully laid out, in a more formal style than I have hitherto seen, with straight, hard gravel walks, and straight avenues of trees. The effect of the clear running water in the immense tanks lined with blue tiles is most agreeable and cool. Continuous rows of orange trees in tubs, and beds of narcissus, irises, and tulips, with a wealth of trellised roses just coming into leaf, are full of the promise of beauty. These great pleasure gardens are admirably kept. I doubt whether a fallen leaf would not be discovered and removed in five minutes.

The great irregular mass of the Palace buildings on

the garden front is very fine, the mangy and forlorn aspect being confined to the side seen by the public. The walls are much decorated, chiefly with glazed and coloured tiles geometrically arranged, and the general effect is striking.

The " Museum," properly the audience chamber, and certainly one among the finest halls in the world, is approached by a broad staircase of cream-coloured alabaster. We were received by the Grand Vizier's two brothers, and were afterwards joined by himself and another high official.

The decorations of this magnificent hall are in blue and white stucco of the hard fine kind, hardly distinguishable from marble, known as *gatch*, and much glass is introduced in the ceiling. The proportions of the room are perfect. The floor is of fine tiles of exquisite colouring arranged as mosaic. A table is overlaid with beaten gold, and chairs in rows are treated in the same fashion. Glass cases round the room and on costly tables contain the fabulous treasures of the Shah and many of the Crown jewels. Possibly the accumulated splendours of pearls, diamonds, rubies, emeralds, sapphires, basins and vessels of solid gold, ancient armour flashing with precious stones, shields studded with diamonds and rubies, scabbards and sword hilts incrusted with costly gems, helmets red with rubies, golden trays and vessels thick with diamonds, crowns of jewels, chains, ornaments (masculine solely) of every description, jewelled coats of mail dating back to the reign of Shah Ismaël, exquisite enamels of great antiquity, all in a profusion not to be described, have no counterpart on earth. They are a dream of splendour not to be forgotten.

One large case contains the different orders bestowed on the Shah, all blazing with diamonds, a splendid display, owing to the European cutting of the stones, which brings out their full beauty. There are many glass cases from two to three feet high and twelve inches or more broad, nearly full of pearls, rubies, diamonds, sapphires, emeralds, flashing forth their many-coloured light—treasures not arranged, but piled like tea or rice. Among the extraordinarily lavish uses of gold and gems is a golden globe twenty inches in diameter, turning on a frame of solid gold. The stand and meridian are of solid gold set with rubies. The equator and elliptic are of large diamonds. The countries are chiefly outlined in rubies, but Persia is in diamonds. The ocean is represented by emeralds. As if all this were not enough, huge gold coins, each worth thirty-three sovereigns, are heaped round its base.

At the upper end of the hall is the Persian throne. Many pages would be needed for a mere catalogue of some of the innumerable treasures which give gorgeousness to this hall. Here indeed is " Oriental splendour," but only a part of the possessions of the Shah ; for many gems, including the Dar-i-nur or Sea of Light, the second most famous diamond in the world, are kept elsewhere in double-locked iron chests, and hoards of bullion saved from the revenues are locked up in vaults below the Palace.

If such a blaze of splendour exists in this shrunken, shrivelled, "depopulated" empire, what must have been the magnificence of the courts of Darius and Xerxes, into which were brought the treasures of almost " all the kingdoms of the world and the glory of them "? Since seeing this treasure-house I think that many of the early descriptions of wealth, which I have regarded as Oriental hyperbole, were literal, and that there was a time in Persia, as in Judea, when " silver was not accounted of." And to come down from the far off-glories of Darius, Xerxes, and Khosroe and the Parthian kings, there have

been within almost modern times Persian sovereigns celebrated among other things for their successful "looting"
of foreign kingdoms—Shah Abbas the great, and Nadir
Shah, who scarcely two hundred years ago returned from
the sack of Delhi with gems valued at twenty millions of
our money.

After we had seen most of what was to be seen
the Vizier left us, and we went to the room in which
stands the celebrated Peacock Throne, brought by Nadir
Shah from Delhi, and which ˉhas been valued at
£2,500,000. This throne is a large stage, with parapets
and a high fan back, and is reached by several steps.
It is entirely of gold enamel, and the back is incrusted
with rubies and diamonds. Its priceless carpet has a
broad border, the white arabesque pattern of which is
formed of pearls closely stitched. You will think that I
am lapsing into Oriental exaggeration!

While we were admiring the beautiful view of the
gardens from the windows of this room, Hassan Ali Khan,
better known as "the Nawab," suggested that we should
retire, as the Shah is in the habit of visiting and enjoying
his treasures at a later hour. However, at the foot of
the stairs on the threshold of the vestibule stood the
Shah, the "King of Kings," the "Asylum of the Universe,"
and that his presence there was not an accident was
shown by the fact that the Grand Vizier was with him.

Sir Henry advanced, attended by "the Nawab," and
presented me, lifting his hat to the king, who neither
then nor when he left us made the slightest inclination
of his head. Hassan Ali Khan, in answer to a question,
mentioned some of my travels, and said that with His
Majesty's permission I wished to visit the Bakhtiari
country.[1] The king pushed up his big horn spectacles

[1] Some of the Bakhtiari khans or princes, with their families, are kept
by the Shah as hostages in and round Tihran for the loyalty of their

and focused his eyes, about which there is something very peculiar, upon me, with a stare which would have been disconcerting to a younger person, asked if I were going to travel alone in his dominions, and if fitting arrangements had been made; if I had been in Pekin, and had visited Borneo and the Celebes; said a few other things, and then without a bow turned round abruptly and walked down the garden with the Amin-es-Sultan.

This accidental and informal presentation was a very pleasant incident. The Shah is not what I expected from his various portraits. His manner (though he was said to be very affable on this occasion) has neither Eastern nor Western polish. He is a somewhat rough-looking man, well on in middle life, rather dark in complexion, and wearing a thick dark moustache, probably dyed, as is the custom. The long twisted moustache conceals the expression of his mouth, and the spectacles with thick horn rims that of his eyes. He was very simply dressed. The diamond aigrette and sword with jewelled hilt with which pictures and descriptions have familiarised us were absent, and this splendid monarch, the heir of splendour, and the possessor of fabulous treasures, wore the ordinary Persian high cap of Astrakan lambskin without any ornament, close-fitting dark trousers with a line of gold braid, a full-skirted coat of dull-coloured Kerman silk brocade, loose and open, under which were huddled one or more coats. A watch-chain composed of large diamonds completed his costume. He did not wear gloves, and I noticed that his hands, though carefully attended to, were those of a man used to muscular exercise, strong and wiry.

As the sovereign and his prime minister walked away,

tribes, the conquest of these powerful nomads not being so complete as it might and possibly will be.

it was impossible not to speculate upon coming events: what will happen, for instance, when Nasr-ed-Din, possibly the ablest man in the country which he rules, and probably the best and most patriotic ruler among Oriental despots, goes "the way of all the earth"? and again, whether Ali Askar Khan, who has held his post for five years, and who at thirty-two is the foremost man in Persia after the king, will weather the storm of intrigue which rages round his head, and resist the undermining influence of Russia?

I have had two interesting conversations with him, and he was good enough to propose success to my journey at a dinner at the Legation; and though, as he does not speak French, the services of an interpreter were necessary, he impressed me very favourably as a man of thought, intelligence, and patriotism.

He made one remark which had a certain degree of pathos in it. After speaking of the severe strictures and harsh criticisms of certain recent writers, which he said were very painful to Persians, he added, "I hope if you write you will write kindly, and not crush the aspirations of my struggling country as some have done."

This Amin-es-Sultan, the faithful or trusted one of the sovereign, the Grand Vizier or Prime Minister, the second person in the empire, who unites in his person at this time the ministries of the Treasury, the Interior, the Court, and Customs, is of humble antecedents, being the son of a man who was originally an inferior attendant on the Shah in his hunting expeditions, and is the grandson of an Armenian captive. Certain persons of importance are bent upon his overthrow, and it can only be by the continued favour and confidence of the Shah that he can sustain himself against their intrigues, combined with those of Russia.

My visit to the Palace terminated with the sight of

another throne-room opening upon the garden in which a few days hence, with surroundings of great magnificence, the Shah will receive the congratulations of the diplomatic corps, and afterwards give a general audience to the people.

This is an annual ceremony at the festival of No Ruz when the Persian New Year begins, at the time of the spring solstice, and is probably a relic of the Zoroastrian worship, though the modern Persians, as Mohammedans, allege that it is observed to celebrate the birthday of the Prophet's mother.[1]

Some hours after the close of a splendid ceremony in the audience chamber, chiefly religious, at which the Shah burns incense on a small brazier, he descends to the garden, and walking alone along an avenue of Royal Guards, with the crown of the Kajārs, blazing with jewels, carried in front of him, he seats himself on an alabaster throne, the foreign ministers having been received previously. This throne is a large platform, with a very high back and parapets of bold stone fretwork, supported on marble lions and other figures, and is ascended by three or four steps.

The populace, which to the number of many thousands are admitted into the garden, see him seated on his throne, their absolute master, the lord of life and death. A voice asks if they are content, and they say they are. A hymn

---

[1] On the eve of the day, the last of a festival of ten days, the common people kindle rows of bonfires and leap over them; and, though not on the same day, but on the night of the 25th of February, sacred in the Armenian Church as the day of the presentation of our Lord in the temple, large bonfires are lighted on the mud roofs of the Armenians of the Persian and Turkish cities, and the younger members of the households dance and sing and leap through the flames. Meanwhile the Moslems close their windows, so that the sins which the Christians are supposed to be burning may not enter. Whether these " Beltane fires " are a relic of the ancient fire worship or of still older rites may be a question. Among the Christians the custom is showing signs of passing away.

of congratulation is sung, a chief of the Kajár tribe offers the congratulations of the people of Persia, the Hakim of the people hands the king a jewelled *kalian*, which he smokes, and showers of gold fall among the populace.

The British Minister is understood to be at this time the most powerful foreigner in Persia ; and as we drove through the crowd which had assembled at the Palace gates, he was received with all Oriental marks of respect.

All my intercourse with Persians here has been pleasant, and if I mention one person particularly, it is owing to a certain interest which attaches to himself and his possible future, and because some hours spent at his splendid palace were among the pleasantest of the many pleasant and interesting ones which I shall here-after recall.

Yahia Khan, Minister of Justice and Commerce, whose official title is Muschir-u-Dowleh, was formerly Minister of Foreign Affairs, but forfeited the confidence of the British Government in supposed connection with the escape of Ayoub Khan, and being suspected of Russian proclivities, which he denies, lost his position. He speaks French perfectly, is credited with very great abilities, and not only has courteous and charming manners, but thoroughly understands the customs of Europe.

As the possessor of one of the most magnificent palaces in Persia, married to the Shah's sister, his son, a youth of eighteen, married to a daughter of the Vali-'ahd, the heir-apparent, and as the brother of Mirza Hussein Khan—for long Grand Vizier and *Sipah Salar*, or Com-mander-in-Chief, whose gorgeous mosque, scarcely finished, the finest mosque built in late years by any but a royal personage, adjoins his house, Yahia Khan is in every way an important personage.

He is the fourth husband of the Shah's sister, who has had a tragic life and is a very accomplished woman.

Her first husband, Mirza Taghi, when Prime Minister,
attempted reforms which would have tended to diminish
the hideous corruption which is the bane of Persian
officialism, and consequently made many enemies, who
induced the Shah, then a young man, to depose him.
Worse than deposition was apprehended, and as it was
not etiquette to murder a husband of a royal princess
in her presence, his wife, who loved him, watched him
night and day with ceaseless vigilance for some weeks.
But the fatal day at last came, and a good and powerful
man, whose loss is said to have been an irreparable one
to Persia, was strangled by the Shah's messengers, it is
said, in the bath.

Her son, who has married the Shah's grand-daughter,
is courteous like his father, but is apparently without his
force.

The Muschir-u-Dowleh invited me to breakfast, along
with General Gordon and Hassan Ali Khan. The
dejeûner was altogether in European style, except that
in the centre of the table, among lilies and irises, a concealed fountain sent up jets of rose-water spray. Sèvres
and Dresden porcelain, the finest damask, and antique
and exquisitely beautiful silver adorned the table. The
cooking was French. The wines and liqueurs, an
innovation on Moslem tables now common, but of recent
date, were both French and Persian. The service was
perfection. The host conversed both thoughtfully and
agreeably, and expressed himself remarkably well in
French.

Afterwards we were invited to go over the palace and
its grounds, which are remarkably beautiful, and then
over the magnificent mosque. Shiah mosques are
absolutely tabooed to Christians; but as this has not
yet been used for worship, our entrance was not
supposed to desecrate it. When quite finished it will

be one of the most magnificent buildings dedicated to religious use in the world, and its four tile-covered minarets, its vast dome, and arches and façades in tiled arabesques and conventional patterns and exquisite colouring, show that the Persian artist when adequately encouraged has not lost his old feeling for beauty.

Besides the mosque there is a fine building, the low roof of which is supported by innumerable columns, all of plain brick, resembling a crypt, which will be used for winter worship. In addition, a lavish endowment has provided on the grounds a theological college and a hospital, with most, if not all, of the funds needed for their maintenance; and on every part of the vast pile of buildings the architect has lavished all the resources of his art.

No houses are to my thinking more beautiful and appropriate to the climate and mode of living than those of the upper classes of Persians, and the same suitability and good taste run down through the trading classes till one reaches the mud hovel, coarse and un-ideal, of the workman and peasant.

My memory does not serve me for the details of the Muschir-u-Dowleh's palace, which, though some of the rooms are furnished with European lounges, tables, and chairs in *marqueterie* and brocade, is throughout distinctively Persian; but the impression produced by the general *coup d'œil*, and by the size, height, and perfect proportion of the rooms, galleries, staircases, and halls, is quite vivid. The rooms have dados of primrose-coloured Yezd alabaster in slabs four feet high by three broad, clouded and veined most delicately by nature. The banqueting hall is of immense size, and the floor is covered with a dark fawn *namad* three-quarters of an inch thick, made, I understood, in one piece eighty feet long by fifty broad. The carpets are the most

beautiful which can be turned out by Persian looms, and
that is saying a great deal.

The roofs, friezes, and even the walls of this house,
like those of others of its class, have a peculiarity of
beauty essentially Persian.   This is the form of *gatch*
or fine stucco-work known as *ainah karee.* I saw it
first at Baghdad, and now at Tihran wonder that such
beautiful and costly decoration does not commend itself
to some of our millionaires.   Arches filled with honeycomb decoration, either pure white or tastefully coloured
and gilded, are among the architectural adornments which
the Alhambra borrowed from Persia.   My impression is
that this exquisite design was taken from snow on the
hillsides, which is often fashioned by a strong wind into
the honeycomb pattern.

But the glory of this form of decoration reaches its
height when, after the *gatch* ceiling and cornice or deep
frieze have been daringly moulded by the workman into
distinct surfaces or facets, he lays on mirrors while the
plaster is yet soft, which adhere, and even at their edges
have scarcely the semblance of a joining.   Sometimes,
as in the new summer palace of the Shah's third son,
the Naib-es-Sultaneh, the whole wall is decorated in
this way; but I prefer the reception-rooms of Yahia
Khan, in which it is only brought down a few feet.
Immense skill and labour are required in this process
of adornment, but it yields in splendour to none, flashing
in bewildering light, and realising the fabled glories of the
palaces of the *Arabian Nights.*   One of the *salons*, about
sixty feet by fifty, treated in this way is about the
most beautiful room I ever saw.

The Persian architect also shows great art in his windows.   He masses them together, and by this means gives
something of grandeur even to an insignificant room.
The beauty of the designs, whether in fretwork of wood

or stone, is remarkable, and the effect is enhanced by the filling in of the interstices with coloured glass, usually amber and pale blue. So far as I have seen, the Persian house is never over-decorated, and however gorgeous the mirror-work, or involved the arrangement of arches, or daring the dreams in *gatch* ceilings and pillars, the fancy of the designer is always so far under control as to give the eye periods of rest.

Under the palace of the Muschir-u-Dowleh, as under many others, is a sort of glorified *serdab*, used in hot weather, partly under ground, open at each end, and finished throughout with marble, the roof being supported on a cluster of slender pillars with capitals picked out in gold, and the air being cooled by a fountain in a large marble basin. But this *serdab* is far eclipsed by a summer hall in the palace of the Shah's third son, which, as to walls and ceiling, is entirely composed of mirror-work, the floor of marble being arranged with marble settees round fountains whose cool plash even now is delicious. The large pleasure gardens which surround rich men's houses in the city are laid out somewhat in the old French style of formality, and are tended with scrupulous care.

I did not see the *andarun* of this or any house here, owing to the difficulty about an interpreter, but it is not likely that the ladies are less magnificently lodged than their lords. The *andarun* has its own court, no one is allowed to open a window looking upon it, it is as secluded as a convent. No man but the master of the house may enter, and when he retires thither no man may disturb him. To all inquirers it is a sufficient answer to say that he is in the *andarun*. To the Shah, however, belongs the privilege of looking upon the unveiled face of every woman in Persia. The domestic life of a Moslem is always shrouded in mystery, and even in the case of the Shah " the fierce light that beats upon a throne " fails to reveal to the outer world the number of wives and women in his *andarun*, which is variously stated at from sixty to one hundred and ninety.

It is not easy in any Eastern city to get exactly what one wants for a journey, especially as a European cannot buy in the bazars ; and the servant difficulty has been a great hindrance, particularly as I have a strong objection to the regular interpreter-servant who has been accustomed to travel with Europeans.

I have now got a Persian cook with sleepy eyes, a portion of a nose, and a grotesquely " hang-dog " look. For an interpreter and personal attendant I have an educated young Brahmin, for some years in British post-office service in the Gulf, and lately a teacher in the American school here. He speaks educated English, and is said to speak good Persian. He has never done any " menial " work, but is willing to do anything in order to get to England. He has a frank, independent manner and "no nonsense about him." Taking him is an experiment.[1]

I. L. B.

---

[1] An experiment I never regretted. Mirza Yusuf was with me for nine months, and I found him faithful, truthful, and trustworthy, very hard-working, minimising hardships and difficulties, always cheerful, and with an unruffled temper, his failings being those of a desk-bred man transplanted into a life of rough out-doorishness.

LETTER X

KÛM, *March 23.*

THIS so far is a delightful journey. All the circumstances are favourable. A friend who was sending his servants, horses, and baggage to Isfahan has lent me a thorough-bred, and with a trustworthy young soldier as my escort I do not trouble myself about the caravan at all, and get over much of the ground at a gallop. The roads have nearly dried up, the country looks cheerful, travellers are numerous, living and dead, the sun is bright but the air is cool and bracing, and the insects are still hybernating, Mirza Yusuf is getting into my "ways," and is very pleasant. I did not think that I could have liked Persian travelling so well. A good horse and a good pace make an immense difference. It is not the custom for European ladies to travel unattended by European gentlemen in Persia, but no objection to my doing so was made in the highest quarters, either English or Persian, and so far there have been no difficulties or annoyances.

I left the British Legation at noon four days ago. The handsome Arab, with a sheepskin coat rolled on the front of the saddle, holsters, and Persian housings, looked like a life-guardsman's horse. I nearly came to grief as soon as I got out of the Legation gate; for he would not stand my English snaffle, and reared and threw himself about, and my spur touching him as he did so made him quite wild, and I endured much apprehension all through Tihran, expecting to find myself on the rough pavement; but I took off the offending spur, and rode him on the sharp bit he is used to, and when we were outside the gate he quietened down, and I had a long gallop.

How different it all looks! No more floundering through mud! The trees of Abdul Azim are green. Caravans are moving fast and cheerily. Even the dead on their last journey look almost cheerful under the sunny skies. We did not reach Husseinabad till long after dark. It was so unspeakably dark that my horse and I fell off the road into deep water, and we passed the caravanserai without knowing that we were near it.

The usual disorder of a first night was somewhat worse than usual. The loads were mixed up, and the servants and *charvadars* were quarrelling, and I did not get my dinner till ten; but things are all right now, and have been since the following morning, when I assumed the reins of government and saw the mules loaded myself, an efficient interpreter making my necessary self-assertion intelligible.

Though the spring has set in, most of the country between this and Tihran looks a complete desert. In February it was a muddy waste — it is now a dusty waste, on which sheep, goats, and camels pick up a gray herbage, which without search is not obvious to the human eye, and consists mostly of wormwood and other bitter and aromatic plants. Off the road a few tulips and dwarf irises coming up out of the dry ground show the change of season.

I came for some distance on one day by a road which caravans avoid because of robbers. It crosses a reddish desert with a few salt streams and much saline efflorescence, a blasted region without a dwelling or patch of cultivation. Yet a four-mile gallop across one part of it was most inspiriting. As the two Arabs, excited by the pace, covering great spaces of ground with each powerful stride, dashed over the level gravel I thought, "They'll have fleet steeds that follow"; but no steed or rider or bird or beast was visible through all that hungry land. We passed also close to a salt lake on the Kavir, seen in the distance on the former journey, near which are now pitched a quantity of Ilyat tents, all black. The wealth of these nomads is in camels, sheep, and goats. Though the camps, five in number, were small, they had over 200 camels among them.

Where four weeks ago there was deep mud there is now the glittering semblance of unsullied snow, and the likeness of frost crystals fills the holes. *Miles* of camels loaded with cotton march with stately stride in single file, the noble mountain camel, with heavy black fur on neck, shoulder, fore-arm, and haunch, and kindly gentle eyes, looking, as he is, the king of baggage animals, not degraded by servitude, though he may carry 800 lbs.

Some of the sights of the road were painful. For instance, just as I passed a caravan of the dead bound for Kûm a mule collided with another and fell, and the loosely-put-together boxes on its back gave way and corpses fell out in an advanced stage of decomposition. A camel just dead lay in a gully. On a ledge of rock above it seven gorged vultures (not the bald-headed) sat in a row. They had already feasted on him to repletion. I passed several dead camels, and one with a pleading pathetic face giving up the ghost on the road.

Yesterday I rode in here from the magnificent caravanserai of Shashgird, sixteen miles in three hours before lunch, and straight through the crowded bazars to the telegraph office unmolested, an Afghan camel-driver's coat, with the wool outside, having proved so good a disguise that the *gholam* who was sent to meet me returned to his master saying that he had not seen a lady, but that a foreign soldier and *sahib* had come into Kûm.

When my visit was over and I had received from Mr. Lyne the route to Isfahan, and such full information about rooms, water, and supplies as will enable me to give my own orders, and escape from the tyranny of the *charvadars*, having sent the horses to the caravanserai I disguised myself as a Persian woman of the middle class in the dress which Mrs. Lyne wears in the city, a thick white *crêpe* veil with open stitch in front of the eyes, a black sheet covering me from head to foot, the ends hanging from the neck by long loops, and held with the left hand just below the eyes, and so, though I failed to imitate the totter and shuffle of a Persian lady's walk, I passed unnoticed through the long and crowded streets of this fanatical city, attended only by a *gholam*, and at the door of my own room was prevented from entering by the servants till my voice revealed my identity.

Twice to-day I have passed safely through the city in the same disguise, and have even lingered in front of shops without being detected. Mr. and Mrs. Lyne have made the two days here very pleasant, by introducing me to Persians in whose houses I have seen various phases of Persian life. On reaching one house, where Mrs. Lyne arrived an hour later, I was a little surprised to be received by the host in uniform, speaking excellent French, but without a lady with him.

He had been very kind to Hadji, who, he says, is rich and has three wives. The poor fellow's lungs have been affected for two years, and the affection was for the time aggravated by the terrible journey. He talked a good deal about Persian social customs, especially polygamy.

He explained that he has only one wife, but that this is because he has been fortunate. He said that he regards polygamy as the most fruitful source of domestic unhappiness, but that so long as marriages are made for men by their mothers and sisters, a large sum being paid to the bride's father, a marriage is really buying "a pig in a poke," and constantly when the bride comes home she is ugly or bad-tempered or unpleasing and cannot manage the house. "This," he said, "makes men polygamists who would not otherwise be so.

"Then a man takes another wife, and perhaps this is repeated, and then he tries again, and so on, and the house becomes full of turmoil. There are always quarrels in a polygamous household," he said, "and the children dispute about the property after the father's death." Had he not been fortunate, and had not his wife been capable of managing the house, he said that he must have taken another wife, "for," he added, "no man can bear a badly-managed house."

I thought of the number of men in England who have to bear it without the Moslem resource.

A lady of "position" must never go out except on Fridays to the mosque, or with her husband's permission and scrupulously veiled and guarded, to visit her female friends. Girl-children begin to wear the *chadar* between two and three years old, and are as secluded as their mothers, nor must any man but father or brother see their faces. Some marry at twelve years old.

"La vie des femmes dans la Perse est très triste," he said. The absence of anything like education for girls, except in Tihran, and the want of any reading-book but the Koran for boys and girls, he regards as a calamity. He may be a pessimist by nature : he certainly has no hope for the future of Persia, and contemplates a Russian occupation as a certainty in the next twenty years.

After a long conversation I asked for the pleasure, not of seeing his wife, but the "mother of his children," and was rewarded by the sight of a gentle and lovely woman of twenty-one or twenty-two, graceful in every movement but her walk, exquisitely refined-looking, with a most becoming timidity of expression, mingled with gentle courtesy to a stranger. She was followed by three very pretty little girls. The husband and wife are of very good family, and the lady has an unmistakably well-bred look.

Though I knew what to expect in the costume of a woman of the upper classes, I was astonished, and should have been scandalised even had women only been present. The costume of ladies has undergone a great change in the last ninety years, and the extreme of the fashion is as lacking in delicacy as it is in comfort. However, much travelling compels one to realise that the modesty of the women of one country must not be judged of by the rules of another, and a lady costumed as I shall attempt to describe would avert her eyes in horror by no means feigned from an English lady in a Court or evening-dress of to-day.

The under garment, very much *en évidence*, is a short chemise of tinselled silk gauze, or gold-embroidered muslin so transparent as to leave nothing to the imagination. This lady wore a skirt of flowered silver brocade, enormously full, ten or twelve yards wide, made to stand nearly straight out by some frills or skirts of very stiffly starched cotton underneath, the whole, not even on a waistband round the waist, but drawn by strings, and suspended over the hips, the skirts coming down to within a few inches of the knee, leaving the white rounded limbs uncovered. The effect of this exaggerated *bouffante* skirt is most singular. White socks are worn. Over the transparent *pirahān*, or chemise, she wore a short velvet jacket beautifully embroidered in gold, with its fronts about ten inches apart, so as to show the flowered chemise. Her eyebrows were artificially curved and lengthened till they appeared to meet above her nose, her eyelashes were marked round with *kohl*, and a band of blue-black paint curving downwards above the nose crossed her forehead, but was all but concealed by a small white square of silk *crêpe* on the head and brow and fastened under the chin by a brooch.

Had she been in another house she would have worn a large square of gold-embroidered silk, with the points in front and behind, and fastened under the chin. Under the *crêpe* square there was a small skull-cap of gold-embroidered velvet, matching her little zouave jacket, with an aigrette of gems at the side. Her arms were covered with bracelets, and a number of valuable necklaces set off the beauty of her dazzlingly white neck.

Persian ladies paint, or rather smear, but her young pure complexion needed no such aids. Her front hair, cut to the level of her mouth, hung down rather straight, and the remainder, which was long, was plaited into many small glossy plaits. Contrary to custom, it was undyed, and retained its jet-black colour. Most Persian ladies turn it blue-black with indigo, or auburn with *henna*, and with the latter the finger-nails and palms of the hands are always stained.

Her jewellery was all of solid gold; hollow gold and silver ornaments being only worn by the poor. She wore a chain with four scent caskets attached to it exhaling attar of roses and other choice perfumes.

She was a graceful and attractive creature in spite of her costume. She waited on her husband and on me, that is, she poured out the tea and moved about the room for hot water and *bonbons* with the feeble, tottering gait of a woman quite unaccustomed to exercise, and to whom the windy wastes outside the city walls and a breezy gallop are quite unknown. The little girls were dressed in the style of adults, and wore tinselled gauze *chadārs* or *chargats*.

After seeing a good deal of home life during some months in Persia, I have come to the conclusion that there is no child life. Swaddled till they can walk, and then dressed as little men and women, with the adult tyrannies of etiquette binding upon them, and in the case of girls condemned from infancy to the seclusion of the *andarun*, there is not a trace of the spontaneity and nonsense which we reckon as among the joys of childhood, or of such a complete and beautiful child life as children enjoy in Japan. There does not appear to be any child talk. The Persian child from infancy is altogether interested in the topics of adults; and as the conversation of both sexes is said by those who know them best to be without reticence or modesty, the purity which is one of the greatest charms of childhood is absolutely unknown. Parental love is very strong in Persia, and in later days the devotion of the mother to the boy is amply returned by the grown-up son, who regards her comfort as his charge, and her wishes as law, even into old age.

When tea was over the host retired with the remark that the ladies would prefer to amuse themselves alone, and then a Princess and another lady arrived attended by several servants. This Princess came in the black silk sheet with a suggestion of gold about its border which is the street disguise of women of the richer classes, and she wore huge bag-like violet trousers, into which her voluminous skirts were tucked.

She emerged from these wrappings a " harmony " in rose colour—a comely but over-painted young woman in rose and silver brocade skirts, a rose velvet jacket embroidered in silver, a transparent white muslin *pirahān* with silver stars upon it, and a *chargat* of white muslin embroidered in rose silk.

She and the hostess sat on a rug in front of a

fire, and servants now and then handed them *kalians*. The three little girls and the guest's little girl were in the background. The doors were then fastened and a number of servants came in and entertained their mistresses. Two sang and accompanied themselves on a sort of tambourine. Tea was handed round at intervals. There was dancing, and finally two or three women acted some little scenes from a popular Persian play. By these amusements, I am told, the women of the upper classes get rid of time when they visit each other; and they spend much of their lives in afternoon visiting, taking care to be back before sunset. After a long time the gentle hostess, reading in my face that I was not enjoying the performances, on which indeed unaccustomed English eyes could not look, brought them to a close, and showed me some of her beautiful dresses and embroidered fabrics.

Putting on my disguise and attended by a servant I walked a third time unrecognised and unmolested through the crowded bazars, through the gate and across the bridge, when a boy looked quite into my shroud, which I was not perhaps clutching so tightly as in the crowd, and exclaiming several times *Kafir*, ran back into the city. I did not run, but got back to the " hotel " as fast as possible.

It is very noisy, and my room being on the ground floor, and having three doors, there is little peace either by day or night. Thirteen days from the *No Ruz* or New Year, which was March 21, are kept as a feast before the severe fast of the Ramazan, and this city of pilgrims is crowded, and all people put on new clothes, the boys being chiefly dressed in green.

To-morrow I begin my journey over new ground.

I. L. B.

LETTER XI

KASHAN, *March 26.*

I HAVE seen the last of Kûm and hotels and made roads for many months. So much the better! I had to ride the whole length of the bazars and the city, a mile and a half, but the camel-driver's coat served again as a disguise, and I heard no remarks except from two boys. Indeed I am delighted to find that the " foreign soldier " who rides in front of me attracts so much curiosity that I pass in his wake unnoticed.

The ruinous condition of Kûm is fearful. Once outside the houses and bazars which surround the shrine of Fatima, the town is mostly rubbish and litter, with forlorn, miserable houses created out of the rubbish, grouped near festering pools ; broken cause-ways infamously paved, full of holes, heaps of pot-sherds, bones obtruding themselves, nothing to please and everything to disgust the eye and sadden the spirit, religious intolerance, a diminished population, and desolation.

The pottery bazar, abounding in blue glazed ware of graceful shapes, and a number of shrines of saints, are the only objects of interest. The domes of the latter were once covered with blue tiles, but these have nearly all peeled off, leaving the universal mud—a mud so self-asserting everywhere that Persia may be called the " Great Mud Land." The cherry and apricot trees are

in full bloom, but as yet there is little greenery round
Kûm, and the area of cultivation is very limited.

I am now on the road which, with the exception of
that from Tihran to Resht, is best known to travellers,[1]
but I cannot help sketching it briefly, though the interests
are few considering the distance travelled, 280 miles
from Tihran to Isfahan.   I now see Persia for the first
time; for traversing a country buried in snow is not
seeing it.   It would be premature to express the opinion
that the less one sees of it the more one is likely to
admire it.

I have been *en route* for a week under the best
possible circumstances—the nights always cool, the days
never too warm, the accommodation tolerable, the caravan
in excellent working order, no annoyances, and no griev-
ances.   The soldier who attends me arranges everything
for my comfort, and is always bright and kind.   I have
no ambition to " beat the record," but long gallops on a
fine Arab horse turn marches of from twenty-two to
thirty miles into delightful morning rides of from three
and a half to four and a half hours, with long pleasant
afternoons following them, and sound sleep at night.   These
are my halcyon days of Persian travelling; and yet I
cannot write that Persia is beautiful.

It is early spring, and tulips and irises rise not out of a
carpet of green but, to use the descriptive phrase of Isaiah,
" as a root out of a dry ground," the wormwood is dressed
in its gray-green, the buds of the wild dwarf-almond
show their tender pink, the starry blossom of the narcissus gleams in moist places, the sky is exquisitely blue,
and shining cloud-masses fleck the brown hillsides with
violet shadows.   Where there is irrigation carpets of
young wheat cover the ground ; but these, like the villages,

[1] It is new to me, however, and may be new to a large proportion of the
"untravelled many" for whom I write.

occur only at long intervals, for the road passes mainly through a country destitute of water, or rather of arrangements for storing it.

As to natural trees there are none, and even the bushes are few and unlovely, chiefly camel thorn and a rigid and thorny tamarisk.   Beyond Kûm there is no made road. A track worn by the caravans of ages exists,—sometimes parallel ruts for a width of half a mile, sometimes not two yards wide, and now and then lapsing into illegibility.   There are large and small caravanserais of an inferior class along the route, and *chapar khanas* at intervals.   Water is often bad and sometimes brackish.   It is usually supplied from small brick *abambars*, or covered reservoirs.   Milk is hard to obtain, often impossible; at some places fowls can be bought for eightpence each, and " flap jacks " everywhere.

Except the snowy cone of Demavend, with purple ranges curtaining his feet, no special object of admiration exists; the plains are reddish, yellowish, barren, gravelly, or splotched with salt; the ranges of hills, which are never far off (for Persia is a land of mountains), are either shapeless and gravelly, or rocky, rugged, and splintered, their hue reddish and purplish, their sides scored by the spring rush of wasted torrents, their aspect one of complete desolation, yet not without a certain beauty at this season—rose-flushed in the early morning, passing through shades of cobalt and indigo through the day, and dying away at sunset in translucent amethyst against a sky of ruddy gold.

But, take away the atmospheric colouring—which the advancing heat will abolish—and the plain English of the route is this, that in every direction, far as the eye can reach, the country is a salt waste or a gravelly waste, with a few limited oases of cultivation on the plains and in the folds of the hills, always treeless, except round a few of the villages, where there are small groves of poplars and willows. The villages are clusters of mud hovels, scarcely distinguishable from the wastes, and many of them are ruined and deserted, oppressive exactions or a failure of water being common reasons for a migration. These dismal ruins are shapeless heaps of mud, the square towers of the square walls alone retaining any semblance of form.

Long lines of choked *kanaats*, denoted by their crumbling shafts, attest the industrious irrigation of a former day. Tracks wind wearily among shrunken villages, or cross ridges of mud or gravel to take their unlovely way over arid stony plains. Unwatered tracts of land, once cultivated, as the *kanaats* show, but now deserts of sand and stones, send up gyrating clouds of gritty dust.

Such is Persia between its two capitals; and yet I repeat that in cool weather, and on a good horse, the journey is a very pleasant one. Most European men ride *chapar*, that is, post; but from what I see of the *chapar* horses, I would not do it for the sake of doubling the distance travelled in the day, and therefore cannot describe either its pleasures or tortures from experience.

On certain roads, as from Tihran to Shiraz, there are post stations (*chapar khana*) with horses and men at distances of from twenty to twenty-five miles, with a charge of one *kran* (eightpence) per *farsakh* (four miles) for each horse engaged, an order having been previously obtained from a government official. Besides your own horse you have to take one for the *shagird chapar*, or post-boy, who has to take the horses back, and one for the servant. The two latter carry the very limited kit, which includes a long cotton bag, which, being filled with chopped straw at night, forms the traveller's bed. The custom is to ride through all the hours of daylight whenever horses are to be got, doing from sixty to

ninety miles a day, always inspired by the hope of
" cutting the record," even by half an hour, and winning
undying fame.

The horses, which are kept going at a canter so long
as they can be thrashed into one, are small and active,
and do wonders ; but from the strain put upon them, bad
feeding, sore backs, and general dilapidation and exhaustion, are constantly tumbling down. Several times I
have seen wretched animals brought into the yards,
apparently " dead beat," and after getting some chopped
straw and a little barley thrashed into a canter again
for twenty-five miles more, because the traveller could
not get a remount. They often fall down dead under
their riders, urged by the heavy *chapar* whip to the last.

Riding *chapar*, journeying in a *taktrawan* or litter, or in
a *kajaweh*, or riding caravan pace, by which only about
thirty miles a day can be covered, are the only modes
of travelling in Persia, though I think that with capable
assistance a carriage might make the journey from Tihran
as far as Kashan.

I lodge in the *chapar khanas* whenever I can. They
consist of mud walls fourteen feet high, enclosing yards
deep in manure, with stabling for the *chapar* horses on
two sides, and recesses in their inner walls for mangers.
The entrance is an arched gateway. There are usually
two dark rooms at the sides, which the servants occupy
and cook in, and over the gateway is the *balakhana*, an
abortive tower, attained by a steep and crumbling stair,
in which I encamp. The one room has usually two
doors, half-fitting and non-shutting, and perhaps a
window space or two, and the ashes of the last traveller's
fire.

Such a breezy rest just suits me, and when my camp
furniture has been arranged and I am enjoying my
" afternoon tea," I feel " monarch of all I survey," even

of the boundless desert, over which the cloud shadows chase each other till it purples in the light of the sinking sun. If there is the desert desolation there is also the desert freedom.

The first halt was delicious after the crowds and fanaticism of Kûm. A broad plain with irrigated patches and a ruinous village was passed; then came the desert, an expanse of camel-brown gravel thickly strewn with stones, with a range of low serrated brown hills, with curious stratification, on the east. A few caravans of camels, and the *haram* of the Governor of Yezd in closely-covered *kajawehs*, alone broke the monotony. Before I thought we were half-way we reached the *abambars*, the small brown caravanserai, and the *chapar khana* of Passanghām, having ridden in three hours a distance on which I have often expended eight.

Cool and breezy it was in my room, and cooler and breezier on the flat mud roof; and the lifting of some clouds in the far distance to the north, beyond the great sweep of the brown desert, revealed the mighty Elburz range, white with new-fallen snow. At Sinsin the next evening it was gloriously cold. There had been another heavy snowfall, and in the evening the Elburz range, over a hundred miles away, rose in unsullied whiteness like a glittering wall, and above it the colossal cone of Demavend, rose-flushed.

The routine of the day is simple and easy. I get the caravan off at eight, lie on the floor for an hour, gallop and walk for about half the march, rest for an hour in some place, where Mahboud, the soldier, always contrives to bring me a glass of tea, and then gallop and walk to the halting-place, where I rest for another hour till the caravan comes in. I now know exactly what to pay, and by giving small presents get on very easily.

There were many uncomfortable prophecies about the

annoyances and rudenesses which a lady travelling alone would meet with, but so far not one has been fulfilled. How completely under such circumstances one has to trust one's fellow-creatures ! There are no fastenings on the doors of these breezy rooms, and last night there was only the longitudinal half of a door, but I fell asleep, fearing nothing worse than a predatory cat.

The last two days' marches have been chiefly over stony wastes, or among low hills of red earth, gray gravel, and brown mud, with low serrated ranges beyond, and farther yet high hills covered with snow, after which the road leaves the hills and descends upon a pink plain, much of the centre of which is snow-white from saline efflorescence. The villages Kasseinabad, Nasrabad, and Aliabad are passed on the plain, with small fruit trees and barley surrounding them, and great mud caravan-serais at intervals, only remarkable for the number of camels lying outside of them in rows facing each other. In the fresh keen air of evening the cone of Demavend was painted in white on the faint blue sky, reddening into beauty as the purple-madder shadows deepened over the yellow desert.

Tea made with saltish water, and salt sheep's milk, have been the only drawbacks of the six days' march.

Not far from Kashan we entered on a great alluvial plain formed of fine brown earth without a single stone—a prolific soil if it had water, as the fruit trees and abundant crops of young wheat round the villages show. So level, and on the whole so smooth, is this plain that it possesses the prodigy of a public conveyance, an omnibus with four horses abreast, which makes its laborious way with the aid of several attendants, who lift the wheels out of holes, prevent it from capsizing, and temporarily fill up the small irrigation ditches which it has to cross. Its progress is less " by leaps and bounds " than by jolts and rolls, and as my Arab horse bounded past I wondered that six men could be found to exchange the freedom of the saddle for such a jerky, stuffy box.

Five hundred yards from the gate of Kashan there is a telegraph station of the Indo-European line, where M. du Vignau and his wife expected me, and' have received me with great kindness and hospitality. The electricians at these stations are allowed to receive guests in what is known as the "Inspectors' Room," and they exercise this liberty most kindly and generously. Many a weary traveller looks back upon the "Inspectors' Room" as upon an oasis in the desert of dirt; and though I cannot class myself just now with "weary travellers," I cordially appreciate the kindness which makes one "at home," and the opportunity of exchanging civilised ideas for a few hours.

I must not go beyond Kashan without giving a few words to the Persian section of the Indo-European telegraph line, one of the greatest marvels of telegraph construction, considering the nature of the country which the line traverses. Tihran is the centre of telegraphic control, and the residence of Colonel Wells, R.E., the Director, with a staff of twenty telegraphists, who work in relays day and night, and a Medical Officer. Julfa is another place of importance on the line, and at Shiraz there is another Medical Officer.

The prompt repair of the wires in cases of interruption is carefully arranged for. At suitable places, such as Kûm, Soh, Kashan, and other towns or villages from fifty to eighty miles apart, there are control or testing stations, each being in charge of a European telegraphist, who has under him two Persian horsemen, who have been well trained as linesmen. At stated hours the clerks place their instruments in circuit, and ascertain if all is right.

If this testing reveals any fault, it can be localised at

once, and horsemen are despatched from the control stations on either side of it, with orders to ride rapidly along the line until they meet at the fault and repair it. As the telegraph crosses passes such as Kuhrūd, at an altitude of over 8000 feet, the duties of both inspectors and linesmen are most severe, full not only of hardship but of danger in terrible winter storms and great depths of snow, yet on their ceaseless watchfulness and fidelity the safety of our Indian Empire may some day depend.

The skill brought to bear upon the manipulation of this Government line from the Gulf, and throughout the whole system of which it is a part, is wonderful. Messages from any part of the United Kingdom now reach any part of India in less than an hour and a half, and in only about one word in two hundred does even the most trifling mistake occur in transmission, a result all the more surprising when it is remembered that the telegrams are almost entirely either in code or cypher, and that over 1000 are transmitted in the course of a day.

Among these are the long despatches continually passing between the Viceroy of India and the India Office on vitally important subjects, and press telegrams of every noteworthy event. The " exhaustive summary " of Indian news which appears weekly in the *Times*, accompanied by a commentary on events, is an altogether un-padded telegram, and is transmitted with punctuation complete, and even with inverted commas for quotations.[1]

The English staff, numbering from fifty to sixty men, is scattered along a line of 1900 miles. Some of them

[1] Major-General Sir R. Murdoch Smith, K.C.M.G., late Director of the Persian section of the Indo-European telegraph, read a very interesting paper upon it before the Royal Scottish Geographical Society on December 13, 1888,—a *Sketch of the History of Telegraphic Communication between the United Kingdom and India.*

are married, and most occupy isolated positions, so far as other Europeans are concerned. It is the universal testimony of Englishmen and Persians that the relations between them have been for many years of the most friendly character, full of good-will and mutual friendly offices, and that the continual contact brought about by the nature of the duties of the electricians has been productive not of aversion and distrust, but of cordial appreciation on both sides.

I. L. B.

LETTER XI (*Continued*)

KASHAN is one of the hottest places on the great Persian plateau, but has the rare luxury of a good water supply brought from a reservoir some distance off in the Kuhrūd mountains.   It has a much-diminished population, said now to number 30,000 souls.   Much of it is in ruins, and much more is ruinous.   It has a thriving colony of Jews.   It is noted for its silks and velvets; but the modern productions are regarded by judges as degenerate. It is still famous for its work in copper and for its great copper bazar.

Silk produced at Resht is brought here to be spun and dyed.   Then it is sent to Sultanabad to be woven into carpets, and is brought back again to have the pile cut by the sharp instruments used for cutting velvet pile, and the finished carpets are sent to Tihran for sale.   They are only made in small sizes, and are more suitable for *portières* than for laying on the floor.   The colouring is exquisite, and the metallic sheen and lustre are unique.   Silk carpets are costly luxuries. The price of even a fairly good one of very small size is £50, the silk alone costing £20.

Kashan is a great place for *curio* buyers, who enlist the Jews in their service.   There are some valuable antiques in this house—embroideries, carpet squares in silk, glass whose greenish colour and grace of form remind me of Venetian glass, enamels on porcelain, tiles, metal inlaying and damascening, pierced brasswork, and many other articles of *vertu*, the art of making which is either lost or has greatly degenerated.

It is unaccountable, but it is certain that the secret of producing the higher types of beauty in various arts, especially the Keramic, died out more than one hundred and fifty years ago, and that there are no circumstances of that date to account for its decease, except that it is recorded that when the Afghan conqueror Mahmoud destroyed Isfahan he massacred the designers of *reflêt* tiles and other Keramic beauties, because they had created works which gave great umbrage to the Sunni sect to which he belonged.

These *reflêts*, for which collectors give fabulous sums, are intrinsically beautiful, both in the elegant conceptions of their designs and the fantastic richness of their colouring. There are designs in shades of brown on a lapis-lazuli ground, or in blue and green on a purple or umber ground, some of them star-shaped, with a pure white border composing the rest of the square, on which are inscribed phrases from the Koran. Looked at from above or frontwise, one exclaims, " What a beautiful tile ! " but it is on turning it to the light that one's stereotyped phrases of admiration are exchanged for silence in presence of a singular iridescence which transfigures the tile, making it seem to gleam from within with golden purples and rosy gold.

The mosaic tiles are also beautiful, especially where the mosaic is on a lapis-lazuli or canary-yellow ground, neither of them reproducible at this day ; and this also refers to other shades of blue, and to various reds and browns of exceeding richness, the art of making which has been lost for a century. But enough of art !

Possibly there may be a resurrection for Persian art ; but in the meantime aniline dyes, tawdry European importations, and Western models without either grace or originality are doing their best to deprave it here, as elsewhere.

Roads from Tihran, Gulpaigan, Yezd, and Isfahan meet here, and it is something of what the Americans call "a distributing point," but it is a most uninviting place, in situation and general aspect, and its unsightly mud ruins, as in other Persian cities, are eloquent of nothing but paralysis and retrogression.

Murcheh Khurt, Palm Sunday, March 30.—Three very pleasant marches, equal to seventy-six miles, have brought me here, and now Isfahan is only two days off, and it will end my palmy days of Persian travelling.

The first day's march from Kashan was only seven *farsakhs* (the *parasang* of Xenophon), twenty-eight miles, but it is equivalent to thirty-five, owing to the roughness of the road and the long ascent. There was scarcely any ground for galloping, the way was lost once, and the march took over eight hours.

The track, for only in places did it attain to the dignity of a bridle-road, lay for hours over a stony desert, and then entered the mountains, where I halted for an hour at the once magnificent caravanserai of Gaberabad, in a romantic situation, but falling fast into ruins, and deserted for no reason, so far as I could make out, but that people used to be robbed and have their throats cut there.

Beyond it the scenery became very wild, and the rocks and mountains highly coloured and snow-patched, and after ascending along the side of a stream and up a causewayed sort of stair past the reservoir which supplies Kashan with water, we entered the rising valley of Kuhrūd, where the snow came nearly down to the road, and every slope was terraced and every level cultivated, and young wheat was springing and fruit orchards flourished, with green sward under the branches, and great poplars in picturesque groups towered above the lower woods.

We lost the way in the snow, and then took to the pebbly river as the safest track, and had an hour of fumbling in water and snow under apple and pear trees for the halting-place. The twilight of a frosty evening was coming on when we reached the village of Kuhrūd— 500 houses in terraces on a mountain side, and clustering round a fort on a projecting spur.

It is surrounded and interpenetrated by groves of walnut, apricot, cherry, peach, plum, apple, pear, poplar, and vine, with roses climbing over everything and planted in rows like vines, and through it passes a fair, bright stream of living water, a stream " whose waters fail not," turning the mountain valley into an oasis. But at that altitude of something like 7000 feet, the buds are only just swelling, and the crimson catkins of the hazels were the only reminder of spring. It is the one place that I should care to revisit.

The snow was piled in great heaps in the village and against the wall of the very wretched, ruinous *chapar khana* in which I sought rest and shelter. Mahboud went up to the loft over the gateway, and came down looking dejected, mustering English enough to say, " No, no, mem Sahib ! " I actually had to occupy one of the two gateway rooms, an inferior stable, without the smallest window hole, and no door except two unconnected boards with which one could cover a part of the doorway. Even when these were not put up a candle was necessary. It was freezing hard, but one could not have a fire because there was no smoke-hole. The walls were slimily and inkily black from the smoke of the fires of people who were less particular than I am. The dust and rubbish of the floor were swept into one corner. If one wanted a place to store boxes in, and looked into that room, one would exclaim dubiously, "Well, it *might* do for glass and china!"

Mahboud put a rug on the floor and brought a bowl of delicious milk, and with an inverted saddle for a pillow I rested quite comfortably, being too tired to be impatient, till Mirza Yusuf arrived with my luxuries, and the news that the caravan could not get in for another hour, for that several of the mules had fallen and the loads were slipping round constantly. Indeed it was ten before I had dinner. It is very fortunate to have an attendant always cheerful, never fussy, caring nothing for personal comfort, and always ready to interpret.

The *ketchuda* called with the usual proffer of service, " I am your sacrifice," etc., and induced me to buy some of the specialties of Kuhrūd, rose-water in bottles without corks, and a paste made of rose-water, pounded walnuts, and sugar. The rose-water is not very clear, but it has much of the overpowering, lingering odour of attar of roses.

Kuhrūd seems prosperous. Besides exporting large quantities of rose-water and walnut paste formed into blocks and done up in white skins, it sends wheat and fruit in abundance to Kashan.

Freedom, good sleep, and satisfactory travelling make up for all annoyances but vermin, and these are still hybernating. In that precarious privacy I slept soundly, and got the caravan off at eight the next morning—a glorious winter morning, the icy roads and the snow-covered valley glittering with frost crystals. We lost the way again among the pretty orchards, then got into a valley between high mud mountains, whose shapeless-ness is now judiciously concealed by snow from one to three feet deep, through which a track has been broken a foot wide. It is six miles from Kuhrūd to the summit of the Kuhrūd Pass, which is over 8000 feet, and it grew very cold and gray, and ragged masses of cloud swept angrily round the mountain-tops.

On the steepest part of the ascent it was extremely slippery, and the horses not being roughed slipped badly, and I was just fearing an accident to my borrowed horse and planning some method of dismounting when down he came on his nose and then on the side of his head, and fell several times again in his struggles to get up, his feet slipping from under him.   When he did succeed in getting on his legs I was convinced that he had cut his knees, and slipped off him somehow to examine them ; but my fears were groundless, and I had great difficulty in getting out of the drift into which I had descended, which was nearly up to my shoulders.   His nose was bleeding a little, but that was all.

There was no way of remounting on a path a foot wide between walls of snow, and besides I was afraid of another accident, so I slipped the snaffle rein over his head and led him.   It was horribly slippery, and having nails in my boots I fell several times just under his feet, but the sweet creature always stopped when I fell.

From the top there was a truly fearful view of " blackness, darkness, and tempest," inky mists, white mountain-tops showing momentarily through them to be lost again, and great sheets of very deep snow.   Soon the gathering storm burst, a " blizzard " in which the snow was quite blinding, snow drifting and hissing as it went by, the wind tempestuous, mountains, valleys, path obliterated, even the soldier in front of me constantly lost to sight.   An hour of this and I could walk no more, and somehow scrambled into the saddle.

At the foot of the descent the sky cleared, the sun shone, and we picked up the caravan, which had had rather a hard time.   The succeeding route was through an absolutely uninhabited and uninhabitable country, clay and mud hills, purple, red, gray, pink, brown, an utter desolation, till we came in sight of the good-sized and at a distance imposing-looking village of Soh in a keen wind with frequent snow showers. Soh is a telegraph testing station.

The electrician was absent, but had kindly left directions that I was to be received, and I found a most comfortable guest-room quite ready. A little later an Englishman riding *chapar* to Isfahan threw a packet of English letters in at my door—a delightful surprise, which made havoc of the rest of the evening.

The desolation of this part of the route may be judged of from the fact that except the village of Kuhrūd there is not an inhabited house for forty-six miles. The country traversed reminds me much of the least interesting part of the route from Lesser Tibet into Kulu.

Yesterday morning there was ice, and the roads were very slippery on the gradual descent from the plain which opens out after passing Bideshk, the *chapar* station, an hour from Soh. The twenty-four miles' ride over this gravelly waste, quite uninhabited, was very pleasant, as it was possible to gallop much of the way, and besides the beauty of the atmospheric colouring the mirage occurring in most remarkable forms rendered monotony impossible.

There were no caravans on the road, but I met several dervishes, and there is one here to whom I have given what he demanded—a night's lodging. He carries a large carved almsholder ; and the panther skin on his shoulders, the knotted club, and his lean, hungry, fanatical face give him a dangerous look. All I have seen on this march have worn long matted bushy hair, often covering their shoulders, an axe in the girdle, and peculiar turbans decorated with phrases from the Koran.

They are the "mendicant friars" of Persia, and are under vows of poverty. Some are said to be learned; but they object to discussing religious matters with infidels, and almost nothing is known as to their beliefs. They hold universally the sanctity of idleness, and the duty of being supported by the community. The lower classes hold them in reverence, and the upper, though they are apt to loathe them, treat them with great respect, for fear of laying themselves open to the charge of laxity in religious matters.

A DERVISH.

Many of them deal in charms, and are consulted as astrologers. Some are professed tellers of stories, to which I am told no European could degrade himself by listening, but which are most palatable to a village audience; and at this moment this unwelcome guest of mine has a crowd listening to a narrative partly told and partly acted.

They are credited with many vices, among the least of which are hazy ideas as to mine and thine, opium and bhang smoking to excess, and drunkenness.

They have recognised heads or chiefs, to whom they show great deference. One of their vows is that of obedience; and besides paying to the chief a part of the alms they receive, he gives them orders as to the houses they are to infest, and though the nuisance is not so common as formerly, a dervish at the door is still a sign of being great or rich, or both. Their cries, and their rude blasts on the buffalo horn, which is a usual part of their equipment, are most obnoxious. In the larger towns, such as Kûm and Kirmanshah, there are shops for the sale of their outfit—the tiger and panther skins, the axes, the knotted clubs, the almsbowls, etc.

Some are respectable, and enjoy much consideration, and I hope that many even of those whom a careful writer has called "disgusting vagabonds" are not humbugs; but the presumption is so much the other way that I am always glad when the ground admits of galloping past them, otherwise the dervish comes forward, with his knotted club much *en évidence*, with many compliments and good wishes, or else silently extends his almsholder, ejaculating *Huk* ("my right"). I usually have the means of appeasing, if not of satisfying him, but on the rare occasions when I have had no money the yells and maledictions have been awful.

The light and profane use of the Divine name is universal. The dervishes curse, but every one uses the name *Allah* wherever they can bring it in. The *Ya Allah*, as an expression of fatigue, or discontent, or interest, or nothing, is heard all day, and the boy who drives a cow, or a team, or a mule in a caravan, cries *Ya Allah* incessantly as an equivalent of "go along," and the gardener pushing his spade into the ground, the chopper with every blow of the axe, the labourer throwing up bricks, ejaculates the same. *Mashallah, Inshallah,* interlard all conversation. When men are building, the perpetual sing-song of phrases such as these is heard, "Brother, in God's name toss me a brick," the other replying, "Brother, in God's name here is a brick.'

The vocabulary of abuse is also very large, and often involves serious reflections on the female relatives of the person abused. I hear such harmless phrases as "son of a burnt father," "son of a dog," "offspring of a pig," etc., on all occasions.

Murcheh Khurt is a large village with a good deal of cultivation about it, a mosque or more, a *hammam*, a *chapar khana*, and a caravanserai. Here again I found that the smart foreign soldier attracted all the notice, and that before the people ceased to wonder at him I had passed them. The *chapar khana* was full of men, so I have had to sink to the level of a recessed den with a manger in front in a ruinous caravanserai crowded with Persian travellers, muleteers, mules, horses, and asses, and the courtyard half-choked with ruins. I had not seen the inside of one of these dens before. Travellers have exhausted the vocabulary of abuse upon them; possibly they deserve it in the "vermin season"; but there is nothing worse than a square and perfectly dark room, with unplastered walls blackened by the smoke and cobwebs of ages, and a door which will not fasten.

The air is cool and the sky blue, and sitting at the open door is very pleasant. Mahboud and two of the servants caught cold at Kuhrūd and are ill, and my Arab has a chill too. He is a very stupid horse. His gentle eyes never change their expression, and his small ears rarely move. He has little sense or affection, but when he is patted his proud neck takes on a loftier arch. Gentle as he is to people he is a brute to other horses. He would like to fight every one of them, to stand on his hind-legs and grapple them round the shoulders with his fore-feet and bite their necks, roaring and squealing all the time. He and Mahboud's horse are inveterate enemies, and one of the few difficulties of the journey is the keeping them from a regular stand-up fight.

This village is an oasis in the desert. I have been through its gates, barely wide enough to admit an ass loaded with brushwood, with the *seraidar* and Mirza, walked through its narrow alleys, and inadvertently stumbled into a mosque where a great crowd of women were listening to a story of one of the twelve Imams told by a *mollah*, looked down upon it and over the adjacent country from a house roof, visited several houses, in which some of the inmates were ill and desired "Feringhi medicine," had a long conversation with the *ketchuda*, who came to see me to ask for eye lotion, and with the *seraidar*, and altogether have had quite a pleasant day.

Chapar Khana, Gez.——I am sitting in one of the three doorless doorways of my loft, grieving that the journey is just over, and that this is the last night of the exhilarating freedom of the desert. I rode twenty-four miles before one o'clock to-day, over a level uncultivated plain, bordered as usual by ranges of mountains. In fact, while I write of levels and plains it must be understood that Persia is chiefly a land of hills rising from a table-land from 3400 feet to 6000 feet in altitude, and that the traveller is rarely, if ever, more than fourteen or fifteen miles from mountains from 2000 to 6000 feet above the plain from which they rise, crowned by Demavend, whose imposing summit is 18,600 feet above the sea. The hills beyond Isfahan have assumed lofty proportions, and some of the snowy mountains of Luristan are to be seen in the far distance.

It is nearly an unmitigated waste between Murcheh Khurt and Gez, destitute even of tufts of wormwood ; but the latter part of the march is through a stoneless alluvial desert of dry friable soil, soft springy galloping ground which water would turn into a paradise of fertility ; and water there has once been, for not far from the road are the remains of some *kanaats*.

The questions naturally arise in a traveller's mind, first, what becomes of the enormous amount of snow which falls on the mountains; and next, how in a country so arid as the plateaus of Central Asia water for irrigation, and for the basins and fountains which abound in rich men's houses, is obtained.

Wells, unless the artesian borings shortly to be begun in the Tihran desert should be successful, are all but unknown, except for supplying drinking water, and there are scarcely any reservoirs, but ingenuity has devised a plan of subterranean water-channels, which besides their other advantages prevent loss by evaporation. Tihran has thirty-five of them, and the water which they distribute is naturally expensive, as the cost of making them is great.

It is on the slope of a hill that the spring is found which is the original source of supply; this is tapped at some depth, and its waters are led along a tunnel about four feet high by two feet wide lined with baked pottery where the ground is soft, and having a slight fall to the next spring or well, which may be from twenty-five to even sixty yards off.

As the labourers dig they draw up the earth and arrange it in a circle round the shaft, and as they come to water they draw up the mud and pour it on the top of the earth, where it dries and hardens, and below, the water is conducted as a running underground stream across great plains, its progress marked by mounds which have been compared to ant-hills and craters, but to my thinking are more like the shafts of disused mines.

Hundreds of these *kanaats* are seen, ruined and dry, and are the resort of porcupines and jackals. To construct a *kanaat* may call a village or series of villages into being. The letting it fall to ruin is one cause of deserted villages. Those which are not lined require annual repairs, which are now going on, but frequently the complete fall of the roof destroys the fall of the water, and the tunnel becomes irreparable.

The peasants are obliged to buy the water, for they cannot steal it, and the making of a *kanaat* is often a lucrative speculation. Pigeons live in them, and many of them are full of fish, which foreigners amuse themselves by poisoning by throwing a mixture of *cocculus indicus* with dough down the wells, when the poisoned but wholesome fish rise to the surface. They usually recover when they are left in the water. Dr. Wills describes them as having a muddy taste. The *kanaats* are a feature of Persia.

Ever since leaving Kûm all the dry and hard parts of the road have been covered with the industrious "road beetle," which works, like the ant, in concert, and carries on its activities at all seasons, removing from the road to its nest all the excreta of animals, except in regions where even animal fuel is so exceptionally scarce that boys with asses and ponies follow caravans for the same purpose. These beetles hover over the road on the wing, and on alighting proceed to roll the ball towards the nest, four or five of them standing on their hind-legs and working it forwards, or else rolling it with their heads close to the ground. Their instinct is wonderful, and they attract the attention of all travellers. They are about the size of a small walnut. Otherwise there is little of animated life to be seen on this route.

No day has had fewer noticeable objects. Two or three *abambars*, several caravanserais in absolute ruins, and a magnificent one in partial ruins are its record.

Gez consists of this post-house and a decaying caravanserai. From the roof as I write I watch the grooming of a whole row of *chapar* horses. As each pad is removed there is a horrid revelation of wounds, deep ulcers, sores often a foot long, and in some cases the white vertebræ of the spine are exposed. These are the wretched animals which often carry men who ride from fourteen to seventeen stone fifty miles in a day. It is hard enough even with ·extreme carefulness to keep the back of a horse all right on a continuous journey, but I never before saw animals ridden in such a state., They wince pitifully when their pads are put on again.

The desert is all around, purpling in the sunset, sweeping up to low broken ridges, and to some higher hills in the north-west covered with new-fallen snow. That the waste only requires water to make it prolific is apparent, for below these walls wheat is growing luxuriantly in some deep pits, irrigated from a dirty ditch out of which the drinking water comes. Nothing can be got, except by sending to a village a mile away.

Four of the men are ill, one with inflammation of the eyes, another with an abscess, and a third, a very strong man, with something like bilious fever, and a *charvadar* with malarial fever. The strong man's moans often become howls. He insists that he shall die to-night. These two afternoons have been much taken up with making poultices and medicines, and I shall be glad for the poor fellows to reach Isfahan and the care of a competent doctor.

Julfa, April 2.—I daresay this journey seems longer to you than it did to me. It was very pleasant, and its goal is pleasant, and a most kind welcome and the refinement of cultured English people go far to compensate for the loss of the desert freedom and the easy stride of the Arab horse.

I started the caravan at nine yesterday, with two men with bandaged eyes, and other two hardly able to sit on their mules ; Mahboud, who is really more seriously ill than any of them, keeping up his pluck and capableness to the last. The man who threatened to die at Gez was very much better the next morning.

Soon after leaving Gez the country changes its aspect, the road becomes very bad, and passes through nine miles of rich cultivation—wheat, barley, opium, and vegetables growing abundantly ; orchards are numerous, villages with trees and gardens succeed each other rapidly, water abounds, and before the gate of Isfahan is reached, domes and minarets rising among cypresses, planes, and poplars indicate the remains of the former capital of Persia.

Inside the shabby gateway the road to Julfa lies among rows of mean mud houses, heaps of ruins, and shabby provision bazars ; and that mile or more of Isfahan was the one disagreeable part of the journey.

It was about the last day of the holidays, and the bazars, alleys, and open spaces were full of men in gay attire, and companies of shrouded women were moving along the quieter roads. It was too warm for the sheep-skin coat which had served me so well at Kûm, and I had dressed with some regard to European sensibilities. The boys began to shout " A Feringhi woman ! a Nazarene woman ! " and then to call bad names ; then men began to make up fiendish laughs,[1] and the howls and outcries gathered strength as I went on at the inevitable foot's pace, spitting being quite common, poor Mahboud con-stantly turning to me a perturbed wretched face, full of annoyance at the insults of his co-religionists, which it would have been dangerous to resent. It was a bad half-hour.

[1] I can imagine now what a hellish laugh that was with which "they laughed Him to scorn."

I was a month in Julfa, but never saw anything more of Isfahan, which is such a fanatical city that I believe even so lately as last year none of the ladies of the European community had visited it, except one or two disguised as Persian women.

Before passing the residence of the Amir-i-Panj (the commander of 5000) near the Julfa gate the uproar died away, and once through the gate and in the *Chahar Bagh* (four gardens) there was peace. A bad road of cobble stones, with a double avenue of once magnificent planes, some once ornamental tanks, very high walls, pierced by storied gates, ornamented with wild designs on plaster in flaring colours, above which a blue dome is a conspicuous object, leads to a handsome bridge of thirty-three arches, with a broad level roadway, and corridors for foot passengers on either side, over the Zainderud, then came fields with springing wheat, a few houses, a narrow alley, and two or three miles from Isfahan the gate of its Armenian suburb, Julfa.

At once on crossing the bridge there was a change. Ruddy, cheery-looking unveiled women in red gowns, and pure white *chadars* completely enveloping their persons, moved freely about, and the men wore neither the becoming turban nor the ominous scowl of Islam. In the quaint narrow streets were churches with open vestibules, through which pictures of the thorn-crowned Christ and of sweet-faced Madonnas were visible; priests in black robes and women in white glided along the narrow roads. There was the fresher, purer air of Christianity, however debased and corrupted. In the low-browed churches divine honours are paid to a crowned and risen Christ, and the white-robed women have been baptized into His name. Never again will the Julfa alleys be so peaceful and lovable as yesterday, when they offered a haven from the howling bigots of Isfahan.

Dr. Bruce has not returned from Baghdad, but Mrs. and Miss Bruce welcomed me very kindly, and I am already forgetting my unpleasant reception. I. L. B.

LETTER XII

JULFA, *April 17.*

MR. GEORGE CURZON wrote of Julfa: " The younger Julfa
is a place wholly destitute of superficial attractions, consisting as it does of a labyrinth of narrow alleys closed
by doors and plentifully perforated with open sewers.
Life there is ' cabined, cribbed, confined' to an intolerable degree, and it is a relief to escape from its squalid
precincts."

I dare not write thus if I would!   It is now the
early spring.   The "sewers" are clear rapid streams,
margined by grass and dandelions, and shaded by ash
trees and pollard willows in their first flush of green.
The "narrow alleys" are scrupulously clean, and there is
neither mud nor dust.   If I go up on the roof I see a
cultivated oasis, gardens prolonged indefinitely concealing
the desert which lies between them and the bold mountain ranges which surround this lofty and breezy plain.
Every breeze is laden with the delicious odour of the
bean blossom.   A rapid river spanned by noble bridges
hurries through the oasis it has helped to create, and on
its other side the domes and minarets of Isfahan rise out
of masses of fine trees, and bridges and mosques, minarets
and mountains, are all seen through a most exquisite pink
mist, for hundreds of standard peach trees are in full
bloom, and look where one may everything is *couleur de
rose.*

I quite admit that Julfa consists of a "labyrinth of alleys." I can never find my way about it. One alley with its shady central stream (or "sewer"), its roughly paved paths on either side, its mud walls pierced by low doors, is very much like another, and however lucky one may be in "happening on" the right road, it is always a weary time before one escapes from between mud walls into the gardens and wheatfields, to the blossoming beans, and the exquisite wild-flowers among the wheat.

As to the "cabined, cribbed, confined" life, I can give no testimony from personal knowledge. All life in European settlements in the East appears to me "cabined, cribbed, confined," and greatly devoid of external interests. Perhaps Julfa is deficient in the latter in an eminent degree, and in a very small foreign community people are interested chiefly in each other's affairs, sayings, and doings. Lawn tennis, picnics, and dinner parties are prevalent, the ordinary etiquette of European society prevails, and in all cases of need the residents are kind to each other both in life and death.

The European society is divided into three circles— the missionaries, the mercantile community, and the telegraph staff. The British agent, Mr. Aganoor, is an Armenian.[1] No Christians, Armenian or European, live in Isfahan, and it is practically *défendu* to European women. This transpontine restriction undoubtedly narrows the life and interests of Julfa. It is aggravating and tantalising to be for ever looking at a city of 60,000 or 70,000 people, the fallen capital of the Sufari dynasty, and never be able to enter it.

This Christian town of Julfa has a certain accessible

[1] Since my visit Mr. Preece, then, and for many previous years, the superintending electrician of this section of the Indo-European telegraph, has been appointed Consul, the increasing dimensions of English interests and the increasing number of resident British subjects rendering the creation of a Consulate at Isfahan a very desirable step.

historic interest. Shah Abbas, justly surnamed the Great, conceived the sagacious project of introducing among his Persian subjects at Isfahan—then, in the latter part of the sixteenth century, a magnificent capital—the Christian habits of trading, sagacity, and thrift, for then as now the Armenians had commercial dealings with China, India, and Europe, and had imported several arts into Persia.

This project he carried out in truly despotic fashion by moving almost the whole population of Julfa on the Araxes, on the modern Russo-Persian frontier, to the banks of the Zainderud, making over to it the best lands in the neighbourhood of Isfahan. Many years later the new Julfa was a place with twenty-four churches, great prosperity, and an estimated population of 40,000. Its agriculturists were prosperous market-gardeners for the huge city of Isfahan, and it had likewise a great trading community, and was renowned for the making of jewellery and watches.

It has now a dwindling population of about 3000, chiefly elderly men, women, and girls, the young men, after receiving a good education in the Church Mission and other schools, flying from its stagnation to India, Java, and even Europe. The twenty-four churches are reduced to twelve, and these with the vast cemetery in the desert at the base of Kuh Sufi are its chief objects of interest, apart from those which are human and living.

April 22.—The peach blossoms have long since fallen, but perhaps I still see Julfa *couleur de rose*, even after three weeks, so very great is the kindness under this roof, and so fully is my time occupied with various interests, and the preparations for a difficult journey.

This, as you know, is the Church Mission House. Dr. Bruce has been here for twenty years, and until lately, when the Archbishop of Canterbury's mission to the Assyrian Christians began its work at Urmi, near the

Turkish frontier in the north-west, this was the only English mission in the Empire. It was contemplated as a mission to the Mohammedans, but in this respect has been an apparent failure. It is true that much prejudice has been disarmed, and, as I have heard from some leading Mohammedans, Dr. Bruce's zeal and good works have won their respect. A large part of the Bible has been translated into Persian and very widely circulated through the adjacent country by means of colporteurs of the British and Foreign Bible Society. His preaching of Christianity is listened to respectfully, and even with interest, wherever he itinerates, and Moslems daily call on him, and show much friendliness, but the results, as results are usually estimated, are *nil*—that is, no Mohammedans openly profess Christianity.

There is actual though not legal toleration, but Moslem children may not attend a mission school, and a Moslem who becomes a Christian loses his means of living, and probably his life is sacrificed to fanaticism.

In consequence of these difficulties, and certain encouragements in another direction, the *ostensible* work of the mission is among Armenians. Dr. Bruce has not been afraid of incurring the stigma of being a proselytiser, and has a large congregation of Armenians worshipping after the English form, ninety-four being communicants of the Church of England. On Easter Eve there was an evening Communion, and the great row of women kneeling at the rail in the pure white robes which cover them from head to foot, and then moving back to their places in the dim light, was very picturesque and beautiful.

Good works have been added one after another, till the mission is now a very large establishment. The C. M. S. has been liberal to this, its only Persian agency, and Dr. Bruce, having private means, has generously expended them largely on missionary work in Julfa.

The chief features of the compounds are the church, which is both simple and ecclesiastical in its exterior and interior, and the library adjoining it, where Dr. Bruce works at the translation of the Old Testament into Persian and the revision of the New, aided by a *munshi*, and where through much of the day he is receiving Moslems, some of whom come to inquire into Christianity, others for religious disputations, and a third and numerous class out of mere friendliness. The latter are generally invited into the Mission House, and are regaled with coffee and *kalians*, in orthodox Persian fashion. Among the latter visitors has been the Amir-i-Panj, who came to ask me to call on his wife, accompanied by a general of cavalry, whose name I cannot spell, and who speaks French remarkably well.

Among the other buildings are those of the Medical Mission, which include a roomy courtyard, where the animals which carry the patients are tethered, rooms for the doctor, a well-arranged dispensary and consulting-room, with waiting-rooms for both sexes, and rooms above in which serious surgical cases are received for treatment, and where at present there are eleven patients, although just now there is no European doctor, and they are being treated by the native assistants, most kindly helped by Dr. Scully of the telegraph staff. This hospital and dispensary are largely taken advantage of by Moslems, who highly appreciate this form of Christian benevolence.

The boys' school, with 205 pupils, has been a great benefit to Julfa. The head-master, Mr. Johannes, was educated in England and was formerly a master of the Nassik School in India. This school provides the education of one of our best middle-class schools, and the teaching is thorough. *Smattering* would be infinitely despised by teachers and pupils. In this thorough fashion Latin, French, the first four books of Euclid, and algebra are taught to the young men of the upper form. The boys have a large playground, with a great tank for bathing, and some of the equipments of a gymnasium, a vaulting pole, parallel bars, etc.

The girls' schools, containing 100 girls, have their own courtyard, and they need enlarging, though the process has been more than once repeated. Mrs. Aidin, an English teacher, is at their head, and exercises that strong influence which love and firmness give. The girls are a mass of red, a cool red, without yellow, and when they disperse they enliven the Julfa alleys with their carnation dresses and pure white *chadars*. The education is solid and suitable, and special attention is given to needlework.

Besides these there is an orphanage, begun for the benefit of those whose parents died in the famine, in which are twenty boys. Outside are many other works, a Bible House, from which colporteurs at intervals proceed on journeys, a Young Men's Christian Association, or something like it, etc. etc.

Now as to the Mission House itself, which has to accommodate Dr., Mrs., and Miss Bruce, Mr. Carless, a clerical missionary, and two English lady missionaries. So much has been written lately about the "style of living" of missionaries, their large houses, and somewhat unnecessary comfort in general, that I am everywhere specially interested in investigating the subject, having formed no definite opinion on the question whether living as natives or living as Europeans is the more likely mode of producing a salutary impression.

The Mission House here is a native building, its walls and ceilings simply decorated with pale brown arabesques on a white ground. There are a bedroom and parlour, with an ante-room between giving access to both from the courtyard, a storeroom, and a kitchen. Across the court are servants' quarters and a guest-room for natives.   Above these, reached by an outside stair, are a good room, occupied by Mr. Carless as study and bedroom, and one small guest-room.   Another stair leads to two rooms above some of the girls' school premises, having enclosed alcoves used as sleeping and dressing rooms. These are occupied by two ladies.   One room serves as eating-room for the whole mission party, at present six in number, and as drawing-room and workroom.   Books, a harmonium, Persian rugs on the floor, and just enough furniture for use constitute its "luxury."

There are two servants, both of course men, and all the ladies do some housework.   At present the only horse is the dispensary horse, a beast of such rough and uneven paces that it is a penance to ride him.   The food is abundant, well cooked, and very simple.

The life, all round, is a very busy one.   Visitors are never refused at any hour.   The long flat mud roofs from which one can see the gardens and the hills are used for exercise, otherwise some of the party would never have anything better than mud walls for their horizon, and life in courtyards is rather depressing for Europeans.   I have told facts, and make no comments, and it must be remembered that both Dr. Bruce and Miss V——— a lady of rare devotion who has lately arrived,[1] are to a certain extent "honorary" missionaries, and have the means, if they had the desire, of surrounding themselves with comforts.

This is about the twenty-third mission circle with which I have become acquainted during the last eight months, and I see in nearly all the same difficulties, many of them of a nature which we can hardly realise at home.

---

[1] A few weeks later she died, her life sacrificed, I think, to over-study of a difficult language, and the neglect of fresh air and exercise.

Women coming to the East as missionaries are by far the greatest sufferers, especially if they are young, for Eastern custom, which in their position cannot be defied with advantage, limits free action and abridges all the comforts of independence. Thus a woman cannot take a walk or a ride or go to a house without a trusty man-servant in attendance on her, and this is often inconvenient, so she does not go out at all, contenting herself with a walk on the roof or in the courtyard.

The wave of enthusiasm on which a lady leaves her own country soon spends its force. The interest which has centred round her for weeks or even months is left behind. The enthusiastic addresses and farewell meetings, the journey "up the country" with its excitement and novelties, and the cordial welcome from the mission circle to which she is introduced, soon become things of the past. The circle, however kind, has its own interests and work, and having provided her with a *munshi*, necessarily goes on its own way more or less, and she is left to face the fearful difficulties of languages with which ours has no affinity, in a loneliness which is all the more severely felt because she is usually, for a time at least, one nominally of a family circle.

Unless she is a doctor or nurse she can do nothing till she has learned the language, and the difficulty of learning is increased by the loss of the flexible mind and retentive memory which are the heritage of extreme youth. The temptation is to "go at it" violently. Then come the aching head, the loss of sleep, the general lassitude and nervousness, and the self-questionings as to whether she was right in leaving her fruitful work in England.

Then, instead of realising the truth of the phrases used at home—"multitudes flocking as the doves to their windows"—"fields white unto the harvest," etc.—she finds that the work instead of seeking her has to be made by her most laboriously, and oftentimes the glowing hope of telling of the Redeemer's love and death to throngs of eager and receptive listeners is fulfilled in the drudgery of teaching sewing and the rudiments of English during the first year.

It is just this first year under which many women succumb. Then how many of the failings and weaknesses of the larger world must be epitomised in a mission group exposed, as Mr. Heyde of Kyelang feelingly said, "to the lowering influence of daily contact with a courteous and non-repulsive Heathenism and Mohammedanism"! Missionaries are not likely to possess, as they certainly are the last to claim, superior sanctity, and the new-comer, dreaming of a circle in all respects consecrated, finds herself among frictions, strong differences as to methods of working, not always gently expressed, and possible jealousies and criticisms, and an exaggeration of the importance of trifles, natural where large events are rare. A venerable American missionary in Turkey said, "Believe me, the greatest trial of missionaries is missionaries."

The small group is frequently destitute of social resources outside itself, it is cut off from friendly visits, services, lectures, music, new books, news, and the many recreative influences which all men regard as innocent. The life-work seems at times thrown away, the heat, the flies, and the mosquitos are depressing and exhausting, and in the case of young women, especially till they can use the language colloquially, there is little if any outside movement. Is it wonderful that supposed slights, tiffs, criticisms which would be utterly brushed away if a good walk in the open or a good gallop were possible, should be brooded over till they attain a magnitude which embitters and depresses life?

A man constantly finds the first year or two very

trying till he has his tools—the language—at command, and even men at times rub each other the wrong way, but a man can take a good walk or a solitary gallop, or better still, a week of itinerating among the villages. People speak of the dangers and privations of missionary life. I think that these are singularly over-estimated. But the trials which I have alluded to, and which, with the hot climates and insufficient exercise, undermine the health of very many female missionaries, cannot be exaggerated, and demand our deep sympathy.

I do not think that the ordinary pious woman, the successful and patient worker in district visiting, Bible classes, mothers' meetings, etc., is necessarily suited to be a foreign missionary, but that a heart which is a well-spring of human love, and a natural "enthusiasm of humanity" are required, as well as love to the Master, the last permeating and sanctifying the others, and giving them a perennial freshness. Fancy G. G—— grumbling and discontented and magnifying unpropitious trifles, when her heart goes out to every Chinawoman she sees in a perfect passion of love![1]

With the *medical* missionary, whether man or woman, the case is different. The work seeks the worker even before he is ready for it, claims him, pursues him, absorbs him, and he is powerful to heal even where he is impotent to convert.

[1] These sentences were written nearly a year ago, but many subsequent visits to missions have only confirmed my strong view of the very trying nature of at least the early period of a lady missionary's life in the East, and of the constant failure of health which it produces ; of the great necessity there is for mission boards to lay down some general rules of hygiene, which shall include the duty of riding on horseback, for more rigorous requirements of vigorous *physique* in those sent out, and above, all, that the *natural characteristics* of those who are chosen to be "epistles of Christ" in the East shall be such as will not only naturally and specially commend the Gospel, but will stand the wear and strain of difficult circumstances.

I have been to the hospital to see a woman from the Kuhrūd mountains, who was brought here to undergo an operation. She had spent all her living on native physicians without result, and her husband has actually sold his house to get money to give his wife a last chance of recovery. Fifteen years ago this man nearly took Dr. Bruce's life. Now, he says, " The fruits of Christianity are good."

Daily the " labyrinth of alleys " becomes denser with leafage, and the sun is hot enough to make the shade very pleasant, while occasional showers keep the greenery fresh. Indeed it is warm enough in my room to make the cool draught from the *bādgīr* very pleasant. These wind-towers are a feature of all Persian cities, breaking the monotony of the flat roofs.

Letters can be sent once a week from Isfahan, and there is another opportunity very safe and much taken advantage of, the " Telegraph *chapar*," a British official messenger, who rides up and down between Bushire and Tihran at stated intervals. The Persian post is a wretched institution, partaking of the general corruption of Persian officialism, and nowhere, unless *registered*, are letters less safe than in Tihran.[1] I shall send this, scrappy as it is, as I may not be here for another week's mail. I. L. B.

[1] Nearly all my non-registered letters to England failed to reach their destination.

LETTER XIII

JULFA, *April 29.*

EACH day has been completely filled up since I wrote, and this is probably the last here. My dear old Cabul tent, a *shuldari*, also Indian, and a servants' tent made here on a plan of my own, are pitched in one of the compounds to exercise the servants in the art, and it really looks like going after many delays.

A few festivities have broken the pleasant monotony of life in this kindly and hospitable house—dinner parties, European and Armenian ; a picnic on the Kuh Sufi, from which there is a very fine panoramic view of the vast plain and its surrounding mountains, and of the immense ruins of Isfahan and Julfa, with the shrunken remains of both ; and a " church picnic."

From Kuh Sufi is seen how completely, and with a sharp line of definition, the arid desert bounds the green oasis of cultivated and irrigated gardens which surround the city, and which are famous for the size and lusciousness of their fruit. From a confusion of ruinous or ragged walls of mud, of ruined and modern houses standing complacently among heaps of rubbish, and from amidst a greenery which redeems the scene, the blue tiled dome of the Masjid-i-Shah, a few minarets, and the great dome of the Medresseh, denuded of half its tiles, rise conspicuously. Long lines of mud streets and caravanserais, gaunt in their ruin, stretch into the desert, and the

city once boasting of 650,000 inhabitants and a splendid
court survives with a population of less than 80,000 at
the highest estimate.

The "church picnic" was held in a scene of decay, but
260 people, with all the women but three in red, enlivened
it. It was in the grounds of the old palace of Haft
Dast, in which Fatteh Ali Shah died, close to one of the
three remarkable bridges of Isfahan, the Pul-i-Kajū.
These bridges are magnificent. Their construction is
most peculiar, and their roadways being flat they are
almost unique in Persia.

The Pul-i-Kajū, though of brick, has stone piers of immense size, which are arched over so as to form a level
causeway. On this massive structure the upper bridge is
built, comprising a double series of rooms at each pier
with doorways overlooking the river, and there are staircases and rooms also in the upper piers.

The Chahar Bagh bridge is also quaint and magnificent,
with its thirty-three arches, some of them very large, its
corridors for foot passengers, and chambers above each
pier, each chamber having three openings to the river.
These bridges have a many-storied look, from their
innumerable windows at irregular altitudes, and form a
grand approach to the city.

As at first, so now at last the most impressive thing to
me about the Zainderud next to its bridges is the extent
to which rinsing, one of the processes of dyeing, is carried
on upon its shingle flats. Isfahan dyed fabrics are famous
and beautiful, heavy cottons of village make and unbleached cottons of Manchester make being brought here
to be dyed and printed.

There is quite a population of dyers, and now that
the river is fairly low, many of them have camped for
the season in little shelters of brushwood erected on the
gravel banks. For fully half-a-mile these banks are

covered with the rinsers of dyed and printed calicoes, and with mighty heaps of their cottons. Hundreds of pieces after the rinsing are laid closely together to dry, indigo and turquoise blue, brown and purple madder, Turkey red and saffron predominating, a vile aniline colour showing itself here and there. Some of the smaller dyers have their colour vats by the river, but most of the cotton is brought from Isfahan, ready dyed, on donkeys' backs, with the rinsers in attendance.

Along the channels among the shingle banks are rows of old millstones, and during much of the day a rinser stands in front of each up to his knees in water. His methods are rough, and the cotton must be good which stands his treatment. Taking in his hands a piece of soaked half-wrung cotton, from fifteen to twenty yards long, he folds it into five feet and bangs it on the millstone with all his might, roaring a tuneless song all the time, till he fails from fatigue. The noise is tremendous, and there will be more yet, for the river is not nearly at its lowest point. When the piece has had the water beaten out of it a boy spreads it out on the gravel, and keeps it wet by dashing water over it, and then the process of beating is repeated. The coloured spray rising from each millstone in the bright sunshine is very pretty. Each rinser has his watchdog to guard the cottons on the bank, and between the banging, splashing, and singing, the barking of the dogs and the shouts of the boys, it is a noisy and cheery scene.

I have heard that certain unscrupulous English makers were in the habit of sending "loaded" cottons here, but that the calico printers have been a match for them, for the calico printer weighs his cloth before he buys it, washes and dries it, and then weighs it again. A man must "get up very early" if he means to cheat a Persian.

The patterns and colours are beautiful. Quilts, "table-cloths" (for use on the floor), and *chadars* are often things of exquisite beauty. Indeed I have yielded to temptation, and to gratify my own tastes have bought some beautiful "table-cloths" for Bakhtiari women, printed chiefly in indigo and brown madder on a white ground.

The temptations are great. I really need many things both for my own outfit and for presents to the Bakhtiaris, and pedlars come every day and unpack their tempting bundles in the small verandah. No Europeans and no women of the upper classes can enjoy the delights of shopping in Persia, consequently the pedlar is a necessary institution.

Here they are of the humbler sort. They have learned that it is useless to display rich Turkestan and Feraghan carpets, gold and silver jewellery, inlaid arms, stuffs worked with gold thread, or any of the things which tempt the travelling Feringhi, so they bring all sorts of common fabrics, printed cambrics, worthless woollen stuffs, and the stout piece cottons and exquisitely-printed cotton squares of Isfahan.

At almost any hour of the day a salaaming creature squatting at the door is seen, caressing a big bundle, which on seeing you he pats in a deprecating manner, looks up appealingly, declares that he is your "sacrifice," and that with great trouble and loss he has got just the thing the *khanum* wants. If you hesitate for one moment the bundle is opened, and on his first visit he invariably shows flaring Manchester cottons first; but if you look and profess disgust, he produces cottons printed here, strokes them lovingly, and asks double their value for them. You offer something about half. He recedes and you advance till a compromise is arrived at representing the fair price.

But occasionally, as about a table-cloth, if they see

that you admire it very much but will not give the price asked, they swear by Allah that they will not abate a fraction, pack up their bundle, and move off in well-simulated indignation, probably to return the next day to offer the article on your own terms. Mrs. Bruce has done the bargaining, and I have been only an amused looker-on. I should prefer doing without things to the worry and tedium of the process of buying them.

The higher class of pedlars, such as those who visit the *andaruns* of the rich, go in couples, with a donkey or servant to carry their bundles.

I mentioned that the Amir-i-Panj had called and had asked me to visit his wife. I sent a message to say that my entrance into Isfahan had been so disagreeable that I should be afraid to pass through its gates again, to which he replied that he would take care that I met with no incivility. So an afternoon visit was arranged, and he sent a splendid charger for me, one of the finest horses I have seen in Persia, a horse for Mirza Yusuf, and an escort of six cavalry soldiers, which was increased to twelve at the city gate. The horse I rode answered the description—" a neck clothed with thunder,"—he was perfectly gentle, but his gait was that of a creature too proud to touch the earth. It was exhilarating to be upon such an animal.

The cavalry men rode dashing animals, and wore white Astrakan high caps, and the *cortège* quite filled up the narrow alley where it waited, and as it passed through the Chahar Bagh and the city gate, with much prancing and clatter, no "tongue wagged" either of dervish or urchin.

At the entrance to the Amir's house I was received by an *aide-de-camp* and a number of soldier-servants, and was "conducted" into a long room opening by many windows upon a beautiful garden full of peach blossom, violets, and irises; the table was covered with very pretty confectionery, including piles of *gaz*, a favourite sweet-meat, made of manna which is chiefly collected within eighty miles of Isfahan. Coffee was served in little cups in filigree gold receptacles, and then the Amir-i-Panj appeared in a white uniform, with a white lambskin cap, and asked "permission to have the honour of accompanying me to the *andarun*."

Persian politeness is great, and the Amir, though I think he is a Turk and not a Persian, is not deficient in it. Such phrases as "My house is purified by your presence, I live a thousand years in this visit," etc., were freely used.

This man, who receives from all a very high character, and whom Moslems speak of as a "saint," is the most interesting Moslem I have met. In one sense a thoroughly religious man, he practises all the virtues which he knows, almsgiving to the extent of self-denial, without distinction of creed, charity in word and deed, truth, purity, and justice.

I had been much prepossessed in his favour not only from Dr. Bruce's high opinion of him but by the unbounded love and reverence which my interpreter has for him. Mirza Yusuf marched on foot from Bushire to Isfahan, without credentials, an alien, and penniless, and this good man hearing of him took him into his house, and treated him as a welcome guest till a friend of his, a Moslem, a general in the Persian army, also good and generous, took him to Tihran, where he remained as his guest for some months, and was introduced into the best Persian society. From him I learned how beautiful and pure a life may be even in a corrupt nation. When he bowed to kiss the Amir's hand, with grateful affection in his face, his "benefactor," as he always calls him, turned to me and said, "He is to me as a dear son, God will be with him."

The garden is well laid out, and will soon be full of flowers. The Amir seemed to love them passionately. He said that they gave rest and joy, and are "the fringes of the garment of God." He could not cut them, he said, "Their beauty is in their completeness from root to petals, and cutting destroys it."

A curtained doorway in the high garden wall, where the curtains were held aside by servants, leads into the court of the *andarun,* where flowers again were in the ascendant, and vines concealed the walls. The son, a small boy, met us and kissed my hand. Mirza had told me that he had never passed through this wall, and had never seen the ladies, but when I proposed to leave him outside, the Amir said he would be welcome, that he wished for much conversation, and for his wife to hear about the position and education of women in England.

The beautiful reception-room looked something like home. The pure white walls and honeycombed ceiling are touched and decorated with a pale shade of blue, and the ground of the patterns of the rich carpets on the floor is in the same delicate colour, which is repeated in the brocaded stuffs with which the divans are covered. A half-length portrait of the Amir in a sky-blue uniform, with his breast covered with orders, harmonises with the general "scheme" of colour. The *takchahs* in the walls are utilised for vases and other objects in alabaster, jade, and bronze. A tea-table covered with sweetmeats, a tea equipage on the floor, and some chairs completed the furnishing.

The Amir stood till his wife came in, and then asked permission to sit down, placing Mirza, who discreetly lowered his eyes when the lady entered, and never raised them again, on the floor.

She is young, tall, and somewhat stout. She was much rouged, and her eyes, to which the arts of the toilet could add no additional beauty, were treated with *kohl*, and the eyebrows artificially extended. She wore fine gray socks, white skin-fitting tights, a black satin skirt, or rather flounce, embroidered in gold, so *bouffante* with flounces of starched crinoline under it that when she sat down it stood out straight, not even touching the chair. A chemise of spangled gauze, and a pale blue gold-embroidered zouave jacket completed a costume which is dress, not clothing. The somewhat startling effect was toned down by a beautiful Constantinople silk gauze veil, sprigged in pale pink and gold, absolutely transparent, which draped her from head to foot.

I did not get away in less than two hours. The Amir and Mirza, used to each other's modes of expression, found no difficulties, and Mirza being a man of education as well as intelligence, thought was conveyed as easily as fact. The lady kept her fine eyes lowered except when her husband spoke to her.

The chief topics were the education and position of women in England, religion, politics, and the future of Persia, and on all the Amir expressed himself with a breadth and boldness which were astonishing. How far the Amir has gone in the knowledge of the Christian faith I cannot say, nor do I feel at liberty to repeat his most interesting thoughts. A Sunni, a liberal, desiring complete religious liberty, absolutely tolerant to the *Bābis*, grateful for the kindness shown to some of them by the British Legation, and for the protection still given to them at the C. M. S. house, admiring Dr. Bruce's persevering work, and above all the Medical Mission, which he regards as " the crown of beneficence " and " the true imitation of the life of the Great Prophet, Jesus," all he said showed a strongly religious nature, and a philosophical mind much given to religious thought. " All true religions aim at one thing," he said, " to make the heart and life pure."

He asked a good deal about my travels, and special objects of interest in travelling, and was surprised when I told him that I nearly always travel alone ; but after a moment's pause he said, " I do not understand that you were for a moment alone, for you had everywhere the love, companionship, and protection of God."

He regards as the needs of Persia education, religious liberty (the law which punishes a Moslem with death for embracing Christianity is still on the statute-book), roads, and railroads, and asked me if I had formed any opinion on the subject. I said that it appeared to me that security for the earnings of labour, and equal laws for rich and poor, administered by incorruptible judges, should accompany education. I much fear that he thinks incorruptible judges a vision of a dim future !

The subject of the position of women in England and the height to which female education is now carried interested him extremely. He wished his wife to understand everything I told him. The success of women in examinations in art, literature, music, and other things, and the political wisdom and absolutely constitutional rule of Queen Victoria, all interested him greatly. He asked if the women who took these positions were equally good as wives and mothers ? I could only refer again to Queen Victoria. An Oriental cannot understand the position of unmarried women with us, or dissociate it from religious vows, and the Amir heard with surprise that a very large part of the philanthropic work which is done in England is done by women who either from accident or design have neither the happiness nor the duties of married life. He hopes to see women in Persia educated and emancipated from the trammels of certain customs, " but," he added, " all reform in this direction must come slowly, and grow naturally out of a wider education, if it is to be good and not hurtful."

He asked me what I should like to see in Isfahan, but when I mentioned the prison he said he should be ashamed to show it, and that except for political offences imprisonment is not much resorted to, that Persian justice is swift and severe—the bastinado, etc., not incarceration.

Afterwards I paid a similar visit to the house of Mirza Yusuf's other "benefactor," also a good and charitable man, who, as he speaks French well, acted as interpreter in the *andarun*.

A few days later the Amir-i-Panj, accompanied by General Faisarallah Khan, called on Dr. Bruce and on me, and showed how very agreeable a morning visit might be made, and the following day the Amir sent the same charger and escort for me, and meeting him and Dr. Bruce in the Chahar Bagh, we visited the *Medresseh*, a combined mosque and college, and the armoury, where we were joined by two generals and were afterwards entertained at tea in the Standard Room, while a military band played outside. The Amir had ordered some artificers skilled in the brass-work for which Isfahan is famous to exhibit their wares in one of the rooms at the armoury, and in every way tried to make the visit more agreeable than an inspection of the jail! He advises me not to wear a veil in the Bakhtiari country, and to be "as European as possible."

The armoury, of which he has had the organising, does not fall within my province. There are many large rooms with all the appliances of war in apparently perfect order for the equipment of 5000 men.

With equal brevity I pass over the *Medresseh*, whose silver gates and exquisite tiles have been constantly described. Decay will leave little of this beautiful building in a few years. The tiles of the dome, which can be seen for miles, are falling off, and even in the

halls of instruction and in the grand mosque under the
dome, which are completely lined and roofed by tiles, the
making of some of which is a lost art, one may augur
the approach of ruin from the loss or breakage here and
there.   In the rooms or cells occupied by the students,
who study either theology or law, there are some very
fine windows executed in the beautiful tracery common
to Persia and Kashmir, but the effect of beauty passing
into preventible decay is very mournful.

Isfahan too I barely notice, for the best of all reasons,
that I have not seen it!   Though a fourth part of it is
in ruins, and its population is not an eighth of what it
was in the days of Shah Abbas, it is a fairly thriving
commercial emporium with an increasing British trade.
Indeed here Russian commercial influence may be said
to cease, and that of England to become paramount.
It is the paradise of Manchester and Glasgow cottons :
woollen goods come from Austria and Germany, glass
from Austria, crockery from England, candles and kerosene
represent Russia.   Our commercial supremacy in Isfahan
cannot be disputed.   I am almost tired of hearing of it.
Opium, tobacco, carpets from the different provinces,
and cotton and rice for native consumption, are the chief
exports.   Opium is increasingly grown round the city,
and up the course of the Zainderud.   Of the 4500 cases
exported, worth £90 a case, three-fourths go to China.
Its cultivation is so profitable and has increased so
rapidly to the neglect of food crops that the Prince
Governor has issued an order that one part of cereals
shall be sown for every four of the opium poppy.

The cotton in the bazars, through which one can walk
under cover for between two and three miles, is of the
best quality, owing to the successful measures taken by
the calico printers to defeat the roguery of the cheating
manufacturers.   All the European necessaries and many

of the luxuries of life are obtainable, and the Isfahan
bazars are the busiest in Persia except those of Tabriz.

It is only fair to this southern capital to say that if one
can walk over two miles under the roofs of its fine
bazars, one can ride for many miles among its ruins,
which have desolation without stateliness, and are chiefly
known for the production of the excellent wild asparagus
which is used lavishly on European tables at this season.

The "Persian Versailles," the Palace of Forty Pillars,
each pillar formed of shafts enriched with colour and
intricate work, and resting on a marble lion, the shaking
Minarets, the Masjid-i-Shah with its fine dome of pea-
cock-blue tiles, all falling into premature decay, remain
to attest its former greatness; the other noble palaces,
mosques, caravanserais, and *Medressehs* are ruinous, the
superb pleasure gardens are overgrown with weeds or
are used for vetches and barley, the tanks are foul or
filled up, the splendid plane trees have been cut down
for fuel, or are dragging out a hollow existence—every
one, as elsewhere in Persia, destroys, no one restores.
The armoury is the one exception to the general law of
decay.

Yet Isfahan covered an area of twenty-four miles in
circumference, and with its population of 650,000 souls
was until the seventeenth century one of the most magnificent cities of the East. Its destruction last century by
an Afghan conqueror, who perpetrated a fifteen days'
massacre, and the removal of the court to Tihran, have
reduced it to a mere commercial centre, a "distributing
point," and as such, its remains may take a new lease of
life. It has a newspaper called the *Farhang,* which
prints little bits of news, chiefly personal. Its editor
moves on European lines so far as to have "interviewed"
me !

There are manufactures in Isfahan other than the

successful printing and dyeing of cottons; viz., earthenware, china, brass-work, velvet, satin, tents, coarse cottons, glass, swords, guns, pistols, jewellery, writing paper and envelopes, silk brocades, satins, gunpowder, bookbinding, gold thread, etc.

The plateau on which Isfahan stands, about seventy miles from east to west and twenty from north to south, and enclosed by high mountains with a striking outline, lies 5400 feet above the sea. The city has a most salubrious climate, and is free from great extremes both of heat and cold. The Zainderud, on whose left bank it is situated, endows much of the plain with fertility on its way to its undeserved doom in a partially-explored swamp.

This Christian town, called a suburb, though it is really two and a half miles from Isfahan, is a well-built and well-peopled nucleus. It is not mixed up with ruins as Isfahan is. They have a region to themselves chiefly in the direction of the Kuh Sufi. My impression of it after a month is that it is clean and comfortable-looking, Mr. Curzon's is that it is "squalid." I prefer mine!

It is a "city of waters." Streams taken from a higher level of the Zainderud glide down nearly all its lanes, shaded by pollard mulberries, ash, elm, and the "sparrow-tongue" willow, which makes the best firewood, and being "planted by the rivers of water," grows so fast that it bears lopping annually, and besides affording fuel supplies the twigs which are used for roofing such rooms as are not arched.

The houses, some of which are more than three centuries old, are built of mud bricks, the roofs are usually arched, and the walls are from three to five feet thick. All possess planted courtyards and vineyards, and gardens into which channels are led from the streams in the streets. These streams serve other purposes: continually a group of Armenian women may be seen washing their clothes in them, while others are drinking or drawing water just below. The lanes are about twenty feet wide and have narrow rough causeways on both sides of the water-channel. It is difficult on horseback to pass a foot passenger without touching him in some of them.

Great picturesqueness is given to these leafy lanes by the companies of Armenian women in bright red dresses and pure white robes, slowly walking through them at all hours of daylight, visions of bright eyes and rosy cheeks. I have never yet seen a soiled white robe! Long blank mud walls, low gateways, an occasional row of mean shops, open porches of churches, dim and cool, and an occasional European on foot or horseback, and groups of male Armenians, whose dress so closely approaches the European as to be without interest, and black-robed priests gliding to the churches are all that is usually to be seen. It sounds dull, perhaps.

Many of the houses of the rich Armenians, some of which are now let to Europeans, are extremely beautiful inside, and even those occupied by the poorer classes, in which a single lofty room can be rented for twopence a week, are very pretty and appropriate. But no evidence of wealth is permitted to be seen from the outside. It is only a few years since the Armenians were subject to many disabilities, and they have even now need to walk warily lest they give offence. As, for instance, an Armenian was compelled to ride an ass instead of a horse, and when that restriction was relaxed, he had to show his inferiority by dismounting from his horse before entering the gates of Isfahan.

They were not allowed to have bells on their churches, (at Easter I wished they had none still), but now the *Egglesiah Wang* (the great church) has a fine campaᵔ ile

over 100 feet high in its inner court.   The ancient mode
of announcing the hours of worship is still affectionately
adhered to, however.   It consists of drumming with a
mallet on a board hanging from two posts, and successfully breaks the sleep of the neighbourhood for the daily
service which begins before daylight.

The Armenians, like the rich Persians, prudently keep
to the low gateways, which, with the absence of windows
and all exterior ornament, give the lanes so mean an
aspect, and tend to make one regard the beauty and even
magnificence within with considerable surprise.

In England a rich man, partly for his own delectation,
and partly, if he be " the architect of his own fortune,"
to impose his position ocularly on his poorer neighbours,
displays his wealth in all ways and on most occasions.
In Persia his chief pleasure must be to hoard it and con-
template it, for any unusual display of it in equipages or
furnishings is certain to bring down upon him a " squeeze,"
at Tihran in the shape of a visit from the Shah with its
inevitable consequences, and in the Provinces in that of
a requisition from the governor.

For a man to " enlarge his gates " is to court destruction.   Poor men have low gates, which involve stooping,
to prevent rich men's servants from entering their houses
on horseback on disagreeable errands.   Christian churches
have remarkably low doors elsewhere than in Julfa, to
prevent the Moslems from stabling their cattle in them.
Rich men affect mean entrances in order not to excite the
rapacity of officialism, according to the ancient proverb,
" He that exalteth his gate seeketh destruction " (Proverbs
xvii. 19).   Only Royal gates and the gates of officials who
represent Royalty are high.

The Armenian merchants have, like the Europeans,
their offices in Isfahan.   The rest of the people get
their living by the making and selling of wine, keeping

small shops, making watches and jewellery, carpentering,
in which they are very skilful, and market-gardening;
they are thrifty and industrious, and there is very little
real poverty.

The selling of wine does not conduce to the peace of
Julfa.   A mixture of sour wine and *arak*, a coarse spirit,
is very intoxicating, and Persians, when they do drink,
drink till they are drunk, and the abominable concealed
traffic in liquor with the Moslems of the town is apt
to produce disgraceful brawls.

Wine can be bought for fourpence a quart, but the
upper classes make their own, and it costs less than this.
Wines are both red and white, and one red wine is said
to be like good Chianti.   The Armenians tipple and also
get drunk, priests included.   It is said that some of the
jars used in fermenting are between 200 and 300 years
old.

The excellent education given in the C. M. S. school
has had the effect of stimulating the Armenian schools
and of producing among the young men a large
emigration to India, Batavia, Constantinople, and even
England.   Only the dullards as a rule remain in Julfa
Some rise high in Persian and even in Turkish employment.

The Armenian women are capital housewives and
very industrious.   In these warm evenings the poorer
women sit outside their houses in groups knitting.
The knitting of socks is a great industry, and a woman
can earn 4s. a month by it, which is enough to live upon.

In Julfa, and it may be partly owing to the presence
of a European community, the Christians have nothing
complain of, and, so far as I can see, they are on terms
equality with the Persians.

However, Isfahan is full of religious intolerance wh
can easily be excited to frenzy, and the arrogance of the

mollahs has increased since the fall from almost regal state of the Zil-i-Sultan, the Shah's eldest son, into the position of a provincial governor, for he curbed them somewhat, and now the restraint is removed. However, it is against the Jews and the *Bābis*, rather than the Christians, that their hostility is directed.

A few weeks ago some *Bābis* were peaceably returning to a neighbouring village, when they were attacked, and seven of their number were massacred under atrocious circumstances, the remainder taking refuge for a time in the British Telegraph office. Several of both sexes who escaped are in concealment here in a room in the Hospital compound, one of them with a broken jaw.

The hiding of these *Bābis* has given great umbrage to the bigots of Isfahan, though the Amir-i-Panj justified it on all grounds, and about the time I arrived it was said that a thousand city fanatics purposed to attack the mission premises. But at one of the mosques there is a mollah, who with Gamaliel-like wisdom urged upon them "that if 300 Moslems were killed nothing would happen, but if a single European were killed, what then ?"[1]

I cannot close this letter without a few words on the Armenian churches, some of which I visited with Mr. and Dr. Aganoor, and others with Dr. Bruce. The ceremony representing the washing of the disciples' feet on the Armenian Holy Thursday was a most magnificent one as regards the antique splendour and extreme beauty of the vestments and jewels of the officiating bishop, but

[1] I have written nothing about this fast-increasing sect of the *Bābis*, partly because being a secret sect, I doubt whether the doctrines which suffered to leak out form really any part of its esoteric teaching, and partly because those Europeans who have studied the *Bābis* most candidly diametrically opposed in their views of their tenets and practice, some holding that their aspirations are after a purer life, while others, and I think a majority, believe that their teachings are subversive of morality and of the purity of domestic life.

the feet, which are washed in rose-water and anointed, are not, as in Rome, those of beggars, but of neophytes costumed in pure white. Incense, embroideries, crowds of white-robed women, and other accessories made the function an imposing one.

The Cathedral, a part of the Monastery, has a narrow winding approach and a thick door, for ecclesiastics were not always as safe as they are now. In the outer court is the campanile before mentioned. The floor is paved with monumental slabs, and among the graves are those of several Europeans. Piles of logs look as if the Julfa carpenters seasoned their wood in this court!

The church is divided by a rail into two compartments. The dome is rich with beaten gold, and the dado is of very fine tiles, which produce a striking effect. The embroideries and the carpets, some of which are worth fabulous sums, are between two and three centuries old. The vestments and ornaments of the priests are very fine, and suggest the attire of the Aaronic priesthood.

It is a striking building, and the amount of gold and colour, toned into a certain harmony by time, produces a gorgeous effect. The outer compartment has a singular interest, for 230 years ago its walls were decorated with religious paintings, on a large scale, of events in Bible history, from the creation downwards. Some are copies, others original, and they are attributed to Italian artists. They are well worth careful study as representing the conceptions which found favour among the Armenian Christians of that day. They are terribly realistic, but are certainly instructive, especially the illustrations of the miracles and parables.

In one of the latter a man with a huge beam sticking out of one eye is represented as looking superciliously with the other at a man with an insignificant spike projecting. The death of Dives is a horrible representation.

His soul, in the likeness of a very small nude figure, is represented as escaping from the top of his head, and is being escorted to the entrance of the lower regions by a flight of small black devils. The idea of the soul emerging from the top of the head is evidently borrowed from the Moslems.

Our Lord is, I think, everywhere depicted as short, dark, and dark-haired, with eyebrows much curved, and a very long upper lip, without beauty or dignity, an ordinary Oriental workman.

The picture of the Cathedral is an enormous canvas, representing the day when " before Him shall be gathered all nations." The three persons of the Trinity are there, and saints and angels are portrayed as worshipping, or as enjoying somewhat earthly but perfectly innocent delights.

In this the conception is analogous to those celebrated circular pictures in which the Buddhistic future is unrolled, and which I last saw in the monasteries of Lesser Tibet. The upper or heavenly part is insignificant and very small, while the torments of the lost in the lower part are on a very large scale, and both the devils and the nude human sufferers in every phase of anguish have the appearance of life size. The ingenuity of torment, however, is not nearly so great, nor are the scenes so revolting as those which Oriental imagination has depicted in the Buddhist hells. A huge mythical monster represents the mouth of hell, and into his flaming and smoking jaws the impenitent are falling. Does any modern Armenian believe that any of those whose bones lie under the huge blocks of stone in the cemetery in the red desert at the foot of Kuh Sufi have passed into " this place of torment "?

The other church which claims one's interest, though not used for worship, is that of St. George, the hero of the

fraudulent contract in bacon, as well as of the dragon
fight, to whom the Armenians as well as ourselves render
singular honour.

This church is a great place for "miracles" of healing,
and cells for the sick who come from a distance are
freely provided.   In a covered court are some large stones
in a group, one of them evidently the capital of a column.
Two of them have cavities at the top, and the sick kneel
before them, and as the voluble women who were there
told us, "they first pray to God and then to the stones,"
and finally pour water into these cavities and drink it.
The cure is either instantaneous or occurs at any time
within fifteen days, and in every case the patient hears
the voice of St. George telling him to go home when it
is complete.

These stones, according to the legend told by the
women and popularly believed by the uneducated, took
it into their heads to come from Etchmiadzin in
Armenia, the residence of the *Catholicos*, in one night,
and deposited themselves where the church now stands.
Seven times they were taken into Faraidan, eighty miles
from Julfa, and as often returned, and their manifest pre-
dilection was at last rewarded by a rest of centuries.
There were a number of sick people waiting for healing,
for which of course fees are bestowed.

The Armenians, especially the women, pay great
attention to the externals of their religion.   Some of its
claims are very severe, such as the daily service before
daylight, winter and summer, and the long fasts, which
they keep with surprising loyalty, *i.e.* among the poor in
towns and in the villages.   For at least one-sixth of the
year they are debarred from the use of meat or even
eggs, and are permitted only vegetable oils, fruits, vegetables, and grain.   Spirits and wine, however, are not
prohibited.

I really believe that their passionate attachment to their venerable church, the oldest of all national churches, is fostered by those among them who have ceased to believe its doctrines, as a necessity of national existence. I doubt very much whether the " Reformed " congregations, which have been gathered out here and elsewhere, would survive the withdrawal of foreign aid. Rather, I think, they would revert to the original type.

Superstitions without number are mixed up with their beliefs, and are countenanced by the priests. The *meron* or holy oil used in baptism and for other purposes has the stamp of charlatanism upon it. It is made in Etchmiadzin.

Rose leaves are collected in an immense vat, which is filled with water, and at a set time the monks and nuns form a circle round it, and repeat prayers till " fermentation" begins. They claim that the so-called fermentation is a miracle due to the prayers offered. Oil, probably attar of roses, rises to the surface, and this precious *meron* is sent to the Armenian churches throughout the world about once in four or five years. In Persia those who bear it are received with an *istikbal* or procession of welcome.

It is used not only in baptism and other rites but at the annual ceremony of washing the Cross at Christmas, when some of it is poured into the water and is drunk by the worshippers. In the villages they make a paste by mixing this water and oil with earth, which is made into balls and kept in the houses for " luck." If a dog licks a bowl or other vessel, and thus renders it unclean, rubbing it round with one of these balls restores it to purity.

At a village in Faraidan there is an ancient New Testament, reputed to be of the sixth century. To this MS. people come on pilgrimage from all quarters, even from Fars, Tihran, and Armenia, to be healed of their diseases, and they make offerings to it, and practically render it worship.

To go and pray on a newly-made grave is a remedy for childlessness much resorted to by childless wives. When two boys fight, and one of them is hurt, or when any one is injured by a dog or by a tree falling, they wash the damaged person in water, and then throw the water over the boy, dog, or tree which has been the cause of the injury, believing that in this way the mischief is transferred.

When any one is ill of fright and the cause is not known, the nuns come to the house, and pour wax into a basin of boiling water, noting the form it takes, such as a snake, a dog, or a frog. In a case lately they went out and killed a snake, for the thing whose form the wax takes ought to be killed; but as this might often be difficult or unsuitable, they compromise the matter by throwing the water (not boiling, I hope) over the nearest dog or toad, or anything else which is supposed to be the culprit.

On the first Monday in Lent the women wash their knitting needles for luck in a stream which runs through Julfa. The children educated in the Mission schools laugh at these and many other superstitions.

The dress of the Armenian women is very showy, but too much of a *huddle*. Red is the dominant colour, a carnation red with white patterns sprawling over it. They wear coloured trousers concealed by a long skirt. The visible under-garment is a long, "shaped" dress of Turkey red. Over this is worn a somewhat scanty gown of red and white cotton, open in front, and very short-waisted, and over this a plain red pelisse or outer garment, often quilted, open in front, gashed up the sides, and falling below the knees. Of course this costume is liable to many modifications in the way of material, and embroidered jackets, heavily trimmed with jewellery and the like.   As fashion is unchanging the acquisition and hoarding of garments are carried to a great extent.

There are two marked features of Armenian dress, one, the massive silver girdle made of heavy chased-silver links four inches long by two deep, often antique and always of antique design, which falls much below the waist in front, and is used to confine the ends of the white sheet which envelops an Armenian woman out of doors, so that it may hang evenly all round.   The other is a skull-cap of embroidered silk or cloth, placed well back on the head above the many hanging plaits in which the hair is worn, with a black velvet coronet in front, from which among the richer women rows of coins depend.   This, which is very becoming to the brilliant complexion and comely face below it, is in its turn covered by a half handkerchief, and over this is gracefully worn, when not gracelessly clutched, a *chadar* or drapery of printed cambric or muslin.   A white band bound across the chin up to the lips suggests a broken jaw, and the *tout ensemble* of the various wrappings of the head a perennial toothache.

I. L. B.

LETTER XIV

JULFA, *April 30.*

YOU will be tired of Julfa though I am not. I fully
expected to have left it a fortnight ago, but unavoidable
delays have occurred. My caravan and servants started
this morning, and I leave myself in a few hours.

Upon my horse I have bestowed the suggestive
name of *Screw*. He is fairly well-bred, big-headed,
big-eared, small-bodied, bright bay, fine-coated, slightly
flat-footed, and with his fore hoofs split in several places
from the coronet nearly to the shoe. He is an un-
doubted *yabu*, and has carried loads for many a day.
He has a long stride, shies badly, walks very fast, canters
easily, and at present shows no tendency to tumble
down.[1]

I have had pleasant rides alone, crossing the definite dividing line between the desert and the oasis of
cultivation and irrigation, watching the daily development of the various crops and the brief life of the wild
flowers, creeping through the green fields on the narrow
margins of irrigating ditches, down to the Pul-i-Kajū,
and returning to the green lanes of Julfa by the

---

[1] *Screw* never became a friend or companion, scarcely a comrade, but
showed plenty of pluck and endurance, climbed and descended horrible
rock ladders over which a horse with a rider had never passed before, was
steady in fords, and at the end of three and a half months of severe
travelling and occasional scarcity of food was in better condition than
when he left Julfa.

bright waters of the Zainderud crimsoning in the setting sun.

For in the late cool and breezy weather, not altogether free from clouds and showers, there have been some gorgeous sunsets, and magnificent colouring of the depth and richness which people call tropical, has blazed extravagantly; and from the violet desert to the indigo storm-clouds on the still snow-patched Kuhrūd mountains, from the vivid green of the oasis to the purple crags in dark relief against a sky of flame, all things have been new.

Two Sundays witnessed two incidents, one the baptism of a young Moslem in a semi-private fashion, who shortly afterwards renounced Christianity, and the other that of a respectable Mohammedan merchant in Isfahan, who has long pleaded for baptism, presenting himself at the altar rails at the Holy Communion, resolved that if he were not permitted to confess Christ as Divine in one way he would in another. He was passed over, to my great regret, if he be sincere, but I suppose the Rubric leaves no choice.[1]

I have written little about my prospective journey because there has been a prolonged uncertainty about it, and even now I cannot give any definite account of the project, except that the route lies through an altogether mountainous region, in that part of the province of Luristan known in Persia colloquially as the "Bakhtiari country," from being inhabited by the Bakhtiari Lurs, chiefly nomads. The pros and cons as to my going have been innumerable, and the two people in Persia who know the earlier part of the route say that the character of the people makes it impossible for a lady to travel

---

[1] He has since been baptized, but for safety had to relinquish his business and go to India, where he is supporting himself, and his conduct is satisfactory.

among them.   On the other hand, I have the consent
and help of the highest authorities, Persian and English,
and shall not go too far, but shall return to Isfahan in
case things should turn out as is feared.   The exploration
of a previously unexplored region will be in itself interesting, but whether there will be sufficient of the human
interests, which I chiefly care for, I doubt ; in that case
the journey will be dull.

At all events I shall probably have to return here in
two months,[1] but such a journey for myself and two servants in such a region requires extensive preparations,
and I have brought all my own travelling "dodges" into
requisition, with a selection of those of other people.

It is considered desirable to carry stores from Isfahan
for forty days, except flour and rice, which can be obtained
a week's march from here.   At the British Legation
I was kindly supplied with many tins of preserved meat,
and milk, and jam, and besides these I am only taking
a quantity of Edwards' Desiccated Soup, portable and
excellent, twelve pounds of tea, and ten pounds of candles.
The great thing in planning is to think of what one can
do without.   Two small bottles of saccharin supply the
place of forty pounds of sugar.

Two *yekdans* contain my stores, cooking and table utensils and personal luggage, a waterproof bag my bedding,
and a divided packing-case, now empty, goes for the flour
and rice.   Everything in the *yekdans* is put up in bags
made of the coarse cotton of the country.   The tents and
tent-poles, which have been socketed for easier transport
on crooked mountain paths, and a camp-bed made from
a Kashmiri pattern in Tihran, are all packed in covers
made from the gunny bags in which sugar is imported,

[1] I never returned, and only at the end of three and a half months
emerged from the "Bakhtiari country" at Burujird after a journey of
700 miles.

and so are double sets of large and small iron tent-pegs.

Presents for the " savages " are also essential, and I have succeeded in getting 100 thimbles, many gross of small china buttons which, it is said, they like to sew on children's caps, 1000 needles, a quantity of Russian thread, a number of boxes with mirror tops, two dozen double-bladed knives, and the same number of strong scissors, Kashmir *kamarbands*, gay handkerchiefs for women's heads, Isfahan printed " table-cloths," dozens of bead bracelets and necklaces, leather purses and tobacco pouches, and many other things.

I take three tents, including a *shuldari*, five feet square, and only weighing ten pounds.   My kit is reduced to very simple elements, a kettle, two copper pots which fit into each other, a frying pan, cooking knife and spoon, a tray instead of a table, a chair, two plates, a teacup and saucer, a soup plate, mug, and teapot, all of course in enamelled iron, a knife, fork, and two spoons.   This is ample for one person for any length of time in camp.

For this amount of baggage and for the sacks of flour and rice, weighing 160 lbs., which will hereafter be carried, I have four mules, none heavily laden, and two with such light loads that they can be ridden by my servants.   These mules, two *charvadars*, and a horse are engaged for the journey at two *krans* (16d.) a day each, the owner stipulating for a *bakhsheesh* of fifty *krans*, if at the end I am satisfied.   This sum is to cover food and all risks.

The animals are hired from a well-known *charvadar*, who has made a large fortune and is regarded as very trustworthy ; Dr. Bruce calls him the " prince of *charvadars*."   He and his son are going on the " trip." He has a quiet, superior manner, and when he came to judge of the weight of my loads, he said they were "very good—very right," a more agreeable verdict than muleteers are wont to pass upon baggage.[1]

The making of the contract with Hadji involved two important processes, the writing of it by a scribe and the sealing of it. The scribe is one of the most important persons in Persia. Every great man has one or more, and every little man has occasion for a scribe's services in the course of a year. He is the trusted depositary of an infinity of secrets. He moves with dignity and deliberation, his "writer's inkhorn" pendent from his girdle, and his physiognomy has been trained to that reticent, semi-mysterious expression common to successful solicitors in England.

Writing is a fine art in Persia. The characters are in themselves graceful, and lend themselves readily to decoration. The old illuminated MSS. are things of beauty; even my contract is ornamental. The scribe holds the paper in his left hand, and uses a reed pen with the nib cut obliquely, writing from right to left. The ink is thick, and is carried with the pens in a *papier-maché* inkhorn.

Hadji tells me with much pride that his son, Abbas Ali, can write "and will be very useful."

Sealing is instead of signing. As in Japan, every adult male has his seal, of agate or cornelian among the rich, and of brass or silver among the poor. The name is carefully engraved on the seal at a cost of from a half-

---

[1] Hadji Hussein deserves a passing recommendation. I fear that he is still increasing his fortune and has not retired. The journey was a very severe one, full of peril to his mules from robbers and dangerous roads, and not without risk to himself. With the exception of a few Orientalisms, which are hardly worth recalling, he was faithful and upright, made no attempt to overreach, kept to his bargain, was punctual and careful, and at Burujird we parted good friends. He was always most respectful to me, and I owe him gratitude for many kindnesses which increased my comfort. It is right to acknowledge that a part of the success of the journey was owing to the efficiency of the transport.

penny to 18s. a letter. Tihran is celebrated for its seal-cutters. No document is authentic without a seal as its signature.

Hadji took the contract and applied it to his fore-head in token of respect, touched the paper with his tongue to make it moist and receptive, waved it in the air to rid it of superfluous moisture, wetted his fingers on a spongy ball of silk full of Indian ink in the scribe's inkstand, rubbed the ink on the seal, breathed on it, and pressed it firmly down on the paper, which he held over the forefinger of his left hand. The smallest acts in Persia are regulated by rigid custom.

The remaining portion of my outfit, but not the least important, consists of a beautiful medicine chest of the most compact and portable make, most kindly given to me by Messrs. Burroughes and Wellcome, containing fifty small bottles of their invaluable "tabloids," a hypodermic syringe, and surgical instruments for simple cases. To these I have added a quantity of quinine, and Dr. Odling at Tihran gave me some valuable remedies. A quantity of bandages, lint, absorbent cotton, etc., completes this essential equipment. Among the many uncertainties of the future this appears certain, that the Bakhtiaris will be clamorous for European medicine.

I have written of my servants. Mirza Yusuf pleases me very much, Hassan the cook seems quiet, but not active, and I picture to myself the confusion of to-night in camp, with two men who know nothing about camp life and its makeshifts !

Whatever the summer brings, this is probably my last letter written from under a roof till next winter. I am sorry to leave Julfa and these kind friends, but the prospect of the unknown has its charms. I. L. B.

NOTES ON THE "BAKHTIARI COUNTRY" OR LURI-BUZURG

In introducing the following journal of a summer spent in Luri-Buzurg or Greater Luristan by a few explanatory notes, I desire to acknowledge the labours of those travellers who have preceded me over some of the earlier portions of the route, and my obligations to those careful explorers of half a century ago, who turned the light of modern research upon the antiquities of Lower Elam and the condition of its modern inhabitants, and whose earnestness and accuracy the traveller in Upper Elam and the Bakhtiari country may well desire to emulate.[1]

For the correction of those portions of my letters which attempt to describe a part of mountainous Luristan previously unexplored, I am deeply indebted

[1] The writers who have dealt with some of the earlier portions of my route are as follows: Henry Blosse Lynch, Esq., *Across Luristan to Ispahan*—*Proceedings of the R. G. S.*, September 1890. Colonel M. S. Bell, V.C., *A Visit to the Karun River and Kûm*—*Blackwood's Magazine*, April 1889. Colonel J. A. Bateman Champain, R.E., *On the Various Means of Communication between Central Persia and the Sea*—*Proceedings of the R. G. S.*, March 1883. Colonel H. L. Wells, R.E., *Surveying Tours in South-Western Persia*—*Proceedings of R. G. S.*, March 1883. Mr. Stack, *Six Months in Persia*, London, 1884. Mr. Mackenzie, *Speech*—*Proceedings of R. G. S.*, March 1883. The following among other writers have dealt with the condition of the Bakhtiari and Feili Lurs, and with the geography of the region to the west and south-west of the continuation of the great Zagros chain, termed in these notes the "Outer" and "Inner"

to a recent unpublished Geographical Report, to which any geographical interest which they may possess is altogether due. For the customs and beliefs of the Bakhtiaris I have had to depend entirely on my own investigations, made through an intelligent and faithful interpreter, whose desire for accuracy was scarcely exceeded by my own.

The accompanying sketch map represents an area of 15,000 square miles, lying, roughly speaking, between Lat. 31° and 34° N., and between Long. 48° and 51° E., and covering a distance of 300 miles from the Khana Mirza to Khuramabad.

The itinerary covers a distance of about 700 miles, a journey of three and a half months, chiefly in the region of the Upper Karun and its affluents, among which must be included the head-waters of the Ab-i-Diz.

During this time the Karun was traced, wherever the nature of its bed admitted of it, from the gorge of Dupulan, below which several travellers have investigated and reported its extraordinary windings, up to the Sar-Cheshmeh-i-Kurang, its reputed scource, a vigorous fountain spring with an altitude of 8000 feet in the steep limestone face of the north-eastern side of the Zard Kuh range, and upwards to its real source in the Kuh-i-Rang or "variegated mountain."

The Ab-i-Diz was found to carry off the water of a larger area than had been supposed; the north-west ranges of the Bakhtiari mountains, their routes touching those of the present writer at Khuramabad : Sir H. Rawlinson, *Notes of a March from Zohab to Khuzistan in 1836—Journal of the R.G.S.*, vol. ix., 1839. Sir A. H. Layard, *Early Adventures in Persia, Susiana, and Babylonia, including a residence among the Bakhtiari and other wild tribes*, 2 vols., London, 1887. Baron C. A. de Bode, *Travels in Luristan and Arabistan*, 2 vols., London, 1845. W. F. Ainsworth (Surgeon and Geologist to the Euphrates Expedition), *The River Karun*, London, 1890. General Schindler travelled over and described the Isfahan and Shuster route, and published a map of the country in 1884.

branches, the Ab-i-Burujird and the Kamandab, which drain the well-watered plain of Silakhor, almost yielding in importance to the Guwa and Gokun, which, uniting to form what, for convenience' sake, was termed the Ab-i-Basnoi, receive the drainage of the upper part of Faraidan, an important district of Persia proper.

A lake of marvellously coloured water, two and a half miles long by one mile wide, very deep, and with a persistent level, was found to occupy a hollow at the inner foot of the grand mountain Shuturun, and this, having no native name, was marked on the map as Lake Irene.

The Bakhtiari mountains are chains of precipitous parallel ranges, generally running north-west and south-east, the valleys which divide them and carry off their waters taking the same directions as far as the Kuh-i-Rang, where a remarkable change takes place, noticed in Letter XVII. This great mountain region, lying between the lofty plateau of Central Persia and the plains of Khuzistan, has continuous ranges of singular steepness, but rarely broken up into prominent peaks, the Kuh-i-Rang, the Kuh-i-Shahan, the Shuturun Kuh, and Dalonak being detached mountains.

The great ranges of the Kuh-i-Sukhta, the Kuh-i-Gerra, the Sabz Kuh, the Kala Kuh, and the Zard Kuh were crossed and recrossed by passes from 8000 to 11,000 feet in altitude; many of the summits were ascended, and the deep valleys between them, with their full-watered, peacock-green streams, were followed up wherever it was possible to do so. The magnificent mountain Kuh-i-Rang was ascertained to be not only a notable water-parting, but to indicate in a very marked manner two distinct mountain systems with remarkable peculiarities of drainage, as well as to form a colossal barrier between two regions which, for, the sake of intelligible description, were called "Upper Elam" and the "Bakhtiari country."

The same authority, for the same purpose, designated the two main and highest chains of mountains by the terms "Outer" and "Inner" ranges, the former being the one nearest the great Persian plateau, the latter the chain nearest to the Khuzistan plains. The conjectural altitudes of the peaks in this hitherto unexplored region have been brought down by some thousands of feet, and the "eternal snow" with which rumour had crested them has turned out a myth, the altitude of the highest summit being estimated at only a trifle over 13,000 feet.

The nearly continuous ranges south-east of the Kuh-i-Rang are pierced for the passage of water by a few remarkable rifts or *tangs*—the Outer range by the Tang-i-Ghezi, the outlet of the Zainderud towards Isfahan, and the Tang-i-Darkash Warkash, by which the drainage of the important districts of the Chahar Mahals passes to the Karun, the Inner range being pierced at the Tang-i-Dupulan by the Karun itself. North-west of the Kuh-i-Rang the rivers which carry the drainage of certain districts of south-west Persia to the sea pierce the main mountain ranges at right angles, passing through magnificent gorges and chasms from 3000 to 5000 feet in depth.

Among the mountains, but especially in the formation south-east of the Kuh-i-Rang, there are many alpine valleys at altitudes of from 7000 to 8500 feet, rich summer pastures, such as Gurab, Chigakhor, Shorab, and Cheshmeh Zarin.

Some of the valleys are of considerable width, many only afford room for narrow tracks above the streams by which they are usually watered, while others are mere rifts for torrents and are inaccessible. Among the limestone ranges fountain springs are of frequent occurrence, gushing out of the mountain sides with great volume and impetuosity—the perennial sources of perennial streams.

Much of the country is absolutely without wood, producing nothing fit even for fuel but the *Astragalus verus* and the *Astragalus tragacantha*. This is especially the case on the outer slopes of the Outer range, which are formed of rocky ribs with a covering of gravel, and are " barren, treeless, waterless, and grassless." From the same crest to the outer slopes of the Inner range, which descend on Khuzistan, there are splendid pasturage, abundant water, and extensive forests in the deep valleys and on the hill slopes.[1]

The trees, however, can rarely be defined as " forest trees." They are small in girth and are usually stunted and wizened in aspect, as if the conditions of their existence were not kindly.

Flowers are innumerable in the months of May and June, beginning with the tulip, the iris, the narcissus, and a small purple gladiolus, and a little later many of the hillsides above an altitude of 7000 feet are aflame with a crimson and terra-cotta *fritillaria imperialis*, and a carnation-red anemone, while the margins of the snowfields are gay with pink patches of an exquisite alpine primula. Chicory, the dark blue centaurea, a large orange and yellow snapdragon, and the scarlet poppy attend upon grain crops there as elsewhere, and the slopes above the upper Karun are brilliant with pink, mauve, and

---

[1] Among the trees and shrubs to be met with are an oak (*Quercus ballota*), which supplies the people with acorn flour, the *Platanus* and *Tamariscus orientalis*, the jujube tree, two species of elm, a dwarf tamarisk, poplar, four species of willow, the apple, pear, cherry, plum, walnut, gooseberry, almond, dogwood, hawthorn, ash, lilac, alder, *Paliurus aculeatus*, rose, bramble, honeysuckle, hop vine, grape vine, *Clematis orientalis*, *Juniperus excelsa*, and hornbeam.

white hollyhocks. But it must be admitted that the chief interest of many of the flowers is botanical only. They are leathery, woolly, thorny, and sticky, adapted rather for arid circumstances than to rejoice the eye.

Among the economic plants observed were the *Centaurea alata*, which grows in singular abundance at a height of from 5500 to 7000 feet, and is cut and stacked for fodder; a species of celery of very strong flavour, which is an important article of food for man and beast, and the flower-stalks of which, six feet high, are woven into booths by some of the tribes; the blue linum, red madder, the *eryngium cœruleum*, which is cut and stacked for fodder; a purple garlic, the bulbs of which are eaten; liquorice, and the *Ferula asafetida* in small quantities.

It is a surprise to the traveller to find that a large area is under cultivation, and that the crops of wheat and barley are clean, and up to the Persian average, and that the removal of stones and a laborious irrigation system are the work of nomads who only occupy their *yailaks* for five months of the year. It may be said that nearly every valley and hill-slope where water is procurable is turned to account for grain crops.

No part of the world in this latitude is fuller of streams and torrents, but three only attain to any geographical dignity—the Zainderud, or river of Isfahan, which after a course full of promise loses itself ignominiously in a partially-explored swamp; the Karun, with its Bakhtiari tributaries of the Ab-i-Bazuft, the Darkash Warkash, the Ab-i-Sabzu, and the Dinarud; and the Ab-i-Diz, which has an important course of its own before its junction with the Karun at Bandakir. None of these rivers are navigable during their course through the Bakhtiari mountains. They are occasionally spanned by bridges of stone or wickerwork, or of yet simpler construction.

With the exception of the small area of the Outer range, which contains the head-waters of the Zainderud, the Bakhtiari country proper consists of the valleys of the upper Karun and its tributaries.

The tracks naturally follow the valleys, and are fairly easy in their gradients to the south-east of the Kuh-i-Rang. To the north-west, however, being compelled to cross rivers which pierce the ranges at right angles to their directions, ascents and descents of several thousand feet are involved at short intervals, formed of rock ladders, which may be regarded as "impassable for laden animals."

The so-called roads are nothing better than tracks worn in the course of centuries by the annual passage of the nomads and their flocks to and from their summer pastures. In addition to the tracks which follow the lie of the valleys, footpaths cross the main ranges where foothold can be obtained.

There are but two bridle tracks which deserve mention as being possible for caravan traffic between Isfahan and Shuster, one crossing the God-i-Murda at a height of 7050 feet and the Karun at Dupulan, the other, which considerably diminishes the distance between the two commercial points, crossing the Zard Kuh by the Cherri Pass at an altitude of 9550 feet and dropping down a steep descent of over 4000 feet to the Bazuft river. These, the Gurab, and the Gil-i-Shah, and Pambakal Passes, which cross the Zard Kuh range at elevations of over 11,000 feet, are reported as closed by snow for several months in winter. In view of the cart-road from Ahwaz to Tihran, which will pass through the gap of Khuramabad, the possible importance of any one of these routes fades completely away.

The climate, though one of extremes, is healthy. Maladies of locality are unknown, the water is usually pure, and malarious swamps do not exist. Salt springs produce a sufficiency of salt for wholesome use, and medicinal plants abound. The heat begins in early June and is steady till the end of August, the mercury rising to 102° in the shade at altitudes of 7000 feet, but it is rarely oppressive; the nights are cool, and greenery and abounding waters are a delightful contrast to the arid hills and burning plains of Persia. The rainfall is scarcely measurable, the snowfall is reported as heavy, and the winter temperatures are presumably low.

There are few traces of a past history, and the legends connected with the few are too hazy to be of any value, but there are remains of bridges of dressed stone, and of at least one ancient road, which must have been trodden by the soldiers of Alexander the Great and Valerian, and it is not impossible that the rude forts here and there which the tribesmen attribute to mythical heroes of their own race may have been built to guard Greek or Roman communications.

The geology, entomology, and zoology of the Bakhtiari country have yet to be investigated. In a journey of three months and a half the only animals seen were a bear and cubs, a boar, some small ibex, a blue hare, and some jackals. Francolin are common, and storks were seen, but scarcely any other birds, and bees and butterflies are rare. It is the noxious forms of animated life which are abundant. There are snakes, some of them venomous, a venomous spider, and a stinging beetle, and legions of black flies, mosquitos, and sand-flies infest many localities.

This area of lofty ranges, valleys, gorges, and alpine pasturages is inhabited by the Bakhtiari Lurs, classed with the savage or semi-savage races, who, though they descend to the warmer plains in the winter, invariably speak of these mountains as "their country." On this journey nearly all the tribes were visited in their own encampments, and their arrangements, modes of living, customs, and beliefs were subjects of daily investigation, the results of which are given in the letters which follow.

Their own very hazy traditions, which are swift to lose themselves in the fabulous, represent that they came from Syria, under one chief, and took possession of the country which they now inhabit. A later tradition states that a descendant of this chief had two wives equally beloved, one of whom had four sons, and the other seven ; and that after their father's death the young men quarrelled, separated, and bequeathed their quarrel to posterity, the seven brothers forming the Haft Lang division of the Bakhtiaris, and the four the Chahar Lang.[1]

The Haft Lang, though originally far superior in numbers, weakened their power by their unending internal conflicts, and in 1840, when Sir A. H. Layard visited a part of Luristan not embraced in this route, and sojourned at Kala-i-Tul, the power and headship of Mehemet Taki Khan, the great chief of their rivals the Chahar Lang, were recognised throughout the region.

The misfortunes which came upon him overthrew the supremacy of his clan, and now (as for some years past) the Haft Lang supply the ruling dynasty, the Chahar Lang being, however, still strong enough to decide any battles for the chieftainship which may be fought among their rivals. Time, and a stronger assertion of the sovereignty of Persia, have toned the feud down into a general enmity and aversion, but the tribes of the two septs rarely intermarry, and seldom encamp near each other without bloodshed.

The great divisions of the Bakhtiaris, the Haft Lang, the Chahar Lang, and the Dinarunis, with the dependencies of the Janiki Garmsir, the Janiki Sardsir, and the Afshar tribe of Gunduzlu, remain as they were half a

[1] In Persian *haft* is seven, and *chahar* four.

century ago, when they were the subject of careful investigation by Sir A. H. Layard and Sir H. Rawlinson.

The tribes (as enumerated by several of the Khans without any divergence in their statements) number 29,100 families, an increase in the last half-century. Taking eight to a household, which I believe to be a fair estimate, a population of 232,800 would be the result.[1]

A few small villages of mud hovels at low altitudes are tenanted by a part of their inhabitants throughout the winter, the other part migrating with the bulk of the flocks; and 3000 families of the two great Janiki divisions are *deh-nishins* or " dwellers in cities," *i.e.* they do not migrate at all; but the rest are nomads, that is, they have winter camping-grounds in the warm plains of Khuzistan and elsewhere, and summer pastures in the region of the Upper Karun and its affluents, making two annual migrations between their *garmsirs* and *sardsirs* (hot and cold quarters).

Though a pastoral people, they have (as has been referred to previously) of late years irrigated, stoned, and cultivated a number of their valleys, sowing in the early autumn, leaving the crops for the winter and early spring, and on their return weeding them very carefully till harvest-time in July.

They live on the produce of their flocks and herds, on leavened cakes made of wheat and barley flour, and on a paste made of acorn flour.

In religion they are fanatical Moslems of the Shiah sect, but combine relics of nature worship with the tenets of Islam.

The tribes, which were to a great extent united under

---

[1] This computation is subject to correction. Various considerations dispose the Ilkhani and the other Khans to minimise or magnify the population. It has been stated at from 107,000 to 275,000 souls, and by a "high authority" to different persons as 107,000 and 211,000 souls!

the judicious and ambitious policy of Mehemet Taki Khan and Hussein Kuli Khan, nominally acknowledge one feudal head, the Ilkhani, who is associated in power with another chief called the Ilbegi. The Ilkhani, who is appointed by the Shah for a given period, capable of indefinite extension, is responsible for the tribute, which amounts to about two *tumans* a household, and for the good order of Luri-Buzurg.

The Bakhtiaris are good horsemen and marksmen. Possibly in inter-tribal war from 10,000 to 12,000 men might take the field, but it is doubtful whether more than from 6000 to 8000 could be relied on in an external quarrel.

The Khan of each tribe is practically its despotic ruler, and every tribesman is bound to hold himself at his disposal.

As concerns tribute, they are under the government of Isfahan, with the exception of three tribes and a half, which are under the government of Burujird.

They are a warlike people, and though more peaceable than formerly, they cherish blood-feuds and are always fighting among themselves. Their habits are predatory by inclination and tradition, but they have certain notions of honour and of regard to pledges when voluntarily given.[1]

They deny Persian origin, but speak a dialect of

[1] Sir. H. Rawlinson sums up Bakhtiari character in these very severe words : "I believe them to be individually brave, but of a cruel and savage character ; they pursue their blood-feuds with the most inveterate and exterminating spirit, and they consider no oath or obligation in any way binding when it interferes with their thirst for revenge ; indeed, the dreadful stories of domestic tragedy that are related, in which whole families have fallen by each other's hands (a son, for instance, having slain his father to obtain the chiefship—another brother having avenged the murder, and so on, till only one individual was left), are enough to freeze the blood with horror.

"It is proverbial in Persia that the Bakhtiaris have been obliged to

Persian. Conquered by Nadir Shah, who took many of them into his service, they became independent after his death, until the reign of Mohammed Shah. Though tributary, they still possess a sort of *quasi* independence, though Persia of late years has tightened her grip upon them, and the Shah keeps many of their influential families in Tihran and its neighbourhood as hostages for the good behaviour of their clans.

Of the Feili Lurs, the nomads of Luri-Kushak or the Lesser Luristan, the region lying between the Ab-i-Diz and the Assyrian plains, with the province of Kirmanshah to the north and Susiana to the south, little was seen. These tribes are numerically superior to the Bakhtiaris. Fifty years ago, according to Sir H. Rawlinson, they numbered 56,000 families.

They have no single feudal chieftain like their neighbours, nor are their subdivisions ruled, as among them, by powerful Khans. They are governed by *Tushmals* (lit. " master of a house ") and four or five of these are associated in the rule of every tribal subdivision. On such occasions as involve tribal well-being or the reverse, these *Tushmals* consult as equals.

Sir H. Rawlinson considered that the Feili Lur form of government is very rare among the clan nations of Asia, and that it approaches tolerably near to the spirit of a confederated republic. Their language, according to the same authority, differs little from that of the Kurds of Kirmanshah.

forego altogether the reading of the *Fâhtihah* or prayer for the dead, for otherwise they would have no other occupation. They are also most dexterous and notorious thieves. Altogeher they may be considered the most wild and barbarous of all the inhabitants of Persia."—" Notes on. a March from Zohab to Khuzistan," *Journal of the R.G.S.*, vol. ix. Probably there is an improvement since this verdict was pronounced. At all events I am inclined to take a much more favourable view of the Bakhtiaris than has been given in the very interesting paper from which this quotation is made.

Unlike the Bakhtiaris, they neglect agriculture, but they breed and export mules, and trade in carpets, charcoal, horse-furniture, and sheep.

In faith they are Ali Ilahis, but are grossly ignorant and religiously indifferent ; they show scarcely any respect to Mohammed and the Koran, and combine a number of ancient superstitions and curious sacrificial rites with a deep reverence for Sultan Ibrahim, who under the name of *Bābā Buzurg* (the great father) is worshipped throughout Luri-Kushak.

For the tribute payable to Persia no single individual is responsible. The sum to be levied is distributed among the tribes by a general council, after which each subdivision apportions the amount to be paid by the different camps, and the *Rish-Sefid* (lit. gray-beard) or head of each encampment collects from the different families according to their means.

The task of the Persian tax-collector is a difficult one, for the tribes are in a state of chronic turbulence, and fail even in obedience to their own general council, and the collection frequently ends in an incursion of Persian soldiers and a Government raid on the flocks and herds. Many of these people are miserably poor, and they are annually growing poorer under Persian mal-administration.

The Feili Lurs are important to England commercially, because the cart-road from Ahwaz to Tihran, to be completed within two years, passes partly through their country,[1] and its success as the future trade route from

---

[1] A report to the Foreign Office (No. 207) made by an officer who travelled from Khuramabad to Dizful in December 1890, contains the following remarks on this route.

"As to the danger to caravans in passing through these hills, I am inclined to believe that the Lurs are now content to abandon robbery with violence in favour of payments and contributions from timid traders and travellers. They hang upon the rear of a caravan ; an accident, a fallen or

the Gulf depends upon their good-will, or rather upon their successful coercion by the Persian Government.

strayed pack animal, or stragglers in difficulty bring them to the spot, and, on the pretence of assistance given, a demand is made for money, in lieu of which, on fear or hesitation being shown, they obtain such articles as they take a fancy to.

"The tribes through whose limits the road runs have annual allowances for protecting it, but it is a question whether these are regularly paid. It can hardly be expected that the same system of deferred and reduced payments; which unfortunately prevails in the Persian public service, should be accepted patiently by a starving people, who have long been given to predatory habits, and this may account for occasional disturbance. They probably find it difficult to understand why payment of taxes should be mercilessly exacted upon them, while their allowances remain unpaid. It is generally believed that they would take readily to work if fairly treated and honestly paid, and I was told that for the construction of the proposed cart-road there would be no difficulty in getting labourers from the neighbouring Lur tribes."

LETTER XIV

KAHVA RUKH, CHAHAR MAHALS, *May 4.*

I LEFT Julfa on the afternoon of April 30, with Miss Bruce as my guest and Mr. Douglas as our escort for the first three or four days. The caravan was sent forward early, that my inexperienced servants might have time to pitch the tents before our arrival.

Green and pleasant looked the narrow streets and walled gardens of Julfa under a blue sky, on which black clouds were heavily massed here and there; but greenery was soon exchanged for long lines of mud ruins, and the great gravelly slopes in which the mountains descend upon the vast expanse of plain which surrounds Isfahan, on which the villages of low mud houses are marked by dark belts of poplars, willows, fruit-trees, and great patches of irrigated and cultivated land, shortly to take on the yellow hue of the surrounding waste, but now beautifully green.

Passing through Pul-i-Wargun, a large and much wooded village on the Zainderud, there a very powerful stream, affording abundant water power, scarcely used, we crossed a bridge 450 feet long by twelve feet broad, of eighteen brick arches resting on stone piers, and found the camps pitched on some ploughed land by a stream, and afternoon tea ready for the friends who had come to give us what Persians call " a throw on the road." I examined my equipments, found that nothing essential was lacking, initiated my servants into their evening duties, especially that of tightening tent ropes and driving tent pegs well in, and enjoyed a social evening in the adjacent camp.

The next day's journey, made under an unclouded sky, was mainly along the Zainderud, from which all the channels and rills which nourish the vegetation far and near are taken. A fine, strong, full river it is there and at Isfahan in spring, so prolific in good works that one regrets that it should be lost sixty miles east of Isfahan in the Gas-Khana, an unwholesome marsh, the whole of its waters disappearing in the *Kavir*. Many large villages with imposing pigeon-towers lie along this part of its course, surrounded with apricot and walnut orchards, wheat and poppy fields, every village an oasis, and every oasis a paradise, as seen in the first flush of spring. On a slope of gravel is the Bagh-i-Washi, with the remains of an immense enclosure, where the renowned Shah Abbas is said to have had a menagerie. Were it not for the beautiful fringe of fertility on both margins of the Zainderud the country would be a complete waste. The opium poppy is in bloom now. The use of opium in Persia and its exportation are always increasing, and as it is a very profitable crop, both to the cultivators and to the Government, it is to some extent superseding wheat.

Leaving the greenery we turned into a desert of gravel, crossed some low hills, and in the late afternoon came down upon the irrigated lands which surround the large and prosperous village of Riz, the handsome and lofty pigeon-towers of which give it quite a fine appearance from a distance.

These pigeon-towers are numerous, both near Isfahan and in the villages along the Zainderud, and are everywhere far more imposing than the houses of the people.

Since the great famine, which made a complete end of pigeon-keeping for the time, the industry has never assumed its former proportions, and near Julfa many of the towers are falling into ruin.

The Riz towers, however, are in good repair. They are all built in the same way, varying only in size and height, from twenty to fifty feet in diameter, and from twenty-five to eighty feet from base to summit. They are "round towers," narrowing towards the top. They are built of sun-dried bricks of local origin, costing about two *krans* or 16d. a thousand, and are decorated with rings of yellowish plaster, with coarse arabesques in red ochre upon them. For a door there is an opening half-way up, plastered over like the rest of the wall.

Two walls, cutting each other across at right angles, divide the interior. I am describing from a ruined tower which was easy of ingress. The sides of these walls, and the whole of the inner surface of the tower, are occupied by pigeon cells, the open ends of which are about twelve inches square. According to its size a pigeon-tower may contain from 2000 to 7000, or even 8000, pairs of pigeons. These birds are gray-blue in colour.

A pigeon-tower is a nuisance to the neighbourhood, for its occupants, being totally unprovided for by their proprietor, live upon their neighbours' fields. In former days it must have been a grand sight when they returned to their tower after the day's depredations. "Who are these that fly as a cloud, and as the doves to their windows?" probably referred to a similar arrangement in Palestine.

The object of the towers is the preservation and collection of "pigeon guano," which is highly prized for the raising of early melons. The door is opened once a year for the collection of this valuable manure. A large pigeon-tower used to bring its owner from £60 to £75

per annum, but a cessation of the great demand for early
melons in the neighbourhood of Isfahan has prevented
the re-stocking of the towers since the famine.

Our experiences of Riz were not pleasant. One of the
party during a short absence from his tent was robbed of
a very valuable scientific instrument. After that there
was the shuffling sound of a multitude outside the tent
in which Miss Bruce and I were resting, and women
concealed from head to foot in blue and white checked
sheets, revealing but one eye, kept lifting the tent
curtain, and when that was laced, applying the one eye
to the spaces between the lace-holes, whispering and
tittering all the time. Hot though it was, their persevering curiosity prevented any ventilation, and the steady
gaze of single eyes here, there, and everywhere was most
exasperating. It was impossible to use the dressing tent,
for crowds of boys assembled, and rows of open mouths
and staring eyes appeared between the *fly* and the
ground. Vainly Miss Bruce, who speaks Persian well
and courteously, told the women that this intrusion on
our privacy when we were very tired was both rude and
unkind. "We're only women," they said, "*we* shouldn't
mind it, we've never seen so many Europeans before."
Sunset ended the nuisance, for then the whole crowd,
having fasted since sunrise, hurried home for food.

The great fast of the month of Ramazan began before
we left Julfa. Moslems are not at their best while it
lasts. They are apt to be crabbed and irritable; and
everything that can be postponed is put off "till after
Ramazan."

Much ostentation comes out in the keeping of it; very
pious people begin to fast before the month sets in. A
really ascetic Moslem does not even swallow his saliva
during the fast, and none but very old or sick people,
children, and travellers, are exempt from the obligation

to taste neither food nor water, and not even to smoke during daylight, for a whole month. The penance is a fearful one, and as the night is the only time for feasting, the Persians get through as much of the day as possible in sleep.

Welcome indeed is the sunset. With joy men fill their pipes and drink tea as a prelude to the meal eaten an hour afterwards. Hateful is the dawn and the cry an hour before it, " Water ! oh, water and opium ! "—the warning to the faithful to drink largely and swallow an opium pill before sunrise. The thirst even in weather like this, and the abstention from smoking, are severer trials than the fasting from food. The Persian either lives to smoke, or smokes to live.

Although travellers are nominally exempt from the fast from water at least, pious Moslems do not avail themselves of the liberty. Hadji Hussein, for instance, is keeping it as rigidly as any one, and, like some others, marches with the end of his *pagri* tucked over his mouth and nose, a religious affectation, supposed to prevent the breaking of the fast by swallowing the animalculæ which are believed to infest the air !

Beyond Riz, everywhere there are arid yellow mountains and yellow gravelly plains, except along the Zainderud, where fruit-trees, wheat, and the opium poppy relieve the eyes from the glare. We took leave of the Zainderud at Pul-i-Kala, where it is crossed by a dilapidated but passable and very picturesque stone bridge of eight arches, and the view from the high right bank of wood, bridge, and the vigorous green river is very pretty.

Little enough of trees or greenery have we seen since. This country, like much of the great Iranian plateau, consists of high mountains with broad valleys or large or small plateaux between them, absolutely treeless, and even now nearly verdureless, with scattered oases wherever a possibility of procuring water by means of laboriously-constructed irrigation canals renders cultivation possible.

Water is scarce and precious; its value may be gathered from the allusions made by the Persian poets to fountains, cascades, shady pools, running streams, and bubbling springs. Such expressions as those in Scripture, "rivers of waters," "a spring of water whose waters fail not," convey a fulness of meaning to Persian ears of which we are quite ignorant. The first inquiry of a Persian about any part of his own country is, "Is there water?" the second, "Is the water good?" and if he wishes to extol any particular region he says "the water is abundant all the year, and is sweet, there is no such water anywhere."

The position of a village is always determined by the water supply, for the people have not only to think of water for domestic purposes, but for irrigating their crops, and this accounts for the packing of hamlets on steep mountain sides where land for cultivation can only be obtained by laborious terracing, but where some perennial stream can be relied on for filling the small canals. The fight for water is one of the hardest necessities of the Persian peasant. A water famine of greater or less degree is a constant peril.

Land in Persia is of three grades, the wholly irrigated, the partially irrigated, and the "rain-lands," usually uplands, chiefly suited for pasturage. The wholly irrigated land is the most productive. The assessments for taxes appear to leave altogether out of account the relative fertility of the land, and to be calculated solely on the supply of water. A winter like the last, of heavy snow, means a plenteous harvest, i.e. "twelve or fourteen grains for one," as the peasants put it; a scanty snowfall means famine, for the little rain which falls is practically of scarcely any use.

The plan for the distribution of water seems to be far

less provocative of quarrels than that of some other regions dependent on irrigation, such as Ladak and Nubra. Where it is at all abundant, as it is in this Zainderud valley, it is only in the great heats of summer that it is necessary to apportion it with any rigidity. It is then placed in the hands of a *mirab* or water officer, who allows it to each village in turn for so many days, during which time the villages above get none, or the *ketchudas* manage it among themselves without the aid of a *mirab*, for the sad truth, which is applicable to all Persian officialism, applies in the *mirab's* case, that if a village be rich enough to bribe him it can get water out of its turn.

The blessedness of the Zainderud valley is exceptional, and the general rule in the majority of districts is that the water must be carefully divided and be measured by "*tashts*," each *tasht* being equivalent to the use of the water supply for eleven minutes.

"This space of time is estimated in a very ancient fashion by floating a copper bowl with a needle hole in the bottom in a large vessel of water. The *tasht* comes to an end as the bowl sinks. The distribution is regulated by the number of *tashts* that each man has a right to. If he has a right to twenty he will receive water for three and three-quarter hours of the day or night every tenth day." Land without water in Persia is about as valuable as the "south lands" were which were given to Caleb's daughter.

So far as I can learn, the Persian peasant enjoys a tolerable security of tenure so long as he pays his rent. A common rate of rent is two-thirds of the produce, but on lands where the snow lies for many months, even when they are "wet lands," it is only one-third; but this system is subject to many modifications specially arising out of the finding or non-finding of the seed by the owner, and there is no uniformity in the manner of holding land or in assessing the taxes or in anything else, though the system established 1400 years ago is still the basis of the whole.[1]

The line between the oasis and the desert is always strongly marked and definite. There is no shading away between the deep green of the growing wheat and the yellow or red gravel beyond. The general impression is one of complete nakedness. The flowers which in this month bloom on the slopes are mostly stiff, leathery, and thorny. The mountains themselves viewed from below are without any indication of green. The usual colouring is grayish-yellow or a feeble red, intensifying at sunset, but rarely glorified owing to the absence of "atmosphere."

It is a very solitary route from Pul-i-Kala, without villages, and we met neither caravans nor foot passengers. The others rode on, and I followed with two of the Bakhtiari escort, who with Rustem Khan, a minor chief, had accompanied us from Julfa. These men were most inconsequent in their proceedings, wheeling round me at a gallop, singing, or rather howling, firing their long guns, throwing themselves into one stirrup and nearly off their horses, and one who rides without a bridle came up behind me with his horse bolting and nearly knocked me out of the saddle with the long barrel of his gun. When the village of Charmi came in sight I signed to them to go on, and we all rode at a gallop, the horsemen uttering wild cries and going through the pantomime of firing over the left shoulders and right flanks of their horses.

The camps were pitched on what might be called the village green. Charmi, like many Persian villages, is

---

[1] The readers interested in such matters will find much carefully-acquired information on water distribution, assessments, and tenure of land in the second volume of the late Mr. Stack's *Six Months in Persia*.

walled, the wall, which is much jagged by rain and frost, having round towers at intervals, and a large gateway. Such walls are no real protection, but serve to keep the flocks and herds from nocturnal depredators. Within the gate is a house called the Fort, with a very fine room fully thirty feet long by fifteen high, decorated with a mingled splendour and simplicity surprising in a rural district. The wall next the courtyard is entirely of very beautiful fretwork, filled in with amber and pale blue glass. The six doors are the same, and the walls and the elaborate roof and cornices are pure white, the projections being "picked out" in a pale shade of brown, hardly darker than amber.

The following morning Miss Bruce left on her return home, and Mr. Douglas and I rode fourteen miles to the large village of Kahva Rukh, where we parted company. It is an uninteresting march over formless gravelly hills and small plains thinly grassed, until the Gardan-i-Rukh, one of the high passes on the Isfahan and Shuster route, is reached, with its extensive view of brown mountains and yellow wastes. This pass, 7960 feet in altitude, crossing the unshapely Kuh-i-Rukh, is the watershed of the country, all the streams on its southern side falling into the Karun. It is also the entrance to the Chahar Mahals or four districts, Lar, Khya, Mizak, and Gandaman, which consist chiefly of great plains surrounded by mountains, and somewhat broken up by their gravelly spurs.

Beyond, and usually in sight, is the snow-slashed Kuh-i-Sukhta range, which runs south-east, and throws out a spur to Chigakhor, the summer resort of the Bakhtiari chiefs. The Chahar Mahals, for Persia, are populous, and in some parts large villages, many of which are Armenian and Georgian, occur at frequent intervals, most of them treeless, but all surrounded by cultivated lands. The Armenian villages possess so-called relics and ancient

copies of the Gospels, which are credited with the power
of working miracles.[1]

The Chahar Mahals have been farmed to the Ilkhani
of the Bakhtiaris for about 20,000 *tumans* (£6000) a
year, and his brother, Reza Kuli Khan, has been appointed
their governor. Thus on crossing the Kahva Rukh pass
we entered upon the sway of the feudal head of the
great Bakhtiari tribes.

We camped outside the village, my tents being pitched
in a ruinous enclosure. The servants are in the habit
of calling me the *Hakīm*, and the report of a Frank *Hakīm*
having arrived soon brought a crowd of sick people, who
were introduced and their ailments described by a blue
horseman, one of the escort.

His own child was so dangerously ill of pneumonia
that I went with him to his house, put on a mustard
poultice, and administered some Dover's powder. The
house was crammed and the little suffering creature had
hardly air to breathe. The courtyard was also crowded,
so that one could scarcely move, all the people being quite
pleasant and friendly. I saw several sick people, and
was surprised to find the village houses so roomy and
comfortable, and so full of "plenishings." It was in vain
that I explained to them that I am not a doctor, scarcely
even a nurse. The fame of Burroughes and Wellcome's

[1] Some of the legends connected with these objects are grossly super-
stitious. At Shurishghan there is a "Holy Testament," regarding which
the story runs that it was once stolen by the Lurs, who buried it under a
tree by the bank of a stream. Long afterwards a man began to cut down
the tree, but when the axe was laid to its root blood gushed forth. On
searching for the cause of this miracle the Gospels were found uninjured
beneath. It is believed that if any one were to take the Testament away it
would return of its own accord. It has the reputation of working miracles
of healing, and many resort to it either for themselves or for their sick
friends, from Northern Persia and even from Shiraz, as well as from the
vicinity, and vows are made before it. The gifts presented to it become
the property of its owners.

medicine chest has spread far and wide, and they think its possessor *must* be a *Hakīm*. The horseman said that medicine out of that chest would certainly cure his child.[1] I was unable to go back to the tea which had been prepared in the horseman's house, on which he expressed great dismay, and said I must be "enraged with him."

Persians always use round numbers, and the *ketchuda* says that the village has 300 Persian houses, and 100 more, inhabited during the winter by Ilyats. It has mud walls with towers at intervals, two mosques, a clear stream of water in the principal street, some very good houses with *balakhanas*, and narrow alleys between high mud walls, in which are entrances into courtyards occupied by animals, and surrounded by living-rooms. The only trees are a few spindly willows, but wheat comes up to the walls, and at sunset great herds of cattle and myriads of brown sheep converge to what seems quite a prosperous village.

May 5.—Yesterday, Sunday, was intended to be a day of rest, but turned out very far from it. After the last relay of "patients" left on Saturday evening, and the last medicines had been "dispensed," my tent was neatly arranged with one *yekdan* for a table, and the other for a washstand and medicine stand. The latter trunk contained some English gold in a case along with some valuable letters, and some bags, in which were 1000 *krans*, for four months' travelling. This *yekdan* was padlocked. It was a full moon, the other camps were quite near, all looked very safe, and I slept until awakened by the sharpness of the morning air.

Then I saw but one *yekdan* where there had been

---

[1] And so it did, though it was then so ill that it seemed unlikely that it would live through the night, and I told them so before I gave the medicine, lest they should think that I had killed it.

two! Opening the tent curtain I found my washing apparatus and medicine bottles neatly arranged on the ground outside, and the trunk without its padlock among some ruins a short distance off. The money bags were all gone, leaving me literally penniless. Most of my store of tea was taken, but nothing else. Two men must have entered my tent and have carried the trunk out. Of what use are any precautions when one sleeps so disgracefully soundly? When the robbery was made known horsemen were sent off to the Ilkhani, whose guest I have been since I entered his territory, and at night a Khan arrived with a message that "the money would be repaid, and that the village would be levelled with the ground!" Kahva Rukh will, I hope, stand for many years to come, but the stolen sum will be levied upon it, according to custom.

The people are extremely vexed at this occurrence, and I would rather have lost half the sum than that it should have happened to a guest. In addition to an escort of a Khan and four men, the Ilkhani has given orders that we are not to be allowed to pay for anything while in the country. This order, after several battles, I successfully disobey. This morning, before any steps were taken to find the thief, and after all the loads were ready, officials came to the camps, and, by our wish, every man's baggage was unrolled and searched. Our servants and *charvadars* are all Moslems, and each of them took an oath on the Koran, administered by a *mollah*, that he was innocent of the theft.

Ardal, May 9.—I left rather late, and with the blue horseman, to whom suspicion generally pointed, rode to Shamsabad, partly over gravelly wastes, passing two mixed Moslem and Armenian villages on a plain, on which ninety ploughs were at work on a stiff whitish soil.

Shamsabad is a most wretched mud village without supplies, standing bare on a gravelly slope, above a clear quiet stream, an affluent of the Karun. This country has not reached that stage of civilisation in which a river bears the same name from mouth to source, and as these streams usually take as many names as there are villages on their course, I do not burden my memory with them. There is a charming camping-ground of level velvety green sward on the right bank of the river, with the towering mass of Jehanbin (sight of the world), 12,000 feet high, not far off. This lawn is 6735 feet above the sea, and the air keen and pleasant. The near mountain views are grand, and that evening the rare glory of a fine sunset lingered till it was merged in the beauty of a perfect moonlight.

After leaving Shamsabad the road passes through a rather fine defile, crosses the Shamsabad stream by a ten-arched bridge between the Kuh-i-Zangun and the Kuh-i-Jehanbin, and proceeds down a narrow valley now full of wild flowers and young wheat to Khariji, a village of fifty houses, famous for the excellent quality of its opium. From Khariji we proceeded through low grassy hills, much like the South Downs, and over the low but very rough Pasbandi Pass into an irrigated valley in which is the village of Shalamzar. I rode through it alone quite unmolested, but two days later the Sahib, passing through it with his servants, was insulted and pelted, and the people said, "Here's another of the dog party." These villagers are afflicted with "divers diseases and torments," and the crowd round my tent was unusually large and importunate. In this village of less than fifty houses nearly all the people had one or both eyes more or less affected, and fourteen had only one eye.

Between Shalamzar and Ardal lies the lofty Gardan-

i-Zirreh, by which the Kuh-i-Sukhta is crossed at a height
of 8300 feet. The ascent begins soon after leaving the
village, and is long and steep—a nasty climb. The upper
part at this date is encumbered with snow, below which
primulas are blooming in great profusion, and lower down
leathery flowers devoid of beauty cover without adorning
the hillside. Two peasants went up with me, and from
time to time kindly handed me clusters of small raisins
taken from the breasts of dirty felt clothing. On reaching the snow I found Rustem Khan's horse half-buried
in a drift, so I made the rest of the ascent on foot. The
snow was three feet deep, but for the most part presented
no difficulties, even to the baggage animals.

At the summit there were no green things except
some plants of *artemisia*, not even a blade of grass, but
among the crevices appeared small fragile snow-white
tulips with yellow centres, mixed with scarlet and mauve
blossoms of a more vigorous make. At that great height
the air was keen and bracing, and to eyes for months accustomed to regions buried in dazzling snow and to glaring
gravelly wastes, there was something perfectly entrancing
about the view on the Bakhtiari side. Though treeless, it
looked like Paradise. Lying at the foot of the pass is the
deep valley of Seligun, 8000 feet high, with the range
of the Kuh-i-Nassar to the south, and of the Kuh-Shah-
Purnar to the north—green, full of springs and streams,
with two lakes bringing down the blue of heaven to earth,
with slopes aflame with the crimson and terra-cotta *Fritillaria imperialis*, and levels one golden glory with a yellow
ranunculus. Rich and dark was the green of the grass,
tall and deep on the plain, but when creeping up the
ravines to meet the snows, short green sward enamelled
with tulips. Great masses of naked rock, snow-slashed,
and ranges of snow-topped masses behind and above,
walled in that picture of cool serenity, its loneliness only

broken by three black tents of Ilyats far away.   So I saw
Seligun, but those who see it a month hence will find
only a brown and dusty plain !

The range we crossed divides the Chahar Mahals from
the true Bakhtiari country, a land of mountains which
rumour crests with eternal snow, of unexplored valleys
and streams, of feudal chiefs, of blood feuds, and of
nomad tribes moving with vast flocks and herds.

Mehemet Ali, a new and undesirable acquisition, was
loaded with my *shuldari*, and we clambered down the
hillside, leading our horses amidst tamarisk scrub and a
glory of tulips, till we reached the level, when a gallop
brought us to the camps, pitched near a vigorous spring
in the green flower-enamelled grass.

That halt was luxury for man and beast.   Later the
air was cool and moist.   The sun-lit white fleeces which
had been rolling among the higher hills darkened and
thickened into rain-clouds, drifting stormily, and only
revealing here and there through their rifts glimpses of
blue.   A few flocks of sheep on the mountains, and the
mules and horses revelling knee-deep in the juicy grass,
were the sole representatives of animated life.   It was
a real refreshment to be away from the dust of mud
villages, and to escape from the pressure of noisy and
curious crowds, and the sight of sore eyes.

Towards evening, a gallop on the Arabs with the
Bakhtiari escort took us to the camp of the lately-arrived
Ilyats.   Orientals spend much of their time in the quiet
contemplation of cooking pots, and these nomads were
not an exception, for they were all sitting round a brushwood fire, on which the evening meal of meat broth with
herbs was being prepared.   The women were unveiled.
Both men and women are of quite a different type from
the Persians.   They are completely clothed and in
appearance are certainly only semi-savages.   These tents

consisted of stones rudely laid to a height of two feet at the back, over which there is a canopy with an open front and sides, of woven goat's-hair supported on poles. Such tents are barely a shelter from wind and rain, but in them generations of Ilyats are born and die, despising those of their race who settle in villages.

There were great neutral-tint masses of rolling clouds, great banks of glistering white clouds, a cold roystering wind, a lurid glow, and then a cloudy twilight. *Hakīm* threw up his heels and galloped over the moist grass, the Bakhtiaris, two on one horse, laughed and yelled—there was the desert freedom without the desert. It was the most inspiriting evening I have spent in Persia. Truth compels me to add that there were legions of black flies.

In the early morning, after riding round the southeast end of the valley, we passed by the lake Seligun or Albolaki, banked up by a revetment of rude masonry. The wind was strong, and drove the foam-flecked water in a long line of foam on the shore. Red-legged storks were standing in a row fishing. Cool scuds of rain made the morning homelike. Then there was a hill ascent, from which the view of snowy mountains, gashed by deep ravines and backed by neutral-tint clouds, was magnificent, and then a steep and rocky defile, which involved walking, its sides gaudy with the *Fritillaria imperialis,* which here attains a size and a depth of colouring of which we have no conception.

In this pass we met a large number of Ilyat families going up to their summer quarters, with their brown flocks of sheep and their black flocks of goats. Their tents with all their other goods were packed in convenient parcels on small cows, and the women with babies and big wooden cradles were on asses. The women without babies, the elder children, and the men walked.

Whatever beauty these women possessed was in the Meg Merrilees style, with a certain weirdness about it. They had large, dark, long eyes, with well-marked eyebrows, artificially prolonged, straight prominent noses, wide mouths with thin lips, long straight chins, and masses of black hair falling on each side of the face. Their dress consisted of enormously full dark blue cotton trousers, drawn in at the ankles, and suspended over the hips, not from the waist (the invariable custom in Persia), and loose sleeved vests, open in front. The adult women all wear a piece of cotton pinned on the head, and falling over the back and shoulders. The men had their hair in many long plaits, hanging from under felt skull-caps, and wore wide blue cotton trousers, white or printed cotton shirts over these, and girdles in which they carried knives, pipes, and other indispensables. All wore shoes or sandals of some kind. These men were very swarthy, but the younger women had rich brunette complexions, and were unveiled.

Some bad horse-fights worried the remainder of the march, which included the ascent of an anemone-covered hill, 7700 feet high, from which we got the first view of the Ardal valley, much cultivated, till it narrows and is lost among mountains, now partly covered with snow. In the centre is a large building with a tower, the spring residence of the Ilkhani, whose goodwill it is necessary to secure. Through a magnificent gorge in the mountains passes the now famous Karun. A clatter of rain and a strong wind greeted our entrance into the valley, where we were met by some horsemen from the Ilkhani.

The great Ardal plateau is itself treeless, though the lower spurs of the Kuh-i-Sabz on the south side are well wooded with the *belut*, a species of oak. There is much cultivation, and at this season the uncultivated ground is covered with the great green leaves of a fodder plant, the *Centaurea alata,* which a little later are cut, dried, and stacked. The rivers of the plateau are the Karun and Sabzu on the south side, and the river of Shamsabad, which brings to the Karun the drainage of the Chahar Mahals, and enters the valley through a magnificent *tang* or chasm on its north side, called Darkash Warkash. The village of Ardal is eighty-five miles from Isfahan, on the Shuster caravan route, and is about 200 from Shuster. Its altitude is 5970 feet, its Long. 50° 50' E. and its Lat. 32° N.

On arriving here the grandeur of the Ilkhani's house faded away. Except for the fortified tower it looks like a second-rate caravanserai. The village, such as there is of it, is crowded on a steep slope outside the "Palace." It is a miserable hamlet of low windowless mud hovels, with uneven mud floors, one or two feet lower than the ground outside, built in yards with ruinous walls, and full of heaps and holes. It is an *olla podrida* of dark, poor, smoky mud huts; narrow dirt-heaped alleys, with bones and offal lying about; gaunt yelping dogs; bottle-green slimy pools, and ruins. The people are as dirty as the houses, but they are fine in physique and face, as if only the fittest survive. There is an *imamzada,* much visited on Fridays, on an adjacent slope. The snow lies here five feet deep in winter, it is said.

When we arrived the roofs and balconies of the Ilkhani's house were crowded with people looking out for us. The Agha called at once, and I sent my letter of introduction from the Amin-es-Sultan. Presents arrived, formal visits were paid, the Ilkhani's principal wife appointed an hour at which to receive me, and a number of dismounted horsemen came and escorted me to the palace. The chief feature of the house is a large audience-chamber over the entrance, in which the chief holds a daily *durbar,* the deep balcony outside being usually thronged by crowds of tribesmen, all having free access to him.   The coming and going are incessant.

The palace or castle is like a two-storied caravanserai, enclosing a large untidy courtyard, round which are stables and cow-houses, and dens for soldiers and servants.   In the outer front of the building are deep recessed arches, with rooms opening upon them, in which the Isfahan traders, who come here for a month, expose

CASTLE OF ARDAL.

their wares.   Passing under the Ilkhani's audience-chamber by a broad arched passage with deep recesses on both sides, and through the forlorn uneven courtyard, a long, dark arched passage leads into a second court-yard, where there is an attempt at ornament by means of tanks and willows.   Round this are a number of living-rooms for the Ilkhani's sons and their families, and here is the *andarun*, or house of the women.   On the far side is the Fort, a tall square tower with loopholes and embrasures.

A Cerberus guards the entrance to the *andarun*, but

he allowed Mirza to accompany me. A few steps lead up from the courtyard into a lofty oblong room, with a deep cushioned recess containing a fireplace. The roof rests on wooden pillars. The front of the room facing the courtyard is entirely of fretwork filled in with pale blue and amber glass. The recess and part of the floor were covered with very beautiful blue and white grounded carpets, made by the women. The principal wife, a comely wide-mouthed woman of forty, advanced to meet me, kissed my hand, raised it to her brow, and sat down on a large carpet squab, while the other wives led me into the recess, and seated me on a pile of cushions, taking their places in a row on the floor opposite, but scarcely raising their eyes, and never speaking one word. The rest of the room was full of women and children standing, and many more blocked up the doorways, all crowding forward in spite of objurgations and smart slaps frequently administered by the principal wife.

The three young wives are Bakhtiaris, and their style of beauty is novel to me—straight noses, wide mouths, thin lips, and long chins. Each has three stars tattooed on her chin, one in the centre of the forehead, and several on the back of the hands. The eyebrows are not only elongated with indigo, but are made to meet across the nose. The finger-nails, and inside of the hands, are stained with henna. The hair hangs round their wild, handsome faces, down to their collar-bones, in loose, heavy, but not uncleanly masses.

Among the "well-to-do" Bakhtiari women, as among the Persians, the hair receives very great attention, although it is seldom exhibited. It is naturally jet black, and very abundant. It is washed at least once a week with a thin paste of a yellowish clay found among the Zard-Kuh mountains, which has a very cleansing effect.

But the women are not content with their hair as it

is, and alter its tinge by elaborate arts. They make a thick paste of henna, leave it on for two hours, and then wash it off. The result is a rich auburn tint. A similar paste, made of powdered indigo leaves, is then plastered over the hair for two hours. On its removal the locks are dark green, but in twenty-four hours more they become a rich blue-black. The process needs repeating about every twenty days, but it helps to fill up the infinite leisure of life. It is performed by the bath attendants.

In justice to my sex I must add that the men dye their hair to an equal extent with the women, from the shining blue-black of the Shah's moustache to the brilliant orange of the beard of Hadji Hussein, by which he forfeits, though not in Persian estimation, the respect due to age.

Some of the Ilkhani's children and grand-children have the hair dyed with henna alone to a rich auburn tint, which is very becoming to the auburn eyes and delicate paleness of some of them.

The wives wore enormously full black silk trousers, drawn tight at the ankles, with an interregnum between them and short black vests, loose and open in front; and black silk sheets attached to a band fixed on the head enveloped their persons. They have, as is usual among these people, small and beautiful hands, with taper fingers and nails carefully kept. The chief wife, who rules the others, rumour says, was also dressed in black. She has a certain degree of comely dignity about her, and having seen something of the outer world in a pilgrimage to Mecca *via* Baghdad, returning by Egypt and Persia, and having also lived in Tihran, her intelligence has been somewhat awakened. The Bakhtiari women generally are neither veiled nor secluded, but the higher chiefs who have been at the capital think it *chic* to adopt the Persian customs regarding women, and the inferior chiefs, when they have houses, follow their example.

My conversation with the " queen " consisted chiefly of question and answer, varied by an occasional divergence on her part into an animated talk with Mirza Yusuf. Among the many questions asked were these : at what age our women marry ? how many wives the Agha has ? how long our women are allowed to keep their boys with them ? why I do not dye my hair ? if I know of anything to take away wrinkles ? to whiten teeth ? etc., if our men divorce their wives when they are forty ? why Mr. —— had refused a Bakhtiari wife ? if I am travelling to collect herbs ? if I am looking for the plant which if found would turn the base metals into gold ? etc.

She said they had very dull lives, and knew nothing of any customs but their own ; that they would like to see the Agha, who, they heard, was a head taller than their tallest men ; that they hoped I should be at Chigakhor when they were there, as it would be less dull, and she apologised for not offering tea or sweetmeats, as it is the fast of the Ramazan, which they observe very strictly.   I told them that the Agha wished to take their photographs, and the Hadji Ilkhani along with them.   They were quite delighted, but it occurred to them that they must first get the Ilkhani's consent.   This was refused, and one of his sons, whose wife is very handsome, said, " We cannot allow pictures to be made of our women.   It is not our custom.   We cannot allow pictures of our women to be in strange hands.   No good women have their pictures taken.   Among the tribes you may find women base enough to be photographed."   The chief wife offered to make me a present of her grandson, to whom I am giving a tonic, if I can make him strong and cure his deafness. He is a pale precocious child of ten, with hazel eyes and hair made artificially auburn.

When the remarkably frivolous conversation flagged, they brought children afflicted with such maladies as ophthalmia, scabies, and sore eyes to be cured, but rejected my dictum that a copious use of soap and water must precede all remedies. Among the adults headaches, loss of appetite, and dyspepsia seem the prevailing ailments. Love potions were asked for, and charms to bring back lost love, with special earnestness, and the woful looks assumed when I told the applicants that I could do nothing for them were sadly suggestive. There could not have been fewer than sixty women and children in the room, many, indeed most of them, fearfully dirty in dress and person. Among them were several negro and mulatto slaves. When I came away the balconies and arches of the Ilkhani's house were full of men, anxious to have a good view of the Feringhi woman, but there was no rudeness there, or in the village, which I walked through afterwards with a courtesy escort of several dismounted horsemen.

After this the Ilkhani asked me to go to see a man who is very ill, and sent two of his retainers with me. It must be understood that Mirza Yusuf goes with me everywhere as attendant and interpreter. The house was a dark room, with a shed outside, in a filthy yard, in which children, goats, and dogs were rolling over each other in a foot of powdered mud. Crowds of men were standing in and about the shed. I made my way through them, moving them to right and left with my hands, with the recognised supremacy of a *Hakīm*! There were some wadded quilts on the ground, and another covered a form of which nothing was visible but two feet, deadly cold. The only account that the bystanders could give of the illness was, that four days ago the man fainted, and that since he had not been able to eat, speak, or move. The face was covered with several folds of a very dirty *chadar*. On removing it I was startled by seeing, not a sick man, but the open mouth, gasping respiration, and glassy eyes of a dying man. His nostrils had been stuffed with moist mud and a chopped aromatic herb The feet were uncovered, and the limbs were quite cold. There was no cruelty in this. The men about him were most kind, but *absolutely ignorant*.

I told them that he could hardly survive the night, and that all I could do was to help him to die comfortably. They said with one clamorous voice that they would do whatever I told them, and in the remaining hours they kept their word. I bade them cleanse the mud from his nostrils, wrap the feet and legs in warm cloths, give him air, and not crowd round him. Under less solemn circumstances I should have been amused with the absolute docility with which these big savage-looking men obeyed me. I cut up a blanket, and when they had heated some water in their poor fashion, showed them how to prepare fomentations, put on the first myself, and bathed his face and hands.

He was clothed in rags of felt and cotton, evidently never changed since the day they were put on, though he was what they call " rich,"—a great owner of mares, flocks, and herds,—and the skin was scaly with decades of dirt. I ventured to pour a little sal-volatile and water down his throat, and the glassy eyeballs moved a little. I asked the bystanders if, as Moslems, they would object to his taking some spirits medicinally ? They were willing, but said there was no *arak* in the Bakhtiari country, a happy exemption ! The Agha's kindness supplied some whisky, of which from that time the dying man took a teaspoonful, much diluted, every two hours, tossed down his throat with a spoon, Allah being always invoked. There was

no woman's gentleness to soothe his last hours. A wife
in the dark den inside was weaving, and once came out
and looked carelessly at him, but men did for him all
that he required with a tenderness and kindness which
were very pleasing. Before I left they asked for directions
over again, and one of the Ilkhani's retainers wrote them
down.

At night the Ilkhani sent to say that the man was
much better and he hoped I would go and see him.
The scene was yet more weird than in the daytime.
A crowd of men were sitting and standing round a fire
outside the shed, and four were watching the dying man.
The whisky had revived him, his pulse was better, the
fomentation had relieved the pain, and when it was re-
applied he had uttered the word "good." I tried to make
them understand it was only a last flicker of life, but
they thought he would recover, and the Ilkhani sent to
know what food he should have.

At dawn "death music," wild and sweet, rang out on
the still air; he died painlessly at midnight, and was
carried to the grave twelve hours later.

When people are very ill their friends give them
food and medicine (if a *Hakīm* be attainable), till, in
their judgment, the case is hopeless. Then they send
for a *mollah,* who reads the Koran in a very loud sing-
song tone till death ensues, the last thirst being alleviated
meantime by *sharbat* dropped into the mouth. Camphor
and other sweet spices are burned at the grave. If they
burn well and all is pure afterwards, they say that the
deceased person has gone to heaven; if they burn feebly
and smokily, and there is any unpleasantness from the
grave, they say that the spirit is in perdition. A
Bakhtiari grave is a very shallow trench.

The watchers were kind, and carried out my directions
faithfully. I give these minute details to show how much

even simple nursing can do to mitigate suffering among a people so extremely ignorant as the Bakhtiaris are not only of the way to tend the sick, but of the virtues of the medicinal plants which grow in abundance around them. A medical man itinerating among their camps with a light hospital tent and some simple instruments and medicines could do a great deal of healing, and much also to break down the strong prejudice which exists against Christianity. Here, as elsewhere, the *Hakīm* is respected. Going in that capacity I found the people docile, respectful, and even grateful. Had I gone among them in any other, a Christian Feringhi woman would certainly have encountered rudeness and worse.

The Ilkhani, who has not been in a hurry to call, made a formal visit to-day with his brother, Reza Kuli Khan, his eldest son Lutf, another son, Ghulam, with bad eyes, and a crowd of retainers. The Hadji Ilkhani,—Imam Kuli Khan, the great feudal chief of the Bakhtiari tribes, is a quiet-looking middle-aged man with a short black beard, a parchment-coloured complexion, and a face somewhat lined, with a slightly sinister expression at times. He wore a white felt cap, a blue full-skirted coat lined with green, another of fine buff kerseymere under it, with a girdle, and very wide black silk trousers.

He is a man of some dignity of deportment, and his usual expression is somewhat kindly and courteous. He is a devout Moslem, and has a finely-illuminated copy of the Koran, which he spends much time in reading. He is not generally regarded as a very capable or powerful man, and is at variance with the Ilbegi, who, though nominally second chief, practically shares his power. In fact, at this time serious intrigues are going on, and some say that the adherents of the two chiefs would not be unwilling to come to open war.

The greatest men who in this century have filled the office of Ilkhani both perished miserably. The fate of Sir H. Layard's friend, Mehemet Taki Khan, is well known to all readers of the *Early Recollections*, but it was possibly less unexpected than that of Hussein Kuli Khan, brother of the present Ilkhani, and father of the Ilbegi Isfandyar Khan. This man was evidently an enlightened

IMAM KULI KHAN.

and able ruler; he suppressed brigandage with a firm hand, and desired to see the Mohammerah-Shuster-Isfahan route fairly opened to trade. He went so far as to promise Mr. Mackenzie, of one of the leading Persian Gulf firms, in writing, that he would hold himself personally responsible for the safety of caravans in their passage through his territory, and would repay any losses by robbery. He agreed to take a third share of the cost of the necessary steamers on the Karun, and to furnish 100 mules for land transport between Shuster and Isfahan.[1]

It appears that Persian jealousy was excited by his enterprising spirit; he fell under the displeasure of the Zil-es-Sultan, and in 1882 was put to death by poison while on his annual visit of homage. The present Ilkhani, who succeeded him, warned possibly by his brother's fate, is said to show little, if any, interest in commercial enterprise, and to have made the somewhat shrewd remark that the English "under the dress of the merchant often conceal the uniform of the soldier."

In 1888 the Shah relented towards Hussein Kuli Khan's sons, the eldest of whom, Isfandyar Khan, had been in prison for seven years, and they with their uncle, Reza Kuli Khan, descended with their followers and a small Persian army upon the plain of Chigakhor, where they surprised and defeated the Hadji Ilkhani. His brother, Reza, was thereupon recognised by the Shah as Ilkhani, and Isfandyar as Ilbegi, with the substance of power. Another turn of the wheel of fortune, and the brothers became respectively Ilkhani and Governor of the Chahar Mahals, and their nephew is reinstated as Ilbegi.[2]

The Ilkhani's word is law, within broad limits, among the numerous tribes of Bakhtiari Lurs who have consented to recognise him as their feudal head, and it has been estimated that in a popular quarrel he could bring from 8000 to 10,000 armed horsemen into the field. He is judge as well as ruler, but in certain cases there is a possible appeal to Tihran from his decisions. He is appointed by the Shah, with a salary of 1000 *tumans* a year, but a strong man in his position could be practically independent.

[1] *Proceedings of R. G. S.*, vol. v. No. 3, New Series.

[2] I am indebted for the information given above to a valuable paper by Mr. H. Blosse Lynch, given in the *Proceedings of the R. G. S.* for September 1890.

It can scarcely be supposed that the present Ilkhani will long retain his uneasy seat against the intrigues at the Persian court, and with a powerful and popular rival close at hand. It is manifestly the interest of the Shah's government to weaken the tribal power, and extinguish the authority and independence of the principal chiefs, and the Oriental method of attaining this end is by plots and intrigues at the capital, by creating and fomenting local quarrels, and by oppressive taxation. It is not wonderful, therefore, that many of the principal Khans, whose immemorial freedom has been encroached upon in many recent years by the Tihran Government, should look forward to a day when one of the Western powers will occupy south-west Persia, and give them security.

The *Hadji* Ilkhani, for the people always prefix the religious title, discussed the proposed journey, promised me an escort of a horseman and a *tufangchi*, or foot-soldier, begged us to consider ourselves here and everywhere as his guests, and to ask for all we want, here and elsewhere. His brother, Reza Kuli Khan, who has played an important part in tribal affairs, resembles him, but the sinister look is more persistent on his face. He was much depressed by the fear that he was going blind, but on trying my glasses he found he could see. The surprise of the old-sighted people when they find that spectacles renew their youth is most interesting.

Another visitor has been the Ilbegi, Isfandyar Khan. Though not tall, he is very good-looking, and has beautiful hands and feet. He is able, powerful, and ambitious, inspires his adherents with great personal devotion, and is regarded by many as the "coming man." He was in Tihran when I was in Julfa, and hearing from one of the Ministers that I was about to visit the Bakhtiari country, he wrote to a general of cavalry in

Isfahan, asking him to provide me with an escort if I needed it.   I was glad to thank him for his courtesy in this matter, and for more substantial help.   Before his visit, his retainer, Mansur, brought me the money of which I had been robbed in Kahva Rukh!   This man absolutely refused a present, saying that his liege lord would nearly kill him if he took one.   Isfandyar Khan welcomed me kindly, regretting much that my first night under Bakhtiari rule should have been marked by a robbery.   He said that before his day the tribesmen not only robbed, but killed, and that he had reduced them to such order that he was surprised as well as shocked at this occurrence.   I replied that it occurred in a Persian village, and that in many countries one might be robbed, but in none that I knew of would such quick restitution be made.

In cases of robbery, the Ilkhani sends round to the *ketchudas* or headmen of the camps or villages of the offending district, to replace the money, as in my case, or the value of the thing taken, after which the thief must be caught if possible.   When caught, the headmen consult as to his punishment, which may be the cutting off of a hand or nose, or to be severely branded.   In any case he must be for the future a marked man.   I gather that the most severe penalties are rarely inflicted.   I hope the fine of 800 *krans* levied on Kahva Rukh may stimulate the people to surrender the thief.   I agreed to forego 200 *krans*, as Isfandyar Khan says that his men raised all they could, and the remaining sum would have to be paid by himself.

After a good deal of earnest conversation he became frivolous!   He asked the Agha his age, and guessed it at thirty-five.   On being enlightened he asked if he dyed his hair, and if his teeth were his own.   Then he said that he dyed his own hair, and wore artificial teeth.   He also asked my age. He and Lutf and Ghulam, the Ilkhani's sons, who accompanied him, possess superb watches, with two dials, and an arrangement for showing the phases of the moon.

Having accepted an invitation from the Ilbegi to visit him at Naghun, a village ten miles from Ardal, accompanied by Lutf and Ghulam, we were ready at seven, the hour appointed, as the day promised to be very hot. Eight o'clock came, nine o'clock, half-past nine, and on sending to see if the young Khans were coming, the servants replied that they had "no orders to wake them." So we Europeans broiled three hours in the sun at the pleasure of "barbarians"!

During the Ramazan these people revel from sunset to sunrise, with feasting, music, singing, and merriment, and then they lie in bed till noon or later, to abridge the long hours of the fast. "Is it such a fast that I have chosen?" may well be asked.

The noise during the night in the Ilkhani's palace is tremendous. The festivities begin soon after sunset and go on till an hour before dawn. Odours agreeable to Bakhtiari noses are wafted down to my tent, but I do not find them appetising. An eatable called *zalabi* is in great request during the Ramazan. It is made by mixing sugar and starch with oil of sesamum, and is poured on ready heated copper trays, and frizzled into fritters. Masses of eggs mixed with rice, clarified butter, and jams, concealing balls of highly-spiced mincemeat, *kabobs*, and mutton stewed with preserved lemon juice and onions are favourite dishes at the Ilkhani's.

Besides the music and singing, the "Court" entertains itself nightly with performing monkeys and dancing men, besides story-tellers, and reciters of the poetry of Hafiz. It is satisfactory to know that the uproarious merriment which drifts down to my tent along with odours of per-

petual frying, owes none of its inspiration to alcohol,
coffee and *sharbat* being the drinks consumed.

We rode without a guide down the Ardal valley, took
the worst road through some deep and blazing gulches,
found the sun fierce, and the treelessness irksome, saw
much ploughing, made a long ascent, and stopped short
of the village of Naghun at a large walled garden on the
arid hillside, which irrigation has turned into a shady
paradise of pear, apricot, and walnut trees, with a
luxurious undergrowth of roses and pomegranates. The
young Khans galloped up just as we did, laughing heartily
at having slept so late. All the village men were
gathered to see the Feringhis, and the Ilbegi and his
brothers received us at the garden gate, all shaking hands.
Certainly this Khan has much power in his face, and his
dignified and easy manner is that of a leader of men.
His dress was becoming, a handsome dark blue cloak
lined with scarlet, and with a deep fur collar, over his
ordinary costume.

So much has been said and written about the Bakhtiaris being " savages " or " semi-savages," that the enter-
tainment which followed was quite a surprise to me.
Two fine canopy tents were pitched in the shade, and
handsome carpets were laid in them, and under a spread-
ing walnut tree a *karsi*, or fire cover, covered with a rug,
served as a table, and cigarettes, a bowl of ice, a glass jug
of *sharbat*, and some tumblers were neatly arranged upon
it. Iron chairs were provided for the European guests,
and the Ilbegi, his brothers, the Ilkhani's sons, and others
sat round the border of the carpet on which they were
placed. There were fully fifty attendants. Into the
midst of this masculine crowd, a male nurse brought the
Ilbegi's youngest child, a dark, quiet, pale, wistful little
girl of four years old, a daintily-dressed little creature,
with a crimson velvet cap, and a green and crimson velvet

frock.   She was gentle and confiding, and liked to remain
with me.

After a long conversation on subjects more or less
worth speaking upon, our hosts retired, to sleep under the
trees, leaving us to eat, and a number of servants brought
in a large *karsi* covered with food.   Several yards of
blanket bread, or " flapjacks," served as a table-cloth, and
another for the dish-cover of a huge *pillau* in the centre.
Cruets, plates, knives and forks, iced water, Russian
lemonade, and tumblers were all provided.   The dinner
consisted of *pillau*, lamb cutlets, a curried fowl, celery
with sour sauce, clotted cream, and sour milk.   The
food was well cooked and clean, and the servants, rough
as they looked, were dexterous and attentive.

After dinner, by the Ilbegi's wish, I paid a visit
to the ladies of his *haram*.   Naghun rivals the other
villages of the tribes in containing the meanest and
worst permanent habitations I have ever seen.   Isfandyar
Khan's house is a mud building surrounding a courtyard,
through which the visitor passes into another, round
which are the women's apartments.   Both yards were
forlorn, uneven, and malodorous, from the heaps of offal
and rubbish lying under the hot sun.   I was received by
fifteen ladies in a pleasant, clean, whitewashed apartment,
with bright rugs and silk-covered pillows on the floor,
and glass bottles and other ornaments in the *takchahs*.

At the top of the room I was welcomed, not by the
principal wife, but by a portly middle-aged woman, the
Khan's sister, and evidently the duenna of the *haram*, as
not one of the other women ventured to speak, or to offer
any courtesies.   A chair was provided for me with a
karsi in front of it, covered with trays of *gaz* and other
sweetmeats.   Mirza and a male attendant stood in the
doorway, and outside shoals of women and children on
tip-toe were struggling for a glance into the room.

Several slaves were present, coal-black, woolly-headed, huge-mouthed negresses. The fifteen ladies held their gay *chadars* to their faces so as to show only one eye, so I sent Mirza behind a curtain and asked for the pleasure of seeing their faces, when they all unveiled with shrieks of laughter.

The result was disappointing. The women were all young, or youngish, but only one was really handsome. The wives are brunettes with long chins. They wore gay *chadars* of muslin, short gold-embroidered jackets, gauze chemises, and bright-coloured balloon trousers. Three of the others wore black satin balloon trousers, black silk jackets, yellow gauze vests, and black *chadars* spotted with white. These three were literally moon-faced, like the representations of the moon on old clocks, a type I have not yet seen. All wear the hair brought to the front, where it hangs in wavy masses on each side of the face. They wore black silk gold-embroidered skull-caps, set back on their heads, and long chains of gold coins from the back to the ear, with two, three, or four long necklaces of the same in which the coins were very large and handsome. One wife, a young creature, was poorly dressed, very dejected-looking, and destitute of ornaments. Her mother has since pleaded for something " to bring back her husband's love." The eyebrows were painted with indigo and were made to meet in a point on the bridge of the nose. Each had one stained or tattooed star on her forehead, three on her chin, and a galaxy on the back of each hand.

Before Mirza reappeared they huddled themselves up in their *chadars* and sat motionless against the wall as before. After tea I had quite a lively conversation with the Khan's sister, who has been to Basrah, Baghdad, and Mecca.

Besides the usual questions as to my age, dyeing my

hair, painting my face, etc., with suggestions on the improvement which their methods would make on my eyes and eyebrows, she asked a little about my journeys, about the marriage customs of England, about divorce, the position of women with us, their freedom, horsemanship, and amusements. She said, "We don't ride, we sit on horses." Dancing for amusement she could not understand. "Our servants dance for us," she said. The dancing of men and women together, and the evening dress of Englishwomen, she thought contrary to the elementary principles of morality. I wanted them to have their photographs taken, but they said, "It is not the custom of our country; no good women have their pictures taken, we should have many things said against us if we were made into pictures."

They wanted to give me presents, but I made my usual excuse, that I have made a rule not to receive presents in travelling; then they said that they would go and see me in my tent at Chigakhor, their summer quarters, and that I could not refuse what they took in their own hands. They greatly desired to see the Agha, of whose imposing *physique* they had heard, but they said that the Khan would not like them to go to the garden, and that their wish must remain ungratified. "We lead such dull lives," the Khan's sister exclaimed; "we never see any one or go anywhere." It seems that the slightest development of intellect awakens them to the consciousness of this deplorable dulness, of which, fortunately, the unawakened intelligence is unaware. As a fact, two of the ladies have not been out of the Ardal valley, and are looking forward to the migration to the Chigakhor valley as to a great gaiety.

They asked me if I could read, and if I made carpets? They invariably ask if I have a husband and children, and when I tell them that I am a widow and childless, they simulate weeping for one or two minutes, a hypocrisy which, though it proceeds from a kindly feeling, has a very painful effect. Their occupation in the winter is a little carpet-weaving, which takes the place of our "fancy-work." They also make a species of *nougat*, from the manna found on the oaks on some of their mountains, mixed with chopped almonds and rose-water. When I concluded my visit they sent a servant with me with a tray of this and other sweetmeats of their own making.

The party in the garden was a very merry one. The Bakhtiaris love fun, and shrieked with laughter at many things. This jollity, however, did not exclude topics of interesting talk. During this time *Karun*, a handsome chestnut Arab, and my horse *Screw* had a fierce fight, and Karim, a Beloochi, in separating them had his arm severely crunched and torn, the large muscles being exposed and lacerated. He was brought in faint and bleeding, and in great pain, and will not be of any use for some time. The Agha asked the Ilbegi for two lads to go with him to help his servants. The answer was, "We are a wandering people, Bakhtiaris cannot be servants, but some of our young men will go with you,"—and three brothers joined us there, absolute savages in their ways. A cow was offered for the march, and on the Agha jocularly saying that he should have all the milk, the Ilbegi said that I should have one to myself, and sent two. He complained that I did not ask for anything, and said that I was their guest so long as I was in their country, and must treat them as brothers and ask for all I need. "Don't feel as if you were in a foreign land" he said; "we love the English."   I. L. B.

LETTER XV

ARDAL, *May 14.*

THE week spent here has passed rapidly. There is much coming and going. My camp is by the side of a frequented pathway, close to a delicious spring, much resorted to by Ilyat women, who draw water in *mussocks* and copper pots, and gossip there. The Ilyats are on the march to their summer quarters, and the steady tramp of their flocks and herds and the bleating of their sheep is heard at intervals throughout the nights. Sometimes one of their horses or cows stumbles over the tent ropes and nearly brings the tent down. Servants of the Ilkhani with messages and presents of curds, celery pickled in sour cream, and apricots, go to and fro. Sick people come at intervals all day long, and the medicine chest is in hourly requisition.

The sick are not always satisfied with occasional visits to the *Hakīm's* tent: a man, who has a little daughter ill of jaundice, after coming twice for medicine, has brought a tent, and has established himself in it with his child close to me, and a woman with bad eyes has also pitched a tent near mine; at present thirteen people come twice daily to have zinc lotion dropped into their eyes. The fame of the "tabloids" has been widely spread, and if I take common powders out of papers, or liquids out of bottles, the people shake their heads and say they do not want those, but " the fine medicines out of the leather box." To such an extent is this preference carried that they reject decoctions of a species of *artemisia*, a powerful tonic, unless I put tabloids of permanganate of potass (Condy's fluid) into the bottle before their eyes.

They have no idea of the difference between curable and incurable maladies. Many people, stone blind, have come long distances for eye-lotion, and to-night a man nearly blind came in, leading a man totally blind for eight years, asking me to restore his sight. The blind had led the blind from a camp twenty-four miles off! Octogenarians believe that I can give them back their hearing, and men with crippled or paralysed limbs think that if I would give them some "Feringhi ointment," of which they have heard, they would be restored. Some come to stare at a Feringhi lady, others to see my tent, which they occasionally say is "fit for Allah," and the general result is that I have very little time to myself.

The Ardal plateau is really pretty at this season, and I have had many pleasant evening gallops over soft green grass and soft red earth. The view from the tent is pleasant: on the one side the green slopes which fall down to the precipices which overhang the Karun, with the snowy mountains, deeply cleft, of the region which is still a geographical mystery beyond them; on the other, mountains of naked rock with grass running up into their ravines, and between them and me billows of grass and wild flowers. A barley slope comes down to my tent. The stalks are only six inches long, and the ears, though ripe, contain almost nothing. Every evening a servant of the Ilkhani brings three little wild boars to feed on the grain. Farther down the path are the servants' and muleteers' camps, surrounded by packing-cases, *yekdans*, mule-bags, nose-bags, gear of all kinds, and the usual litter of an encampment.

The men, whether Indian, Persian, Beloochi, or

Bakhtiari, are all quiet and well-behaved. The motto of the camps is "Silence is golden." Hadji Hussein is quiet in manner and speech, and though he has seven muleteers, yells and shouts are unknown.

There is something exciting in the prospect of travelling through a region much of which is unknown and unmapped, and overlooked hitherto by both geographical and commercial enterprise; and in the prospective good fortune of learning the manners and customs of tribes untouched by European influence, and about whose reception of a Feringhi woman doleful prophecies have been made.

Tur, May 18.—The last day at Ardal was a busy one. Several of the Khans called to take leave. I made a farewell visit to the Ilkhani's *haram*; people came for medicines at intervals from 5 A.M. till 9 P.M.; numberless eye-lotions had to be prepared; stores, straps, ropes, and equipments had to be looked to; presents to be given to the Ilkhani's servants; native shoes, with webbing tops and rag soles, to be hunted for to replace boots which could not be mended, and it was late before the preparations were completed. During the night some of my tent ropes were snapped by a stampede of mules, and a heavy thunderstorm coming on with wind and rain, the tent flapped about my ears till dawn.

It was very hot when we left the next morning. The promised escort was not forthcoming. The details of each day's march have been much alike. I start early, taking Mirza with me with the *shuldari*, halt usually half-way, and have a frugal lunch of milk and biscuits, read till the caravan has passed, rest in my tent for an hour, and ride on till I reach the spot chosen for the camp. Occasionally on arriving it is found that the place selected on local evidence is unsuitable, or the water is scanty or bad, and we march farther.

The greatest luxury is to find the tent pitched, the camp bed put up, and the kettle boiling for afternoon tea. I rest, write, and work till near sunset, when I dine on mutton and rice, and go to bed soon after dark, as I breakfast at four. An hour or two is taken up daily with giving medicines to sick people.

There are no villages, but camps occur frequently. The three young savages brought from Naghun are very amusing from the savage freedom of their ways, but they exasperate the servants by quizzing and mimicking them. The cows are useless. Between them they give at most a teacupful of milk, and generally none. Either the calves or the boys take it, or the marches are too much for them. In the Ilyat camps there is plenty, but as it is customary to mix the milk of sheep, goats, and cows, and to milk the animals with dirty hands into dirty copper pots, and almost at once to turn the milk into a sour mass, like whipped cream in appearance, by shaking it with some " leaven " in a dirty goat-skin, a European cannot always drink it. Indeed, it goes through every variety of bad taste.

The camps halt on Sundays, and the men highly appreciate the rest. They sleep, smoke, wash and mend their clothes, and are in good humour and excellent trim on Monday morning, and the mules show their unconscious appreciation of a holiday by coming into camp kicking and frolicking.

The baggage animals are fine, powerful mules and horses, with not a sore back among them. The pack saddles and tackle are all in good order. The caravan is led by a horse caparisoned with many bells and tassels, a splendid little gray fellow, full of pluck and fire, called Cock o' the Walk. He comes in at the end of a long march, arching his neck, shaking his magnificent mane, and occasionally kicking off his load. Sometimes he

knocks down two or three men, dashes off with his load at
a gallop, and even when hobbled manages to hop up to the
two Arabs and challenge them to a fight.   These handsome
horses have some of the qualities for which their breed is
famous, and are as surefooted as goats, but they are very
noisy, and they hate each other and disturb the peace of
the camp by their constant attempts to fight.   My horse,
Screw, can go wherever a mule can find foothold.   He
is ugly, morose, a great fighter, and most uninteresting.
The donkeys and a fat retriever are destitute of "salient
points."

Hadji Hussein, the *charvadar,* has elevated his profession into an art.   On reaching camp, after unloading,
each muleteer takes away the five animals for which he
is responsible, and liberates them, with the saddles on, to
graze.   After a time they drive them into camp, remove the
saddles, and groom them thoroughly, while the saddler goes
over the equipments, and does any repairs that are needed.
After the grooming each muleteer, having examined the
feet of his animals, reports upon them, and Hadji replaces
all lost shoes and nails.   The saddles and the *juls* or
blankets are then put on, the mules are watered in
batches of five, and are turned loose for the night to feed,
with two muleteers to watch them by turns.   Hadji, whose
soft voice and courteous manners make all dealings with
him agreeable, receives his orders for the morrow, and he
with his young son, Abbas Ali, and the rest of the muleteers, camp near my tent, cook their supper of blanket
bread with *mast* or curds, roll their heads and persons in
blankets, put their feet to the fire, and are soon asleep,
but Hadji gets up two or three times in the night to look
after his valuable property.

At 4 A.M. or earlier, the mules are driven into camp,
and are made fast to ropes, which are arranged the previous
night by pegging them down in an oblong forty feet by

twenty. Nose-bags with grain are put on; and as the loads are got ready the mules are loaded, with Hadji's help and supervision. No noise is allowed during this operation.

After an hour or more the caravan moves, led by Cock o' the Walk, usually with two men at his head to moderate his impetuosity for a time, with a guide; and Hadji on his fine-looking saddle mule looks after the safety of everything. He is punctual, drives fast and steadily, and always reaches the camping-ground in good time. When he gets near it he dismounts, and putting on the air of " your most obedient servant," leads in Cock o' the Walk. He is really a very gentlemanly man for his position, but is unfortunately avaricious, and though he has amassed what is, for Persia, a very large fortune, he wears very poor clothes, and eats sparingly of the poorest food. He is a big man of fifty, wears blue cotton clothing and a red turban, is very florid, and having a white or very gray beard, has dyed it an orange red with henna.

My servants have fallen fairly well into their work, but are frightfully slow. All pitch the tents, and Hassan cooks, washes, packs the cooking and table equipments, and saddles my horse. Mirza Yusuf interprets, waits on me, packs the tent furnishings, rides with me, and is always within hearing of my whistle. He is good, truthful, and intelligent, sketches with some talent, is always cheerful, never grumbles, is quite indifferent to personal comfort, gets on well with the people, is obliging to every one, is always ready to interpret, and though well educated has the good sense not to regard any work as " menial." Mehemet Ali, the " superfluity," is a scamp, and, I fear, dishonest. The servants feed themselves on a *kran* (8d.) a day, allowed as " road money." Sheep are driven with us, and are turned into mutton as required. Really, they follow us, attaching themselves to the gray horses, and feeding almost among their feet.

My food consists of roast mutton, rice, *chapatties*, tea, and milk, without luxuries or variety. Life is very simple and very free from purposeless bothers. The days are becoming very hot, but the nights are cool. The black flies and the sand-flies are the chief tormentors.

On leaving Ardal we passed very shortly into a region little traversed by Europeans, embracing remarkable gorges and singularly abrupt turns in ravines, through which the Karun, here a deep and powerful stream, finds its way. A deep descent over grassy hills to a rude village in a valley and a steep ascent took us to the four booths, which are the summer quarters of our former escort, Rustem Khan, who received us with courteous hospitality, and regaled us with fresh cow's milk in a copper basin. He introduced me to twelve women and a number of children, nearly all with sore eyes. There is not a shadow of privacy in these tents, with open fronts and sides. The carpets, which are made by the women, serve as chairs, tables, and beds, and the low wall of roughly-heaped stones at the back for trunks and wardrobe, for on it they keep their "things" in immense saddle-bags made of handsome rugs. The visible furniture consists of a big copper bowl for food, a small one for milk, a huge copper pot for clarifying butter, and a goat-skin suspended from three poles, which is jerked by two women seated on the ground, and is used for churning butter and making curds.

A steep ascent gives a superb view of a confused sea of mountains, and of a precipitous and tremendous gorge, the Tang-i-Ardal, through which the Karun passes, making a singularly abrupt turn after leaving a narrow and apparently inaccessible cañon or rift on the south side of the Ardal valley. A steep zigzag descent of 600 feet in less than three-quarters of a mile brings the path down to the Karun, a deep bottle-green river, now swirling in drifts of foam, now resting momentarily in quiet depths, but always giving an impression of volume and power. Large and small land turtles abound in that fiercely hot gorge of from 1000 to 2000 feet deep. The narrow road crosses the river on a bridge of two arches, and proceeds for some distance at a considerable height on its right bank. There I saw natural wood for the first time since crossing the Zagros mountains in January, and though the oak, ash, and maple are poor and stunted, their slender shade was delicious. Roses, irises, St. John's wort, and other flowers were abundant.

The path ascends past a clear spring, up steep zigzags to a graveyard in which are several stone lions, rudely carved, of natural size, facing Mecca-wards, with pistols, swords, and daggers carved in relief on their sides, marking the graves of fighting men. On this magnificent point above the Karun a few hovels, deserted in summer, surrounded by apricot trees form the village of Duashda Imams, which has a superb view of the extraordinary and sinuous chasm through which the Karun passes for many miles, thundering on its jagged and fretted course between gigantic and nearly perpendicular cliffs of limestone and conglomerate. Near this village the pistachio is abundant, and planes, willows, and a large-leaved clematis vary the foliage.

Leaving the river at this point, a somewhat illegible path leads through " park-like " scenery, fair slopes of grass and flowers sprinkled with oaks singly or in clumps, glades among trees in their first fresh green, and evermore as a background gray mountains slashed with snow.

In the midst of these pretty uplands is the Ilyat encampment of Martaza, with its black tents, donkeys, sheep, goats, and big fierce dogs, which vociferously rushed upon *Downie*, the retriever, and were themselves rushed upon and gripped by a number of women. The people, having been informed of our intended arrival by Reza Kuli Khan, had arranged a large tent with carpets and cushions, but we pitched the camps eventually on an oak-covered slope, out of the way of the noise, curiosity, and evil odours of Martaza. Water is very scarce there, three wells or pools, fouled by the feet of animals, being the only supply.

I rested on my *dhurrie* under an oak till the caravan came up. It was a sweet place, but was soon invaded, and for the rest of the day quiet and privacy were out of the question, for presently appeared a fine, florid, buxom dame, loud of speech, followed by a number of women and children, all as dirty as it is possible to be, and all crowded round me and sat down on my carpet. This *Khanum Shirin* is married to the chief or headman, but being an heiress she " bosses " the tribe. She brought up bolsters and quilts, and begged us to consider themselves, the whole region, and all they had as *pishkash* (a present from an inferior to a superior), but when she was asked if it included herself, she blushed and covered her face. After two hours of somewhat flagging conversation she led her train back again, but after my tent was pitched she reappeared with a much larger number of women, including two betrothed girls of sixteen and seventeen years old, who are really beautiful.

These maidens were dressed in clean cotton costumes, and white veils of figured silk gauze enveloped them from head to foot. They unveiled in my tent, and looked more like *houris* than any women I have seen in the East; and their beauty was enhanced by the sweetness and maidenly modesty of their expression. I wished them to be photographed, and they were quite willing, but when I took them outside some men joined the crowd and said it should not be, and that when their betrothed husbands came home they would tell them how bold and bad they had been, and would have them beaten. Although these beauties had been most modest and maidenly in their behaviour, they were sent back with blows, and were told not to come near us again. The Agha entertained the *Khanum Shirin* for a long time, and the conversation was very animated, but when he set a very fine musical box going for their amusement the lady and the rest of the crowd became quite listless and apathetic, and said they much preferred to talk. When their prolonged visit came to an end the *Khanum* led her train away, with a bow which really had something of graceful dignity in it.

The next morning her husband, the *Mollah-i-Martaza*, and his son, mounted on one horse, came with us as guides, and when we halted at their camp the *Khanum* took the whip out of my hand and whipped the women all round with it, except the offending beauties, who were not to be seen. The *mollah* is a grave, quiet, and most respectable - looking man, more like a thriving merchant than a nomad chief, though he does carry arms. He is a devout Moslem, and is learned, *i.e.* he can read the Koran.

In a short time the woodland beauty is exchanged for weedy hills and slopes strewn with boulders. Getting other guides at an Ilyat camp, we ascended Sanginak, a mountain 8200 feet high, from the top of which a good idea of the local topography is gained. The most striking features are the absence of definite peaks and the tremendous gorges and abrupt turns of the Karun, which swallows in its passage all minor streams. Precipitous ranges of great altitude hemmed in by ranges yet loftier, snow-covered or snow-patched, with deep valleys between them, well grassed and often well wooded, great clefts, through which at some seasons streams reach the Karun ; mountain meadows spotted with the black tents of Ilyats, and deserted hovels far below, with patches of wheat and barley, make up the land-scape.

These hills are covered with celery of immense size. The leaves are dried and stacked for fodder, and the underground stalks, which are very white, are a great article of food, both fresh and steeped for a length of time in sour milk. After resting in some Ilyat tents, where the people were friendly and dirty, we had a most tiresome march over treeless hills covered with herbs, and down a steep descent into the Gurab plain, on which a great wall of rocky mountains of definite and impressive shapes descends in broken spurs. My guide, who had never been certain about the way, led me wrong. No tents were visible, the nomads I met had seen neither tents nor caravan. Two hours went by in toiling round the bases of green hills, and then there was the joyful surprise of coming upon my tent pitched, the kettle boiling, the mules knee-deep in food, close by the Chesmeh-i-Gurab, a copious spring of good water, of which one could safely drink.

This Gurab plain, one of very many lying high up among these Luristan mountains, is green and pretty now— a sea of bulbs and grass, but is brown and dusty from early in June onwards. It is about four miles long by nine or ten broad, and is watered by a clear and wonder-fully winding stream, which dwindles to a thread later on. The nomads are already coming up.

The rest was much broken by the critical state of Karim's arm, which was swelled, throbbing, and inflamed all round the wound inflicted by *Karun* on May 13, and he had high fever. It was a helpless predicament, the symptoms were so like those of gangrene. I thought he would most likely die of the hot marches. It was a very anxious night, as all our methods of healing were exhausted, and the singular improvement which set in and has continued must have been the work of the Great Physician, to whom an appeal for help was earnestly made. The wound is daily syringed with Condy's fluid, the only antiseptic available, and has a drainage tube. To-day I have begun to use eucalyptus oil, with which the man is delighted, possibly because he has heard that it is very expensive, and that I have hardly any left!

Yesterday I had the amusement of shifting the camps to another place, and Hadji was somewhat doubtful of my leadership. On arriving at the beautiful crystal spring which the guide had indicated as the halting-place for Sunday, I found that it issued from under a mound of grass-grown graves, was in the full sun blaze, and at the lowest part of the plain. The guide asserted that it was the only spring, but having seen a dark stain of vegetation high among the hills, I halted the caravan and rode off alone in search of the water I hoped it indicated, disregarding the suppressed but unmistakably sneering laughter of the guide and *charvadars*. In less than a mile I came upon the dry bed of a rivulet, a little higher up on a scanty, intermittent trickle, higher still on a gurgling streamlet fringed by masses of blue scilla, and still higher on a small circular spring of very cold water, with two flowery plateaux below it just large enough for the camps, in a green quiet corrie, with the mountains close behind. Hadji laughed, and the guide insisted that the spring was not always there. A delightful place it is in which to spend Sunday quietly, with its musical ripple of water, its sky-blue carpet of scilla, its beds of white and purple irises, its slopes ablaze with the *Fritillaria imperialis*, and its sweet, calm view of the green Gurab plain and the silver windings of the Dinarud.

Above the spring is the precipitous hill of Tur, with

the remains of a rude fort on its shattered rocky summit. Two similar ruins are visible from Tur, one on a rocky ledge of an offshoot of the Kuh-i-Gerra, on the other side of the Dinarud valley, the other on the crest of a noble headland of the Sanganaki range, which is visible throughout the whole region. The local legend concerning them is that long before the days of the Parthian kings, and when bows and arrows were the only weapons known, iron being undiscovered, there was in the neighbourhood of Gurab a king called Faruk Padishah, who had three sons, Salmon, Tur, and Iraj. It does not appear to be usual among the Bakhtiaris for sons to "get on" together after their father's death, and the three youths quarrelled and built these three impregnable forts—Killa Tur, the one I examined, Killa Iraj, and Killa Salmon.

The beautiful valley was evidently too narrow for their ambition, and leaving their uncomfortable fastnesses they went northwards, and founded three empires, Salmon to the Golden Horn, where he founded Stamboul, Tur to Turkistan, and Iraj became the founder of the Iranian Empire.

Killa Tur is a stone building mostly below the surface of the hill-top, of rough hewn stone cemented with lime mortar of the hardness of concrete. The inner space of the fort is not more than eighty square yards. The walls are from three to six feet thick.

Chigakhor, May 31.—The last twelve days have been spent in marching through a country which has not been traversed by Europeans, only crossed along the main track. On leaving the pleasant camp of Tur we descended to the Gurab plain, purple in patches with a showy species of garlic, skirted the base of the Tur spur, and rode for some miles along the left bank of the Dinarud, which, after watering the plain of Gurab, sparkles and rushes down a grassy valley bright with roses and lilies, and well wooded with oak, elm, and hawthorn. This river, gaining continually in volume, makes a turbulent descent to the Karun a few miles from the point where we left it. This was the finest day's march of the journey. The mountain forms were grander and more definite, the vegetation richer, the scenery more varied, and a kindlier atmosphere pervaded it. In the midst of a wood of fine walnut trees, ash, and hawthorn, laced together by the tendrils of vines, a copious stream tumbles over rocks fringed with maiden-hair, and sparkles through grass purple with orchises. This is the only time that I have seen the one or the other in Persia, and it was like an unexpected meeting with dear friends.

Crossing the Dinarud on a twig bridge, fording a turbulent affluent, which bursts full fledged from the mountain side, and ascending for some hours through grassy glades wooded with oak and elm, we camped for two days on the alpine meadow of Arjul, scantily watered but now very green. Oak woods come down upon it, the vines are magnificent, and there is some cultivation of wheat, which is sown by the nomads before their departure in the late autumn, and is reaped during their summer sojourn. There are no tents there at present, yet from camps near and far, on horseback and on foot, people came for eye-lotions, and remained at night to have them dropped into their eyes.

The next morning I was awakened at dawn by Mirza's voice calling to me, " Madam, Hadji wants you to come down and sew up a mule that's been gored by a wild boar." Awfully gored it was. A piece of skin about ten inches square was hanging down between its forelegs, and a broad wound the depth of my hand and fully a foot long extended right into its chest, with a great piece taken out. I did what I could, but the animal had to be left behind to be cured by the Mollah-i-Martaza, who

left us there.   Another misfortune to Hadji was the loss
of the fiery leader of the caravan, Cock o' the Walk, but
late at night he was brought into camp at Dupulan quite
crestfallen, having gone back to the rich pastures which
surround the Chesmeh-i-Gurab.   The muleteer who went
in search of him was attacked by some Lurs and stripped
of his clothing, but on some men coming up who said
his master was under the protection of the Ilkhani, his
clothes and horse were returned to him.

The parallel ranges with deep valleys between them,
which are such a feature of this country, are seen in perfection near Arjul.   Some of the torrents of this mountain region are already dry, but their broad stony beds,
full of monstrous boulders, arrest the fury with which at
times they seek the Karun.   One of these, the Imamzada,
passes through the most precipitous and narrow gorge
which it is possible to travel, even with unloaded mules.
The narrow path is chiefly rude rock ladders, threading a
gorge or chasm on a gigantic scale, with a compressed
body of water thundering below, concealed mainly by
gnarled and contorted trees, which find root-hold in every
rift.   Where the chasm widens for a space before
narrowing to a throat we forded it, and through glades
and wooded uplands reached Arjul, descending and
crossing the torrent by the same ford on the march to
Dupulan the next day.

Owing to the loss of two baggage animals and the
necessary re-adjustment of the loads, I was late in starting from Arjul, and the heat as we descended to the
lower levels was very great, the atmosphere being misty
as well as sultry.   Passing upwards, through glades
wooded with oaks, the path emerges on high gravelly
uplands above the tremendous gorge of the Karun, the
manifold windings of which it follows at a great height.
From the first sight of this river in the Ardal valley to

THE KARUN AT DUPULAN.

its emergence at Dupulan, just below these heights, it has come down with abrupt elbow-like turns and singular sinuosities—a full, rapid, powerful glass-green volume of water, through a ravine or gorge or chasm from 1000 to 2000 feet in depth, now narrowing, now widening, but always *the* feature of the landscape.   It would be natural to use the usual phrase, and write of the Karun having " carved " this passage for itself, but I am more and more convinced that this is not the case, but that its waters found their way into channels already riven by some of those mighty operations of nature which have made of this country a region of walls and clefts.

A long, very steep gravelly descent leads from these high lands down to the Karun, and to one of the routes —little used, however—from Isfahan to Shuster.   It is reported as being closed by snow four months of the year. The scenery changed its aspect here, and for walls and parapets of splintered rock there are rounded gravelly hills and stretching uplands.

The three groups of most wretched mud hovels which form the village of Dupulan ("Two Bridge Place") are on an eminence on the left bank of the Karun, which emerges from its long imprisonment in a gorge in the mountains by a narrow passage between two lofty walls of rock so smooth and regular in their slope and so perfect a gateway as to suggest art rather than nature.   This river, the volume of which is rapidly augmenting on its downward course, is here compressed into a width of about twenty yards.

At this point a stone bridge, built by Hussein Kuli Khan, of one large pointed arch with a smaller one for the flood, and a rough roadway corresponding to the arch in the steepness of its pitch, spans the stream, which passes onwards gently and smoothly, its waters a deep cool green.   Below Dupulan the Karun, which in that direction has been explored by several travellers, turns to the south-west, and after a considerable bend enters the levels above Shuster by a north-westerly course. Near the bridge the Karun is joined by the Sabzu, a very vigorous torrent from the Ardal plain, which is crossed by a twig bridge, safer than it looks.

The camps were pitched in apricot orchards in the Sabzu ravine, near some *elægnus* trees, which are now bearing their sweet gray and yellow blossoms, which will be succeeded by auburn tresses of a woolly but very pleasant fruit. Dupulan has an altitude of only 4950 feet, and in its course from the Kuh-i-Rang to this point the Karun has descended about 4000 feet. Though there was a breeze, and both ends of my tent and the *kanats* were open, the mercury was at 86° inside, and at 5 A.M. at 72° outside (on May 21). There were no supplies, and even milk was unattainable.

The road we followed ascends the Dupulan Pass, which it crosses at a height of 6380 feet. The path is very bad, hardly to be called a path. The valley which it ascends is packed with large and small boulders, with round water-worn stones among them, and such track as there is makes sharp zigzags over and among these rocks. *Screw* was very unwilling to face the difficulties, which took two hours to surmount. The ascent was hampered by coming upon a tribe of Ilyats on the move, who at times blocked up the pass with their innumerable sheep and goats and their herds of cattle. Once entangled in this migration, it was only possible to move on a few feet at a time. It straggled along for more than a mile,—loaded cows and bullocks, innumerable sheep, goats, lambs, and kids ; big dogs ; asses loaded with black tents and short tent-poles on the loads ; weakly sheep tied on donkeys' backs, and weakly lambs carried in shepherds' bosoms ; handsome mares, each with her foal, running loose or ridden by women with babies seated on the tops of loaded saddle-bags made of gay rugs ; tribesmen on foot with long guns slung behind their shoulders, and big two-edged knives in their girdles ; sheep bleating, dogs barking, mares neighing, men shouting and occasionally firing off their guns, the whole ravine choked up with the ascending tribal movement.

Half-way up the ascent there is a most striking view of mountain ranges cleft by the great chasm of the Karun. The descent is into the eastern part of the Ardal valley, over arid treeless hillsides partially ploughed, to the village of Dehnau, not yet deserted for the summer. Fattiallah Khan expected us, and rooms were prepared for me in the women's house, which I excused myself from occupying by saying that I cannot sleep under a roof. I managed also to escape partaking of a huge garlicky dinner which was being cooked for me.

The Khan's house or fort, built like all else of mud, has a somewhat imposing gateway, over which are the men's apartments. The roof is decorated with a number of ibex horns. Within is a rude courtyard with an uneven surface, on which servants and negro slaves were skinning sheep, winnowing wheat, clarifying butter, carding wool, cooking, and making cheese. The women's apartments are round the courtyard, and include the usual feature of these houses, an *atrium*, or room without a front, and a darkish room within. The floor of the *atrium* was covered with brown felts, and there was a mattress for me to sit upon. The ruling spirit of the *haram* is the Khan's mother, a comely matron of enormous size, who occasionally slapped her son's four young and comely wives when they were too " forward." She wore a short jacket, balloon-like trousers of violet silk, and a black coronet, to which was attached a black *chadar* which completely enveloped her.

The wives wore figured white *chadars*, print trousers,

and strings of coins.   Children much afflicted with
cutaneous maladies crawled on the floor.   Heaps of
servants, negro slaves, old hags, and young girls crowded
behind and around, all talking at once and at the top of
their voices, and at the open front the village people
constantly assembled, to be driven away at. intervals
by a man with a stick.   A bowl of cow's milk and
some barley bread were given to me, and though a
remarkably dirty negress kept the flies away by flapping
the milk bowl with a dirty sleeve, I was very grateful
for the meal, for I was really suffering from the heat and
fatigue.

A visit to a *haram* is not productive of mutual
elevation.   The women seem exceedingly frivolous, and
are almost exclusively interested in the adornment of
their persons, the dress and ailments of their children,
and in the frightful jealousies and intrigues inseparable
from the system of polygamy, and which are fostered by
the servants and discarded wives.   The servile deference
paid by the other women to the reigning favourite before
her face, and the merciless persistency of the attempts
made behind her back to oust her from her position,
and the requests made on the one hand for charms or
potions to win or bring back the love of a husband, and
on the other for something which shall make the favourite hateful to him, are evidences of the misery of heart
which underlies the outward frivolity.

The tone of Fattiallah Khan's *haram* was not higher
than usual.   The ladies took off my hat, untwisted my
hair, felt my hands, and shrieked when they found that
my gloves came off; laughed immoderately at my Bakhtiari shoes, which, it seems, are only worn by men; put
their rings on my fingers, put my hat on their own
heads, asked if I could give them better hair dyes than
their own, and cosmetics to make their skins fair; paid

the usual compliments, told me to regard everything as *pishkash*, asked for medicines and charms, and regretted that I would not sleep in their house, because, as they said, they "never went anywhere or saw anything."

They have no occupation, except occasionally a little embroidery. They amuse themselves, they said, by watching the servants at work, and by having girls to dance before them. They find the winter, though spent in a warm climate, very long and wearisome, and after dark employ female professional story-tellers to entertain them with love stories. At night the elder lady sent three times for a charm which should give her daughter the love of her husband. She is married to another Khan, and I recalled her as the forlorn-looking girl without any jewels who excited my sympathies in his house.

Marriages are early among these people. They are arranged by the parents of both bride and bridegroom. The betrothal feast is a great formality. The "settlements" having been made by the bridegroom's father and mother, they distribute sweetmeats among the members of the bride's family, and some respectable men who are present tie a handkerchief round the head of the bride, and kiss the hands of her parents as a sign of the betrothal. The engagement must be fulfilled by the bride's parents under pain of severe penalties, from which the bridegroom's parents are usually exempt. But, should he prove faithless, he is a marked man. It appears that "breach of promise of marriage" is very rare. The betrothal may take place at the tenderest age, but the marriage is usually delayed till the bride is twelve years old, or even older, and the bridegroom is from fifteen to eighteen.

The "settlements" made at the betrothal are paid at the time of marriage, and consist of a sum of money or

cattle, mares, or sheep, according to the circumstances
of the bridegroom's parents. It is essential among all
classes that a number of costumes be presented to the
bride. After the marriage is over her parents bestow a
suit of clothes on her husband, but these are usually of
an inferior, or, as my interpreter calls them, of a "trivial"
description.

A Bakhtiari marriage is a very noisy performance.
For three days or more, in fact as long as the festivities
can be afforded, the relations and friends of both parties
are assembled at the tents of the bride's parents, feasting
and dancing (men and women on this occasion dancing
together), performing feats of horsemanship, and shooting
at a mark. The noise at this time is ceaseless. Drums,
tom-toms, reeds, whistles, and a sort of bagpipe are all
in requisition, and songs of love and war are chanted.
At this time also is danced the national dance, the
chapi, of which on no other occasion (except a burial)
can a stranger procure a sight for love or money. It is
said to resemble the *arnaoutika* of the modern Greeks;
any number of men can join in it. The dancers form
in a close row, holding each other by their *kamarbands*,
and swinging along sidewise. They mark the time by
alternately stamping the heel of the right and left foot.
The dancers are led by a man who dances apart, waving
a handkerchief rhythmically above his head, and either
singing a war song or playing on a reed pipe. After
the marriage feast the bride follows her husband to his
father's tent, where she becomes subject to her mother-
in-law.

The messenger, after looking round to see that there
were no bystanders, very mysteriously produced from his
girdle a black, flattish oval stone of very close texture,
weighing about a pound, almost polished by long handling. He told me that it was believed that this stone, if

kept in one family for fifty years and steadily worn by father and son, would then not only turn to gold, but have the power of transmuting any metal laid beside it for five years, and he wanted to know what the wisdom of the Feringhis knew about it.

I went up to my camp above the village and tried to rest there, but the buzz of a crowd outside and the ceaseless lifting of curtains and *kanats* made this quite impossible. When I opened the tent I found the crowd seated in a semicircle five rows deep, waiting for medicines, chiefly eye-lotion, quinine, and cough mixtures. These daily assemblages of " patients " are most fatiguing. The satisfaction is that some " lame dogs " are " helped over stiles," and that some prejudice against Christians is removed.

After this Fattiallah Khan, with a number of retainers, paid a formal visit to the Agha, who kindly sent for me, as I do not receive any but lady visitors in my tent. The Khan is a very good-looking and well-dressed man of twenty-eight, very amusing, and ready to be amused. He was very anxious to be doctored, but looked the opposite of a sick man. He and Isfandyar Khan were in arms against the Ilkhani two years ago, and a few men were shot. He looked as if he were very sorry not to have killed him.

The Bakhtiaris have an enormous conceit of themselves and their country. It comes out in all ways and on all occasions, and their war stories and songs abound in legends of singular prowess, one Bakhtiari killing twenty Persians, and the like. They represent the power of the Shah over them as merely nominal, a convenient fiction for the time being, although it is apparent that Persia, which for years has been aiming at the extinction of the authority of the principal chiefs, has had at least a partial success.

At such interviews a private conversation is impossible. The manners are those of a feudal *régime*. Heaps of retainers crowd round, and even join in the conversation. A servant brought the Khan a handsome *kalian* to smoke three times. He also took tea. A great quantity of opium for exportation is grown about Dehnau, and the Khan said that the cultivation of it is always increasing.

From Dehnau the path I took leads over gravelly treeless hills, through many treeless gulches, to the top of a great gorge, through which the Sabzu passes as an impetuous torrent. The descent to a very primitive bridge is long and difficult, a succession of rocky zigzags. Picturesqueness is not a usual attribute of mud villages, but the view from every point of Chiraz, the village on the lofty cliffs on the other side of the stream, is strikingly so. They are irregularly covered with houses, partly built on them and partly excavated out of them, and behind is a cool mass of greenery, apricot orchards, magnificent walnut and mulberry trees, great standard hawthorns loaded with masses of blossom, wheat coming into ear, and clumps and banks of canary-yellow roses measuring three inches across their petals. Groups of women, in whose attire Turkey red predominated, were on the house roofs. Wild flowers abounded, and the sides of the craggy path by which I descended were crowded with leguminous and umbelliferous plants, with the white and pink dianthus, and with the thorny *tussocks* of the gum tragacanth, largely used for kindling, now in full bloom.

As I dragged my unwilling horse down the steep descent, his bridle was taken out of my hands, and I was welcomed by the brother of Fattiallah Khan, who, with a number of village men escorted me over the twig bridge, and up to an exquisite halting-place under a large mulberry tree, where the next two hours were spent in receiving visitors. It is evident that these fine orchards must have been the pleasure-ground of some powerful ruler, and the immense yellow roses are such as grow in one or two places in Kashmir, where they are attributed to Jehangir.

The track from Chiraz for many miles follows up the right bank of the Sabzu at a great height, descends occasionally into deep gulches, crosses the spurs of mountains whose rifts give root-hold to contorted "pencil cedars," and winds among small ash trees and hawthorns, or among rich grass and young wheat, which is grown to a considerable extent on the irrigated slopes above the river. It is a great surprise to find so much land under cultivation, and so much labour spent on irrigation channels. Some of these canals are several miles in length, and the water always runs in them swiftly, and the right way, although the "savages" who make them have no levels or any tools but spades.

Mountains, much scored and cañoned by streams, very grand in form, and with much snow still upon them, rise to a great height above the ranges which form the Sabzu valley. From Chaharta, an uninteresting camping-ground by the river, I proceeded by an elevated and rather illegible track in a easterly direction to the meeting of two streams, forded the Sabzu, and camped for two days on the green slope of Sabz Kuh, at a height of 8100 feet, close to a vigorous spring whose waters form many streamlets, fringed by an abundance of pink primulas, purple and white orchises, white tulips, and small fragrant blue irises.

Lahdaraz is in the very heart of mountain ranges, and as the Ilyats have not yet come up so high, there were no crowds round my tent for medicine, but one sick woman was carried thither eleven miles on the back of her husband, who seemed tenderly solicitous about her.

On Monday I spent most of the day 1000 feet higher, in most magnificent scenery on an imposing scale of grandeur. The guide took us from the camp through herbage, snow, and alpine flowers, up a valley with fine mountains on either side, terminating on the brink of a gigantic precipice, a cloven ledge between the Kuh-i-Kaller and a stupendous cliff or headland, Sultan Ibrahim, over 12,000 feet, which descends in shelving masses to an abyss of tremendous depth, where water thunders in a narrow rift. The Sabz Kuh, or "green mountain" range, famous for the pasturage of its higher slopes, terminates in Sultan Ibrahim, and unites at its eastern end with the Kuh-i-Kaller, a range somewhat higher. On the east side of this huge chasm rises another range of peaks, with green shelves, dark rifts, and red precipices, behind which rise another, and yet another, whose blue, snow-patched summits blended with the pure cool blue of the sky. In the far distance, in a blue veil, lies the green-tinted plain of Khana Mirza, set as an emerald in this savage scenery, with two ranges beyond, and above them the great mountain mass of the Riji, whose snowy peaks were painted faintly on a faint blue heaven.

That misty valley, irrigated and cultivated, with 100 villages of the Janiki tribe upon it, is the only fair spot in the savage landscape. Elsewhere only a few wild flowers and a gnarled juniper here and there relieve the fierce, blazing verdurelessness of these stupendous precipices. Never, not even among the Himalayas, have I seen anything so superlatively grand, though I have always imagined that such scenes must exist somewhere on the earth. A pair of wild sheep on a ledge, a serpent or two, and an eagle soaring sunwards represented animate nature, otherwise the tremendous heights above, the awful depths below, the snowy mountains, and the valley

with its smile, were given over to solitude and silence,
except for the dull roar of the torrent hurrying down
to vivify the Khana Mirza plain.

After leaving Lahdaraz the path followed the course of
the Sabzu through grass and barley for a few miles. Then
there is an abrupt and disagreeable change to yellow
mud slopes and high mud mountains deeply fissured,
the scanty herbage already eaten down by Ilyat flocks—
a desolate land, without springs, streams, or even Ilyat
tents. Then comes a precipice at an altitude of 7500
feet, through a cleft in which, the Tang-i-Wastagun, the
road passes, and descends to the plain of Gandaman as
something little better than a sheep track on a steep hillside above a stream. The heat was fierce. A pair of
stout gardening gloves does not preserve the hands from
blistering. Spectacles with wire gauze sides have to be
abandoned as they threaten to roast the eyes. In this
latitude, 32°, the heat of the sun at noon is tremendous.
At the precipice top I crept into a hole at the base of a
rock, for " the shadow of a great rock in a weary land,"
till the caravan staggered up. It was difficult to brave
the sun's direct rays. He looked like a ball of magnesium
light, white and scintillating, in the unclouded sky.

On crossing the Tang-i-Wastagun we left behind
the Bakhtiari country proper for a time, and re-entered
the Chahar Mahals, with their mixed village population
of Persians and Armenians. The descent from the
Tang-i-Wastagun is upon a ruined Armenian village with a
large graveyard. The tombstones are of great size, ten feet
long by three feet broad and three feet high, sarcophagus-
shaped, and on each stone are an Armenian epitaph and a
finely-engraved cross. The plain of Gandaman or Wastagun
is a very large one, over 7000 feet in altitude, and is surrounded mainly by high mountains still snow-patched,
but to the north by low rocky hills. Much of it is

irrigated and under cultivation, and grows heavy crops of
wheat and barley.   The pasturage is fine and abundant,
and the people breed cattle and horses.   The uncultivated
slopes are now covered with red tulips and a purple

ALI JAN.

allium, and even the
dry gravel added largely
to the daily increasing
botanical collection.

The   camps   were
pitched on green turf
near three springs, a
quiet place, but there
was little rest.   We
were hardly settled
before there was a
severe fight among the
horses, my sour-tem-
pered *Screw* being the
aggressor.   This was
hardly quieted when
there was a sharp
"scrimmage" between
the *charvadars* and the
Agha's three young
savages, in which one
of them, Ali Jan, was
badly beaten, and came
to me to have a bleed-
ing face and head
dressed.   After that the
people began to come
in from the villages
for eye-washes and medicines.   They have no bottles, nor
have I, and the better-off bring great copper jugs and
basins for an ounce or two of lotion!   A very poor old

woman much afflicted with ophthalmia said she had three sisters all blind, that she had nothing for lotion, nothing in the world but a copper cooking pot, and she cried piteously. I had nothing to give her, and eventually she returned with an egg-shell, with the top neatly chipped off. It is the custom to raise the hands to heaven and invoke blessings on the *Hakīm's* head, but I never received so many as from this poor creature.

The ride to the village of Gandaman, where we halted for two days, was an agreeable one. After being shut up among mountains and precipices, space and level ground to gallop over are an agreeable change, and in the early morning the heat was not excessive. The great plain was a truly pastoral scene. Wild-looking shepherds with long guns led great brown flocks to the hills; innumerable yokes of black oxen, ploughing with the usual iron-shod, pointed wooden share, turned over the rich black soil, making straight furrows, and crossing them diagonally; mares in herds fed with their foals; and shepherds busily separated the sheep from the goats.

Close to the filthy walled Armenian village of Kunak there is a conical hill with a large fort, in ruinous condition, upon it, and not far off are the remains of an Armenian village, enclosed by a square wall with a round tower at each corner. This must have been until recently a place of some local importance, as it is approached by a paved causeway, and had an aqueduct, now ruinous, carried over the river on three arches. Not only the plain but the hill-slopes up to a great height are cultivated, and though the latter have the precariousness of rain-lands, the crops already in ear promise well.

Crossing a spur which descends upon the north side of the plain, we reached Gandaman, a good-looking walled Moslem village of 196 houses, much planted, chiefly with willows, and rejoicing in eight springs, close together, the overflow of which makes quite a piece of water. It has an *imamzada* on an eminence and is fairly prosperous, for besides pastoral wealth it weaves and exports carpets, and dyes cotton and woollen yarn with madder and other vegetable dyes. The mountain view to the south-west is very fine.

I was in my tent early, but there was little rest, for crowds of people with bad eyes and woful maladies besieged it until the evening. At noon a gay procession crossed the green camping-ground, four mares caparisoned in red trappings, each carrying two women in bright dresses, but shrouded in pure white sheets bound round their heads with silver chains. The *ketchuda* of the Armenian village of Libasgun, two miles off, accompanied them, and said that they came to invite me to their village, for they are Christians. Then they all made the sign of the Cross, which is welcome in this land as a bond of brotherhood.

Cleanly, comely, large-eyed, bright-cheeked, and wholesome they looked, in their pure white *chadars*, gay red dresses, and embroidered under-vests. They had massive silver girdles, weighing several pounds, worn there only by married women, red coronets, heavy tiaras of silver, huge necklaces of coins, and large filigree silver drops attached down the edges of their too open vests. Their heavy hair was plaited, but not fastened up. Each wore a stiff diamond-shaped piece of white cotton over her mouth and the tip of her nose. They said it was their custom to wear it, and they would not remove it even to eat English biscuits! They managed to drink tea by veiling their faces with their *chadars* and passing the cup underneath, but they turned their faces quite away as they did it. They had come for the day, and had brought large hanks of wool to wind, but the headman had the tact to take them away after arranging for me to return the visit in the evening,

He seemed an intelligent man. Libasgun, with its 120 houses, is, according to his account, a prosperous village, paying its tax of 300 *tumans* (£100) a year to the Amin-ud-Daulat, and making a present only to the Ilkhani. It has 2000 sheep and goats, besides mares and cattle. It has an oil mill, and exports oil to Isfahan. The women weave carpets, and embroider beautifully on coarse cotton woven by themselves, and dyed indigo blue and madder red by their Gandaman neighbours. This man is proud of being a Christian. Among the Armenians Christianity is as much a national characteristic as pride of race and strict monogamy. He remarked that there are no sore eyes in Libasgun, and attributed it to the greater cleanliness of the people and to the cross signed in holy oil upon their brows in baptism!

I rode to this village in the late afternoon, and was received with much distinction in the *balakhana* of the *ketchuda's* house, where I was handed to the seat of honour, a bolster at the head of the handsomely-carpeted room. It soon filled with buxom women in red, with jackets displaying their figures, or want of figures, down to their waists. From the red velvet coronets on their heads hung two graduated rows of silver coins, and their muslin *chadars* were attached to their hair with large silver pins and chains. Magnificent necklaces of gold coins were also worn.

Forty women sat on the floor in rows against the wall. Each had rosy cheeks, big black eyes, and a diamond-shaped white cloth over her mouth. The uniformity was shocking. They stared, not at me, but at nothing. They looked listless and soulless, only fit to be what they are — the servants of their husbands. When they had asked me my age, and why I do not dye

my hair, the conversation flagged, for I could not get any
information from them even on the simplest topics.
Hotter and hotter grew the room, more stolid the vacancy
of the eyes, more grotesque the rows of white diamonds
over the mouths, when the happy thought occurred to

ARMENIAN WOMEN OF LIBASGUN.

me to ask to see the embroidered aprons, which every
girl receives from her mother on her marriage. Two
mountains of flesh obligingly rolled out of the room, and
rolled in again bringing some beautiful specimens of
needlework. This is really what is known as " Russian
embroidery," cross stitch in artistic colours on coarse red
or blue cotton. The stomachers are most beautifully

worked. The aprons cover the whole of the front and the sides of the dress. The mothers begin to embroider them when their daughters are ten. The diamond-shaped cloth is put on by girls at eight or nine. The women would not remove it for a moment even to oblige a guest. The perpetual wearing of it is one of their religious customs, only prevailing, however, in some localities. They say that when our Lord was born His mother in token of reverence took a cloth and covered her mouth, hence their habit.

When the *ketchuda* arrived he found the heat of the room unbearable and proposed an adjournment to the lower roof, which was speedily swept, watered, and carpeted.

An elaborate banquet had been prepared in the hope that the Agha would pay them a visit, and they were much mortified at his non-appearance. The great copper basins containing the food were heaped together in the middle of the carpets, and the guests, fifty in number, sat down, the men on one side, and the women on the other, the wives of the *ketchuda* and his brothers serving. There were several *samovars* with tea, but only three cups. A long bolster was the place of honour, and I occupied it alone till the village priests arrived,—reverend men with long beards, high black head-dresses, and full black cassocks with flowing sleeves. All the guests rose, and remained standing till they had been ceremoniously conducted to seats. I found them very agreeable and cultured men, acquainted with the varying "streams of tendency" in the Church of England, and very anxious to claim our Church as a sister of their own. This banquet was rather a gay scene, and on a higher roof fully one hundred women and children dressed in bright red stood watching the proceedings below.

I proposed to see the church, and with the priests,

most of the guests, and a considerable following of the onlookers, walked to it through filthy alleys. This ancient building, in a dirty and malodorous yard, differs externally from the mud houses which surround it only in having two bells on a beam. The interior consists of four domed vaults, and requires artificial light. A vault with a raised floor contains the altar and a badly-painted altar-piece representing the B. V.; a rail separates the men, who stand in front, from the women, who stand behind. A Liturgy and an illuminated medieval copy of the Gospels, of which they are very proud, are their only treasures. They have no needlework, and the altar cloth is only a piece of printed cotton. Nothing could well look poorer than this small, dark, vacant building, with a few tallow candles without candlesticks giving a smoky light.

They have two daily services lasting from one to two hours each, and Mass on Sunday is protracted to seven hours! The priests said that all the men, except two who watch the flocks, and nearly all the women are at both services on Sunday, and that many of the men and most of the women are at both daily services, one of which, as is usual, begins before daylight. There is no school. The fathers teach their boys to read and write, and the mothers instruct their girls in needlework.

After visits to the priests' houses, a number of villagers on horseback escorted me back to Gandaman. The heat of those two days was very great for May, the mercury marking 83° in the shade at 10 A.M. One hundred and thirteen people came for medicines, and in their eagerness they swarmed round both ends of the tent, blocking out all air. The ailments were much more varied and serious than among the Bakhtiaris.

The last march was a hot and tedious one of eighteen miles, along an uninteresting open valley, much ploughed,

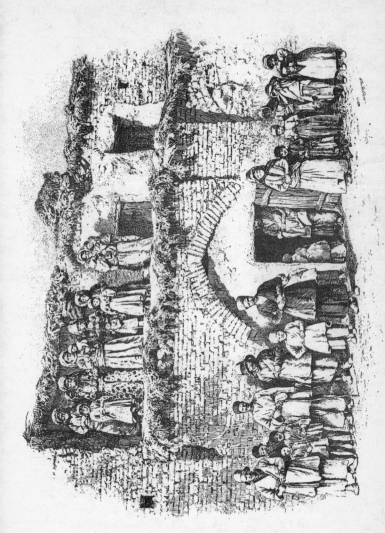

WALL AND GATE OF LIBASGUN.

bounded by sloping herbage-covered hills, surmounted by
parapets of perpendicular rock.   After passing the large
Moslem village of Baldiji, we re-entered the Bakhtiari
country, ascended to the Bakhtiari village of Dastgird,
descended to the plain of Chigakhor, skirted its southern
margin, and on its western side, on two spurs of the
great Kuh-i-Kaller range, with a ravine between them,
the camps were pitched.   In two days most of the tents
were blown down, and were moved into two ravines
with a hill between them, on which the Sahib on his
arrival pitched his camp.

My ravine has a spring, with exactly space for my
tent beside it, and a platform higher up with just room
enough for the servants.   A strong stream, rudely brawl-
ing, issuing from the spring, disturbs sleep.   There is
no possibility of changing one's position by even a six-
feet stroll, so rough and steep is the ground.   Mirza
bringing my meals from the cooking tent has a stick to
steady himself.   At first there was nothing to see but
scorched mountains opposite, and the green plain on
which the ravine opens, but the *Hakīm's* tent was soon
discovered, and I have had 278 " patients '!   Before I
am up in the morning they are sitting in rows one
behind another on the steep ground, their horses and
asses grazing near them, and all day they come.   One of
the chiefs of the Janiki tribe came with several saddle
and baggage horses and even a tent, to ask me to go
with him to the great plain of Khana Mirza, three days'
march from here, to cure his wife's eyes, and was
grieved to the heart when I told him they were beyond
my skill.   He stayed while a great number of sick
people got eye-lotions and medicines, and then asked me
why I gave these medicines and took so much trouble.
I replied that our Master and Lord not only commanded
us to do good to all men as we have opportunity, but

Himself healed the sick. "You call Him Master and Lord," he said; "He was a great Prophet. *Send a Hakīm to us in His likeness.*"

I have heard so much of Chigakhor that I am disappointed with the reality. There are no trees, most of the snow has melted, the mountains are not very bold in their features, the plain has a sort of lowland look about it, and though its altitude is 7500 feet, the days and even nights are very hot. The interest of it lies in it being the summer resort of the Ilkhani and Ilbegi, a fact which makes it the great centre of Bakhtiari life. As many as 400 tents are pitched here in the height of the season, and the coming and going of Khans and headmen with tribute and on other business is ceaseless.

The plain, which is about seven miles long by three broad, is quite level. Near the south-east end is a shallow reedy mere, fringed by a fertile swampiness, which produces extraordinary crops of grass far out into the middle of the level.

Near the same end is a rocky eminence or island, on which is the fortress castle of the Ilkhani. The "season" begins in early June, when the tribes come up from the warm pastures of Dizful and Shuster, to which they return with their pastoral wealth in the autumn, after which the plain is flooded and frozen for the winter. At the north end are the villages of Dastgird and Aurugun, and a great deal of irrigated land producing wheat. Except at that end the plain is surrounded by mountains; on its southern side, where a part of the Sukhta range rises into the lofty peak of Challeh Kuh, with its snow-slashes and snow-fields, they attain an altitude of 12,000 or 13,000 feet.

It is not easy, perhaps not possible, to pass through the part of the Bakhtiari country for which we are bound,

without some sort of assistance from its feudal lords, a
responsible man, for instance, who can obtain supplies
from the people.   Therefore we have been detained here
for many days waiting for the expected arrival of the
Ilkhani.   A few days ago a rumour arrived, since un-
happily confirmed, that things were in confusion below,
owing to the discovery of a plot on the part of the
Ilkhani to murder the Ilbegi.   Stories are current of the
number of persons " put out of the way " before he attained his present rank for the second time, and it is not
" Bakhtiari custom" to be over-scrupulous about human
life.   No doubt his nephew, the Ilbegi, is a very dangerous
rival, and that his retainers are bent on seeing him in a
yet higher position than he now occupies.

A truce has been patched up, however, and yesterday
the Ilkhani and Isfandyar Khan arrived together, with
their great trains of armed horsemen, their *harams*, their
splendid studs, their crowds of unmounted retainers, their
strings of baggage mules and asses laden with firewood,
and all the " rag, tag, and bobtail " in attendance on
Oriental rulers.   Following them in endless nocturnal
procession come up the tribes, and day breaks on an ever-
increasing number of brown flocks and herds, of mares,
asses, dogs, black tents, and household goods.   When we
arrived there were only three tents, now the green bases
of the mountains and all the platforms and ravines where
there are springs are spotted with them, in rows or semi-
circles, and at night the camp fires of the multitude look
like the lights of a city.   Each clan has a prescriptive
right to its camping-ground and pasture (though both are
a fruitful source of quarrels), and arrives with its *ketchuda*
and complete social organisation, taking up its position
like a division of an army.

When in the early morning or afternoon the tribe
reaches the camping-ground, everything is done in the

most orderly way.   The infants are put into their cradles, the men clear the ground if necessary, drive the pegs and put up the poles, and if there be wood—of which there is not a stick here—they make a fence of loose branches to contain the camp, but the women do the really hard work. Their lords, easily satisfied with their modicum of labour, soon retire to enjoy their pipes and the endless gossip of Bakhtiari life.

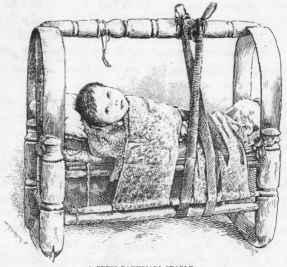

A PERSO-BAKHTIARI CRADLE.

After the ground has been arranged the tents occupy invariably the same relative position, whether the camp is in a row, a semicircle, a circle, or streets, so that the cattle and flocks may easily find their owners' abodes without being driven.   The tents, which are of black goats' hair cloth, are laid out and beaten, and the women spread them over the poles and arrange the rest, after which the inside is brushed to remove the soot.   In a good tent, reed screens are put up to divide the space into two or more

portions, and some of the tribes fence round the whole
camp with these screens, leaving one opening, and use the
interior for a sheepfold.   The small bushes are grubbed
up for fuel.   The women also draw the water, and the
boys attend to the flocks.   Many of the camps, however,
have neither fences nor environing screens, and their inmates dwell without any attempt at privacy, and rely for
the safety of their flocks on big and trustworthy dogs,
of which every camp has a number.

When they move the bulk of the labour again falls
on the women.   They first make the baggage into neat
small packages suited for the backs of oxen; then they
take up the tent pegs, throw down the tents, and roll
them up in the reed screens, all that the men undertake
being to help in loading the oxen.   It is only when a
division halts for at least some days that this process is
gone through.   In fine weather, if a tribe is marching
daily to its summer or winter camping - grounds, the
families frequently sleep in the open.

The chief's tent is always recognisable by its size, and
is occasionally white.   I have seen a tent of a wealthy
Khan fully sixty feet long.   A row of poles not more than
ten feet high supported the roof, which was of brown
haircloth, the widths united by a coarse open stitch.
On the windward side the roof was pinned down nearly
to the top of a loosely-laid wall of stones about three feet
high.   The leeward side was quite open, and the roof,
which could be lowered if necessary, was elevated and extended by poles six feet high.   If the tent was sixty feet
long, it was made by this arrangement twenty feet broad.
At the lower end was a great fire-hole in the earth, and
the floor of the upper end was covered with rugs, quilts,
and pillows, the household stuff being arranged chiefly on
and against the rude stone wall.

The process of encamping for a camp of seventy tents

takes about two hours, and many interruptions occur, especially the clamorous demands of unweaned infants of mature years. De-camping the same number of tents takes about an hour. A free, wild life these nomads lead, full of frays and plots, but probably happier than the average lot.

Below the castle is the great encampment of the chiefs, brown tents and white bell tents, among which the tall white pavilion of the Ilkani towers conspicuously. The Ilkhani and Ilbegi called on me, and as they sat outside my tent it was odd to look back two years to the time when they were fighting each other, and barely two weeks to the discovery of the plot of the dark-browed Ilkhani to murder his nephew. The Ilkhani's face had a very uncomfortable expression. Intrigues against him at Tihran and nearer home, the rumoured enmity of the Prime Minister, the turbulence of some of the tribes, the growing power of the adherents of Isfand-yar Khan, and his own baffled plot to destroy him must make things unpleasant. Several of the small Khans who have been to see me expect fighting here before the end of the summer. The Ilkhani had previously availed himself of the resources of my medicine chest, and with so much benefit that I was obliged to grant a request which deprived me of a whole bottle of " tabloids."

In the evening I visited the ladies who are in the castle leading the usual dull life of the *haram*, high above the bustle which centres round the Ilkhani's pavilion, with its crowds of tribesmen, mares and foals feeding, tethered saddle horses neighing, cows being milked, horsemen galloping here and there, firing at a mark, asses bearing wood and flour from Ardal being unloaded—a bustle masculine solely.

Isfandyar Khan, with whose look of capacity I am more and more impressed, and Lutf received us and led

us to the great pavilion, which is decorated very hand-
somely throughout with red and blue *appliqué* arabesques,
and much resembles an Indian *durbar* tent. A brown
felt carpet occupied the centre.   The Ilkhani, who rose
and shook hands, sat on one side and the Ilbegi on the
other, and sons, Khans, and attendants to the number
of 200, I daresay, stood around.   We made some fine
speeches, rendered finer, doubtless, by Mirza; repeated
an offer to send a doctor to itinerate in the country
for some months in 1891, took the inevitable tea, and
while the escorts were being arranged for I went to the
fort.

It is the fortress of the Haft Lang, one great
division of the Bakhtiari Lurs, which supplies the ruling
dynasty.   The building is a parallelogram, flanked by four
round towers, with large casemates and a keep on its
southern side.   It has two courtyards, surrounded by
stables and barracks, but there is no water within the
gates, and earthquakes and neglect have reduced much
of it to a semi-ruinous condition.   Over the gateway and
along the front is a handsome suite of well-arranged
balconied rooms, richly decorated in Persian style,
the front and doors of the large reception-room being
of fretwork filled in with amber and pale blue glass,
and the roof and walls are covered with small mirrors
set so as to resemble facets, with medallion pictures of
beauties and of the chase let in at intervals.   The effect
of the mirrors is striking, and even beautiful.   There
were very handsome rugs on the floor, and divans
covered with Kashan velvet; but rugs, divans, and squabs
were heaped to the depth of some inches with rose petals
which were being prepared for rose-water, and the principal wife rose out of a perfect bed of them.

These ladies have no conversation, and relapse into
apathy after asking a few personal questions.   Again

they said they wished to see the Agha, of whose height and prowess many rumours had reached them, but when I suggested that they might see him from the roof or balcony they said they were afraid. Again they said they had such dull lives, and regretted my departure, as they thought they might come and see my tent. I felt sorry for them, sorrier than I can say, as I realised more fully the unspeakable degradation and dulness of their lives. A perfect rabble of dirty women and children filled the passages and staircase.

On one of my last evenings I rode, attended only by Mirza, to the village of Dastgird to see two women whose husband desired medicines for them. This village is piled upon the hillside at the north end of the valley and a traveller can be seen afar off. I had never visited any of the camps so slenderly escorted, and when I saw the roofs covered with men and numbers more running to the stream with long guns slung behind their backs and big knives in their girdles, I was much afraid that they might be rude in the absence of a European man, and that I should get into trouble. At the stream the *ketchuda*, whose wives were ill, and several of the principal inhabitants met me. They salaamed, touched their hearts and brows, two held my stirrups, others walked alongside, and an ever-increasing escort took me up the steep rude alley of the village to the low arch by which the headman's courtyard—all rocks, holes, and heaps—is entered.

Dismounting was a difficulty. Several men got hold of *Screw*, one made a step of his back, another of his knee, one grasped my foot, two got hold of my arms, all shouting and disputing as to how to proceed, but somehow I was hauled off, and lifted by strong arms up into the *atrium*, the floor of which was covered with their woven rugs, across which they led me to an improvised place of

honour, a *karsi* covered with a red blanket. A brass
samovar was steaming hospitably on the floor, surrounded
by tea-glasses, trays, and sugar. The chief paid me the
usual Persian compliment, "Your presence purifies the
house;" men crowded in, shrouded women peeped through
doorways; they served me on bended knees with tea
à la Russe, and though they shouted very loud, and often
all together, they made me very cordially welcome.
They send their flocks with some of their people to
warmer regions for the winter, but the chief and many
families remain, though the snow is from seven to nine
feet deep, according to their marks on a post.

I rode to the camp where the wives were, with the
Khan and a number of men on foot and on horseback,
a messenger having been sent in advance. In the village
the great sheep-dogs, as usual, showed extreme hostility,
and one, madder than the rest, a powerful savage, attacked
me, fixing his teeth in my stirrup guard, and hanging on.
The Khan drew a revolver and shot him through the
back, killing him at once, and threatened to beat the
owner. *Screw* was quite undisturbed by the incident.

The power of the *ketchuda* or headman of a group of
families is not absolute even in this small area. His
duties are to arrange the annual migrations, punish small
crimes summarily, to report larger crimes to the Khan, to
collect the tribute, conjointly with the Khan, and to carry
out his orders among the families of his group. Private
oppression appears to be much practised among the
ketchudas, and under the feeble rule of Imam Kuli
Khan to be seldom exposed. The *ketchuda's* office,
originally elective, has a great tendency to become hereditary, but at any moment the Ilkhani may declare it elective in a special case.

Though the offices of Ilkhani and Ilbegi are held only
annually at the pleasure of the Shah, and the *ketchudas*

are properly elective, the office of Khan or chief is strictly
hereditary, though it does not necessarily fall to the eldest
son. This element of permanence gives the Khan almost
supreme authority in his tribe, and when the Ilkhani is
a weak man and a Khan is a strong one, he is practically
independent, except in the matter of the tribute to the
Shah.

It was in curbing the power of these Khans by steer-
ing a shrewd and even course among their feuds and conflicts, by justice and consideration in the collection of
the revenues, and by rendering it a matter of self-interest
for them to seek his protection and acknowledge his
headship, that Sir A. H. Layard's friend, Mohammed
Taki Khan, succeeded in reducing these wild tribes to
something like order, and Hussein Kuli Khan, " the last
real ruler of the Bakhtiaris," pursued the same methods
with nearly equal success.

But things have changed, and a fresh era of broils
and rivalries has set in, and in addition to tribal feuds
and jealousies, the universally-erected line of partisanship
between the adherents of the Ilkhani and Ilbegi produces
anything but a pacific prospect. These broils, and the
prospects of fighting, are the subjects discussed at my tent
door in the evenings.

The Dastgird encampment that evening was the
romance of camp life. On the velvety green grass there
were four high black canopies, open at the front and sides,
looking across the green flowery plain, on which the
Ilkhani's castle stood out, a violet mass against the sunset gold, between the snow-streaked mountains. There
were handsome carpets, mattresses, and bolsters ; *samovars*
steaming on big brass trays, an abundance of curds, milk,
and whey, and at one end of the largest tent there were
two very fine mares, untethered, with young foals, and
children rolling about among their feet. I was placed,

A DASTGIRD TENT.

as usual, on a bolster, and the tent filled with people, all shouting, and clamouring together, bringing rheumatism (" wind in the bones "), sore eyes, headaches (" wind in the head "), and old age to be cured. The Khan's wife, a handsome, pathetic-looking girl, had become an epileptic a fortnight ago. This malady is sadly common. Of the 278 people who have come for medicines here thirteen per cent have had epileptic fits. They call them "faintings," and have no horror of them. Eye diseases, including such severe forms as cataract and glaucoma, rheumatism, headaches, and dyspepsia are their most severe ailments. No people have been seen with chest complaints, bone diseases, or cancer.

In the largest tent there was a young mother with an infant less than twenty-four hours old, and already its eyebrows, or at all events the place where eyebrows will be, were deeply stained and curved. At seven or eight years old girls are tattooed on hands, arms, neck, and chest, and the face is decorated with stars on the forehead and chin.

Though children of both sexes are dearly loved among these people, it is only at the birth of a son that there is anything like festivity, and most of the people are too poor to do more even then than distribute sweetmeats among their friends and relations. The "wealthier" families celebrate the birth of a firstborn son with music, feasting, and dancing.

At the age of five or six days the child is named, by whispering the Divine name in its ear, along with that chosen by the parents.

After a long visit the people all kissed my hand, raising it to their foreheads afterwards, and the Khan made a mounting block of his back, and rode with me to the main path. It was all savage, but the intention was throughout courteous, according to their notions. It became pitch dark, and I lost my way, and should have pulled *Screw* over a precipice but for his sagacious self-will. One of the finest sights I have seen was my own camp in a thunderstorm, with its white tents revealed by a flash of lightning, which lighted for a second the black darkness of the ravine.

The next morning the Khan of Dastgird's servants brought fifteen bottles and pipkins for eye-lotions and medicines. In spite of the directions in Persian which Mirza put upon the bottles, I doubt not that some of the eye-lotions will be swallowed, and that some of the medicines will be put into the eyes!

June 8.—The last evening has come after a busy day. The difficulties in the way of getting ready for the start to-morrow have been great. The iron socket of my tent-pole broke, there was no smith in the valley, and when one arrived with the Ilkhani, the Ilkhani's direct order had to be obtained before he would finish the work he had undertaken. I supplied the iron, but then there was no charcoal. I have been tentless for the whole day. Provisions for forty days have to be taken from Chigakhor, and two cwts. of rice and flour have been promised over and over again, but have only partially arrived to-night. Hassan has bought a horse and a cow, and they have both strayed, and he has gone in search of them, and Mirza in search of him, and both have been away for hours.

Of the escorts promised by the Ilkhani not one man has arrived, though it was considered that the letter to him given me by the Amin-es-Sultan would have obviated any difficulty on this score. An armed sentry was to have slept in front of my tent, and a *tufangchi* was to have been my constant attendant, and I have nobody. Of the escort promised to the Agha not one man has appeared. In this case we are left to do what General

Schindler and others in Tihran and Isfahan declared to be impossible, viz. to get through the country without an escort and without the moral support of a retainer high in the Ilkhani's service. Whether there have been crooked dealings; or whether the Ilkhani, in spite of his promises, regards the presence of travellers in his country with disfavour; or whether, apprehending a collision, both the Ilkhani and Ilbegi are unwilling to part with any of their horsemen, it is impossible to decide.

I. L. B.

END OF VOL. I